RATIONAL-EMOTIVE
CONSULTATION IN
APPLIED SETTINGS

SCHOOL PSYCHOLOGY

RATIONAL-EMOTIVE CONSULTATION IN APPLIED SETTINGS

Edited by

MICHAEL E. BERNARD
Florida Institute for Rational-Emotive Therapy
RAYMOND DIGIUSEPPE
St. John's University

LAWRENCE ERLBAUM ASSOCIATES, PUBLISHERS
1994   Hillsdale, New Jersey   Hove and London

Lawrence Erlbaum Associates, Inc., Publishers
365 Broadway
Hillsdale, New Jersey 07642

Library of Congress Cataloging-in-Publication Data

Rational-emotive consultation in applied settings / edited by Michael
E. Bernard, Raymond DiGiuseppe.
    p.   cm.
    Includes bibliographical references and index.
    ISBN 0-8058-0578-8
    1. Psychological consultation. 2. Rational-emotive psychotherapy.
  I. Bernard, Michael Edwin, 1950–   II. DiGiuseppe, Raymond.
BF637.C56R37   1994
158′.9—dc20   93-8116
                                        CIP

Printed in the United States of America
10 9 8 7 6 5 4 3 2 1

Contents

Contributors

Michael E. Bernard is Executive Director of the Florida Institute for Rational-Emotive Therapy. He is former Director of the graduate program in Educational Psychology at the University of Melbourne, Australia, and former Director of the Australian Institute for Rational Emotive Therapy.

Raymond DiGiuseppe is an Associate Professor of Psychology and Director of the graduate program in School Psychology at St. John's University. He is the Director of Professional Education at the Institute for Rational Emotive Therapy in New York.

Susan Forman is a Professor of Psychology and teaches in the graduate program in School Psychology at the University of South Carolina.

Marie Joyce is a Principal Lecturer in the Department of Behavioral and Social Sciences at the Catholic University of Australia.

John McInerney is Director of McInerney and Associates, a private psychological therapy and consulting service in Cape May County, New Jersey.

Alfred Miller is a Co-Director of the Institute for Cognitive Development, a private psychological therapy and consulting service in Suffolk County, New York.

Marilyn Rothchild is a School Psychologist in the Aurora Colorado School District.

Ann Vernon is a Professor of Counselor Education at the University of Northern Iowa, and the Director of the Midwest Institute for Rational Emotive Therapy.

Virginia Waters is a psychologist in private practice in Manhattan and New Jersey.

Preface

Albert Ellis is primarily known as the founder of an active, directive, and effective form of psychotherapy. Ellis and rational-emotive therapy (RET) are usually not associated with consultation. However, since its inception, the Institute for Rational-Emotive Therapy developed and offered public education workshops to teach people the emotional self-management skills that are at the heart of RET. The Institute was one of the first organizations to offer self-help workshops. Today workshops offering the application of psychological principles to self-management are now part of the standard tools of consultants.

Over the past 25 years there has been a growing increase in the use of RET in consultation. Professionals have been using it at all levels of consultation and in many industries and sectors of public service. RET principles have been used to increase the effectiveness of managers, teachers, and professionals. It has been used to help senior supervisors more efficiently direct organizations. And it has been used as a model for numerous effective stress management programs.

In this volume, we and our contributing authors take the position that almost all consultees when faced with negative events that over a long period of time frustrate them from achieving their goals, experience inappropriately intense emotional reactions such as extreme frustration and anger, panic, or feelings of inadequacy. Such emotional reactions are most often inappropriate because they lead to goal-defeating behavior such as withdrawal or aggression.

The collective experience of contributors of this volume in working with parents, teachers, and managers suggests that consultees have a great deal of difficulty learning how to solve problems differently and make changes in the way in which a family or organization operates because they experience a range of intense emotions which block them from thinking clearly and taking effective action. We have greatly increased our consultative-effectiveness, including our use of behavioral and organizational consultation methods through the concomitant use of RET as a system of emotional self-management.

Simply stated, unless the consultant engages in emotional problem solving with consultees at all the different levels of consultation, practical problem solving and overall consultation progress will be inhibited.

As RET has become more accepted in the professional community, the consultation applications have increased. However, one of the things lacking until now has been RET consultation literature. This volume attempts to fill that void. We have asked many of the pioneers in RET consultation in applied settings to share their knowledge and expertise. Each chapter in this text focuses on one aspect of RET consultation. Each contributor has written from experience in the application of RET in new areas. It has been our hope that this volume will enable readers to apply RET principles in new ways that they had not considered.

We would like to thank Albert Ellis for his inspiration and perspiration in discussing aspects of this volume with us.

Michael E. Bernard
Raymond DiGiuseppe

Dedicated to
Jonathon and Alexandra,
Matthew and Daniel

1 Rational-Emotive Consultation: The Missing Link to Successful Consultation

Michael E. Bernard
Florida Institute for Rational-Emotive Therapy

Raymond DiGiuseppe
St. John's University, Institute for Rational-Emotive Therapy

Sometime in the not so distant future, scholars writing about the development of the theory and practice of consultation will scratch their heads with some perplexity. They will be surprised about a singular sin of omission in the field circa 1990 committed by all but a small group of practitioners sitting out on a lonely isle of consultative practice. The sin of omission they will ponderously note was the failure of consultation models and methods of the late 20th century to consider the dysfunctional and facilitative roles of human emotions as they influence the ability of individuals (consultees) to solve problems and function effectively.

Accompanying their observations and learned hypotheses to explain this anomaly, will appear a photograph of the smiling face of the creator of a theory and practice of mental health who was often controversial in presentation (he was known to utter profanity). His theory maintained that human beings, when faced with events and problems, often experience extremely intense emotional reactions that block their ability to achieve goals. These emotional reactions make it very difficult for them to function effectively and to solve problems. The founder of rational-emotive therapy (RET), Albert Ellis, worked in conjunction with a group of consultants who worked in a variety of educational, business, and governmental agencies around the world. These consultants, who despite resistance emanating from many different quarters, employed rational-emotive consultation (REC) methods to resolve the many and varied problems that troubled most of the individuals and organizations they consulted.

This chapter makes the case that effective consultation requires consultants to examine the role of emotions as impediments or facilitators in the consultation process. The case we make in this chapter, which is reinforced and illustrated

1

throughout this book, is exceptionally simple and straightforward. When individuals (consultees) seek or require the services of an expert (consultant) to help them solve a long-standing, chronic problem, it is likely that they experience strong, negative emotional reactions to such problems. These emotions may be causing, exacerbating, or preventing them from thinking clearly about and solving these problems. No matter the type of consultation intervention decided on or agreed to between the expert and the individual seeking help, unless these emotional entanglements are directly addressed and reduced, the impact and effectiveness of the consultation, both in the short term and long term, will be greatly reduced.

This chapter provides a RET model of consultation consistent with other contemporaneous views. The application of RET methods at different levels of consultation (e.g., client-centered, consultee-centered, systemic centered) is then illustrated. RET's unique contribution to consultation is then presented in a discussion that distinguishes emotional from practical problem solving. Similarities between mental health consultation and rational-emotive consultation, two primary forms of consultation that directly address the emotional involvement of the consultee are examined. The rational emotive theory of consultation, which highlights the role of the *belief system* of the consultee, is then presented. The central importance of what we call the "consultative alliance" in maximizing the effectiveness of REC is introduced followed by a discussion of the different RET consultation methods. The chapter concludes with a look at ways in which RET consultation has been evaluated.

RET MODEL OF CONSULTATION

RET's view of consultation in applied settings is consistent with other current viewpoints (e.g., Bergan & Kratochwill, 1990; Brown, Pryzwansky, & Schulte, 1987; Curtis & Meyers, 1985; Gutkin & Curtis, 1990; Kratochwill, Elliott, & Rotto, 1990; Zins & Ponti, 1990). For example, rational emotive theory of consultation sits comfortably within the following parameters of school-based consultation as defined by Zins and Ponti:

> School based consultation is defined as a method of providing preventatively oriented psychological and educational services in which a consultant and consultee(s) form a collaborative partnership in a systems context to engage in a reciprocal and systematic problem-solving process to empower consultee systems, thereby enhancing students' well-being and performance. (p. 674)

REC conceptualizes consultation as a collaborative problem solving activity between a *consultant,* who is a professionally trained authority in the area of human relations, mental health, or organizational dynamics and a *consultee,* generally another professional, paraprofessional, or parent who has direct responsibility for teaching, managing, supervising or parenting one or more *clients* who may present a variety of learning, adjustment, academic, or work-related problems.

Consultation offers a more efficient and economical form of support service than the traditional one-to-one service delivery system that characterizes traditional counseling and psychotherapy. Consultation as *indirect service delivery* presents a process that involves consultants helping consultees to improve their interpersonal, client management, and problem solving skills and their complete mental health. Through the transmission of knowledge, and the use of professional skills and mental health techniques, the outcomes of consultation are seen as multifold: (a) an improvement in the ability of the consultee to function in the discharge of responsibilities for clients; (b) an improvement in the general skill level and mental health of the consultee; (c) an improvement in the communication skill, decision-making and problem-solving skills as well as the interpersonal relationships of members of an organization or family in order to bring about an enhancement of overall functioning of the system.

Proponents of REC (e.g., Bernard & Joyce, 1984; Forman, 1990; Joyce, 1990; Vernon, 1990) view the rational emotive model as distinctive from, yet compatible with other current models of consultation (behavioral, process, organizational, advocacy). As discussed in a separate section, REC shares much in common with mental health consultation. In addition, *REC offers a distinctive cognitive technology of emotional self-management that provides a vital adjunct to all forms and levels of consultation.*

As argued throughout this chapter and this book, RET is an important self-help technology by itself or as an adjunct to consultation employed whenever consultees' level of emotional involvement with issues prevents them solving problems and profiting from the skills and knowledge imparted in consultation.

A BRIEF HISTORY OF RET CONSULTATION

Rational training can help people function more effectively at work by actively teaching them certain basic principles of interpersonal relations which promote better self-understanding as well as increase insight into others. It is applicable to all levels of management in business and industry and to individuals working in the area of "people contact," including labor officials, sales representatives, teachers, clergymen, and military officers. Ellis and Blum (1967).

Ellis (personnel communication) traces the beginning of RET consultation to 1957, the year he published *How to live with a neurotic at work and home.* In this book, he (consultant) showed how RET could help someone (consultee) who was living or working with a difficult person (client) to relate with that person more successfully. This is done largely by consultees learning how not to disturb themselves about the other's neurotic behavior.

Ellis' (Ellis, Wolfe, & Moseley, 1966) book *How to raise an emotionally, healthy, happy child,* illustrates how parents could raise children and solve problems by teaching children to behave appropriately, but also by teaching parents to not upset themselves about their child's problems.

In the 1970s, because of his book *Executive leadership,* Ellis (1972) began to receive invitations by businesses and, in particular, banking groups in the United States and overseas (e.g., Kuwait). These groups wanted to learn how RET could be used to increase work effectiveness and boost work efficiency rather than an improvement in the mental or stress levels of employees. Ellis has commented on how business people appreciate the logic of his ABC model in learning how to manage difficult work situations.

The 1980s and 1990s saw the proliferation of RET's ideas and methods appearing into many commercial business training programs. Not only was RET being borrowed by trainers to increase work effectiveness, but it was in the forefront in the 1980's tidal wave of stress management programs. Due to the antipathy of business to therapy, all too often RET's direct contribution to different programs has failed to be acknowledged. In the 1990s, RET is increasingly being used in employee assistance programs, in training and development, management leadership development and in the training of human resource personnel.

RET has increasingly been applied in the education arena as epitomized in Bernard's (1990) book *Taking the Stress Out of Teaching*. Since the 1970s, RET has appeared in a variety of educational, parenting, teacher training, and human service professional development programs. It is recognized as having something unique to say in the area of enhancing consultee effectiveness.

EMOTIONAL VERSUS PRACTICAL PROBLEM SOLVING

For sometime now, rational-emotive therapy has distinguished between two different types of problems people can experience (e.g., McInerney, 1985; Walen, DiGiuseppe, & Dryden, 1992): practical problems and emotional problems.

Our motivations for using RET in consultation resulted from our frustration over the years in the lack of skilled application and maintenance of the behavioral strategies we have employed with consultees in collaborative problem solving. Our collective experience of over 30 years of working with parents, teachers, and managers suggests that consultees have a great difficulty learning to solve problems differently because they experience a range of intense emotions such as anxiety, depression, and anger. We have greatly enhanced our consultative effectiveness, including the use of behavioral and organizational consultation methods, through the concomitant use of RET as a system of emotional self-management.

Practical problems are defined as demanding, frustrating, challenging situations, people, or tasks that a consultee faces. Practical problems result from the lack of skills or knowledge required to meet, solve, eliminate, or reduce the frustration or problem.

A common example of a practical problem encountered in parent consultation is the parent of a child diagnosed with an attention deficit disorder (ADD) who lacks the knowledge and skill to manage the child successfully. An example from education is a principal who supervises a teacher with a poorly controlled class who has failed to increase his or her effectiveness after several meetings with the principal. An example from business is the manager who is increasingly expected to participate more fully in and take responsibility for strategic planning and yet fails to do so.

Practical problems require practical solutions that often are the outcome of the consultative problem-solving process. In the scenarios just discussed, the parent could receive constructive advice from a consultant on how best to deal with a child with attention deficits. These might include training in contingency management, structured learning techniques, or receiving up-to-date information on psychopharmacotherapy. The principal faced with a staff member who fails at classroom discipline would benefit from a consultative process that provides the latest information on classroom management technology, peer support and supervision methods. The manager faced with strategic planning would profit from participating in a training program designed to eliminate barriers to creative thinking and provide instruction in the steps of writing such a plan.

Distinct from practical problems, *emotional problems* consist of the negative disturbed emotions people experience in the face of negative, challenging and demanding experiences, people, situations and problems. People frequently experience *emotional problems about practical problems*. Examples include the teacher who experiences extreme stress about a disruptive class and who also lacks classroom management skills.

Common emotional problems assessed in REC include anxiety, depression, anger and low frustration tolerance. Emotional problems can be quantified along a continuum of intensity and severity. For example, parents with attention deficit disorder children vary in the degree of frustration tolerance and depression they experience regarding their child's learning and behavior. Principals faced with teachers who lack adequate classroom management skills and who fail to respond to guidance, vary greatly in the degree of anger they experience toward the "offending" teacher. Managers faced with strategic planning and preparing future goals, objectives and plans to achieve them, experience emotions varying from mild apprehension to panic.

When individuals, groups, families, or organizations require the services of a consultant to deal with past, present, or potential future problems or issues, it is sometimes because they lack certain practical skills and knowledge. It is usually the case that they have intense emotional involvements. These emotions constitute central problems requiring the consultant's attention.

These same emotional difficulties often impede professional functioning. For example, the increasing requirement for principals to provide performance supervision of teachers can be sabotaged by the principals' emotions (extreme anger, anxiety, low frustration tolerance) toward teachers who fail to achieve satisfactory levels of performance (e.g., Cayer, DiMattia, & Wingrove, 1988).

The goal of REC is the reduction in the intensity, duration, and frequency in the emotional reactions of consultees, which exacerbate the problem and prevent the consultee from solving the problem. The goal of RET consultation is not the removal of all negative emotions. Extreme anger and rage, panic and depression are seen as inappropriate negative emotional states since they most often lead to self-defeating behavior. Irritation, concern, and sadness are adaptive negative emotional states, which motivate individuals to make changes in their own behavior that could cause changes in their outside world.

When used preventatively (e.g., parent education), REC equips consultees with a range of rational beliefs and emotional problem-solving strategies that will help to inoculate them against the impact of negative events. That is, consultees will not get too upset in the face of bad events.

LEVELS OF RET CONSULTATION

The four-level model of consultation developed by Meyers, Parsons, and Martin (1979) can be used to illustrate the various ways that RET can be employed in consultation and integrated with other forms of consultation.

Level I: RET Direct Client-Centered Consultation

Level I consultation most closely resembles the traditional one-to-one form of mental health service delivery. At this level, the consultant works *directly with the client* (e.g., student, employee) providing psychoeducation or counseling/therapy. However, it differs from the traditional service delivery method because this service is provided in the presence of the consultee (parent, teacher, other).

Pioneered by Virginia Waters (see chapter 2), RET at Level I involves inviting the client's significant other (e.g., parent, teacher) to become an observer–participant in the one-to-one counseling/therapy session. The consultation at this level involves the consultee learning how the client's emotional problems can be understood by RET theory, how the client's irrational beliefs can be assessed, and how to use disputing to correct faulty inferences and irrational beliefs. The consultee learns to understand, diagnose, and treat problems of children in general by observing the consultant conducting RET with a particular client.

A second benefit of being an observer-participant is that the consultee may overcome their own emotional problems toward the client by observing the manner in which the consultant interacts with the client. The consultant models unconditional positive regard, nonblaming, nonawfulizing, and an objective distance from the problem and teaches the client to be more rational. In this way the consultee learns to be more accepting of clients and their problem.

Also, during the counseling/consultation session, the consultee can be used to help the consultant dispute the client's faulty conceptions of reality. The following case illustration demonstrates the process. This mother, participating as an observer-participant learned from the consultant to dispute her child's irrational beliefs.

Case Illustration

Gary, age 10, was referred by his mother for a variety of concerns including noncompliance at home, but, more importantly, for repeated difficulties at school. Gary, a bright, precocious boy consistently arrived at the nurse's office at school with a variety of physical complaints including a twisted ankle, head-aches, and nausea. All of his ills required his mother to leave work to pick him up. Gary was described as having few friends because of his tendency to brag and initiate fights.

When interviewed alone Gary was presented as an overactive, anxious boy with well-developed verbal skills. Assessment of his school-related problems resulted in defensiveness and denial. However, a discussion about his mother elicited openness and initially anger. In particular, Gary was angry about how his mother treated him at home. She frequently argued with him. He believed that she did not offer him enough attention. Gary's mother was invited in at the end of the session. Gary's concerns were shared and discussed. She agreed to get less upset with Gary. Gary agreed to try to get along better and to behave more compliantly. He agreed to do what was fair and reasonable.

The second session, 1 week later revealed some improvement in their rela-tionship. Gary spoke about his recent visit to the nurse's office at school because of his illness. Assessment by the counselor, of concerns surrounding friends and school which may have precipitated his visit revealed little. On this day, Gary's mother had become extremely upset because the school called for her to get Gary early when she was in an important meeting. While she tried to get Gary to stay at school until the end of the day, Gary refused. An assessment of Gary's emotions revealed surface anger and low frustration tolerance ("She should help me when I need it. I can't stand having to wait for her."). A careful assessment of emotions also revealed anxiety and depression about his mother's unwillingness to pick him up immediately from school. He experienced the irrational beliefs "My mother doesn't love me. If she did, she would always come and pick me up. She wouldn't still be at home when I come home from school. She wouldn't have started to work again."

At this point of the session, the RET counselor disputed Gary's conclusions that his mother didn't love him. In addition, he was asked if it was okay to invite his mother into the session to discuss the problem and he agreed.

The counselor explained to Gary's mother the reason Gary was experiencing certain physical symptoms at school as well as why he frequently experienced feelings of anger and ("consequences"). It was explained to Gary's mother that he was not only upset because she was working, ("activating events"), but also because of the way he thought about and interpreted her behavior. "She doesn't love me" ("beliefs"). Gary's mother was shown that to understand Gary's behav-ior, it was necessary for her to become aware of his feelings. Also she needed to discover the way he interpreted situations and other's behaviors toward him.

The counselor then asked Gary's mother an important question. "What do you think Gary is thinking about when he gets so upset with you at school and home?" When clearly she didn't know, Gary repeated his belief that she didn't love him. His mother helped to dispute Gary's inference. "Is it true that when you get angry with Gary for being difficult at home you don't love him?" "Is the reason you took a job and are not home for him when he gets home from school because you do not love him?" Gary's mother told Gary in a warm, caring voice that she always loved him, but that now that he was old enough she needed to work again. She said she thought he understood this. Gary seemed ready to accept this explanation and became visibly relaxed. Equally important, Gary's mother understood for the first time not only the role of Gary's beliefs in causing his emotional unrest, but how she could use disputing to changing Gary's beliefs to reduce his emotional upset. This interchange led to a dramatic breakthrough in the relationship between Gary and his mother which maintained itself into the future.

Level II: RET Indirect Client-Centered Consultation

At Level II, the RET consultant works collaboratively with a consultee to resolve a problem the consultee is having with a specific client. RET assumes that in most situations, consultees, be they parents, teachers, or managers, will experience personal reactions toward a student or employee that prevents them from thinking through and effectively dealing with the problem.

In providing indirect service to a client, the RET focus is on the consultee's emotional reactions and irrational attitudes toward the client, rather than on providing practical solutions to the problem itself. The goals of Level II consultation are: (a) to reduce the emotional involvement of the consultee in order to improve problem solving skills; (b) where the consultee cannot solve the problem (e.g., modify student's misbehavior), he or she will feel less upset and stressed; (c) for the consultee to acquire a set of rational, emotional management strategies as well as rational attitudes (e.g., long-term hedonism, nonapproval seeking, self-acceptance), which are then taught to the client.

At Level II, the RET consultant is careful to assess the range of emotional reactions the consultee has about the presenting practical problem including guilt, anxiety, self-downing, low frustration tolerance and anger. Once dysfunctional emotions are detected, the RET consultant, conscious of the need for a consultative alliance (see below), employs a variety of RET methods to change the consultee's interpretations and evaluations, which according to RET theory, cause the emotional upset.

Level III: RET Consultee-Centered Consultation

At Level III, consultation has as its primary focus the overall mental health of the consultee as well as the consultee's repertoire of practical, problem-solving, interpersonal and other skills in order for the consultee to effectively function in their particular role (e.g., Bernard, 1989a; DiMattia, 1987, 1989, 1991). It is assumed that targeting and enhancing consultee mental health and functioning will ultimately result in an improvement in the welfare and well-being of clients.

As discussed below, Level III consultation can be employed with individuals or groups and can be oriented towards prevention or remediation.

When employed as prevention, rational-emotive consultation is designed to teach one or more consultees the emotional self management skills necessary for them to better handle problematic situations they encounter (Bernard, 1989b; Forman, 1990; Forman & Forman, 1980). For example, when REC is integrated within a parent education program, it attempts to teach parents how to better manage their anxiety, guilt, anger, and low frustration so that they are better prepared to deal with the multifaceted activities involved in parenting (Hauck, 1967; Joyce, 1990).

As a problem-solving intervention REC is employed with one or more individuals who are experiencing wide ranging difficulties in managing and coping with the demands of their role. Rather than having difficulty with a particular client, the consultee is seen as lacking a range of skills which are preventing them from successfully discharging their responsibilities. The consultee at this level will frequently experience a large amount of stress concerning their failure to come to grips with aspects of their role and responsibilities.

A recent example of how REC can be employed to improve the overall functioning of a consultee can be seen in the example of the young, inexperienced fifth-grade teacher who was not discharging her teaching responsibilities due to her inability to manage the variety of discipline problems. The RET consultant assessed that not only was the teacher lacking in classroom management skills, but also that her lack of effective strategies were a function of her emotional reactions to the task of discipline and her ambivalence concerning her position of friend to her students versus authority figure. The fact that her reputation was being questioned by parents, colleagues, principal and students alike added increased emotional stress.

Over six sessions of work, the RET consultant helped the teacher to recognize the ways in which her emotions such as anxiety as well her attended need for approval were preventing her from becoming firmer in her management of discipline in her classroom. RET's emotional management skills were also successfully employed by the teacher to not only become less approval-seeking and more assertive with her class, but also to manage her overall level of job stress.

When working with individual consultees at Level III, the RET consultant assesses the range of emotional and practical problems and designs interventions to increase practical and emotional management skills. Emotional management is seen as distinctive to RET.

What has been popularly known as in-service training or professional training courses is seen as synonymous with the goals of Level III consultation. Groups of employees, parents, or teachers who attend courses designed to upgrade their client management and other professional skills can be considered recipients of Level III consultation. Typical workshops which incorporate RET include stress management, burnout, conflict resolution, communication and assertiveness, decision making, risk taking, time management, procrastination, giving and receiving performance appraisals, and self-promotion. The use of RET as either an adjunct to these courses or as a distinct stress management component can be seen as a way of all consultants adding value to their ongoing professional development courses. REC is also being used to upgrade skills of consultees in order that they are better informed about how to prevent or resolve client problems (rational-emotive education, Vernon, 1989a, 1989b, 1990; student motivational programs, Ash & Bernard, 1990).

Level IV: RET Systemic-Centered Consultation

Level IV consultation has its objective the improvement in the functioning of a system be it an organization or family (e.g., DiGiuseppe, 1988; Huber & Baruth, 1989; Woulff, 1983). RET systemic consultation shares much in common with traditional organizational development and family therapy approaches. At this level REC has a primary assumption that disturbances in the way a system operates including interpersonal tensions, rigidities in decision-making, poor channels of communication will be manifested in maladaptive behavior, poor learning, work ineffectiveness and poor morale and stress of clients in the system. Most importantly, breakdowns in the way a family or organization operates will impair the ability of the system at the level of policy as well as consultees at the level of management to resolve ongoing problems. Simply stated, REC sees some client problems as accounted for by systemic factors (Level IV) as well as interpersonal (Levels II and III) and intrapersonal factors (Level I).

The distinctiveness of REC at Level IV is in identifying emotional blockages as well as irrational beliefs which are locking individuals into ways of interacting and functioning which not only inhibit their organization or family from functioning effectively, but also prevent systemic change. REC methods at Level IV concentrate on working with individuals but with an eye to how their individual functioning (e.g., lack of support; back-stabbing) impinges on the greater system.

The dividing line between Level III and Level IV RET consultation can be seen in the goals of the consultation, its focus of assessment, rather than distinctive training methods or workshops. At Level IV, the REC consultant assesses the current functioning of the system including norms, structures, functions, staff culture as well as the system's preparedness and resources to cope with the changes with outside circumstances as well as the changing needs of its members (consultees and clients). Out-dated, inflexible and rigid expectations and beliefs which a system imposes on or indoctrinates its members with concerning ways they should be thinking and acting are of particular interest to the RET consultant.

At this level, the RET consultant specifically targets the chief decision-makers (e.g., CEO, general manager, administrator, principal, parent) with a view to ascertaining the ways in which their beliefs about the way their organization or family should operate are interfering or facilitative. Persons with primary responsibility exert a large influence on staff culture, ways in which new members are socialized, problem solving and disciplinary practices as well as they prepare themselves and their members for change.

Level IV RET consultation can take place at the individual or group level. For example, we recently worked with a general manager of a large insurance company who was very concerned with his division's inability to continue to attract high quality sales people who lasted more than one year. Great expense went into training, but with inadequate returns. After several discussions, it became apparent that the general manager subscribed to a number of beliefs about the way agents should be recruited and trained which worked for his organization in the 1970s, but were leading to restricted practices today. Questioning him about the problems of his employees produced a great deal of resentment and hostility about the way they should be. Helping him to identify his unspoken, but deeply held beliefs about organizational practices rather than on the employees themselves led to a more reasonable discussion and subsequent willingness to trial new practices on current circumstances.

Level IV RET consultation with groups still focusses on the responsibility of the individual to change before expecting the organization or family to change. Many of the workshops mentioned as appropriate to Level III consultation can be employed at Level IV with differing goals of consultation in mind. Additional workshops germane to Level IV include executive leadership, strategic planning and managing change.

RET AND MENTAL HEALTH CONSULTATION

At one level, RET consultation has much in common with mental health consultation (Caplan, 1970; Meyers et al., 1979). Both types of consultation are directly applicable to what Caplan called "consultee-centered" consultation. In this type of consultation, the consultee (e.g., teacher, principal, manager, senior executive, administrator, mental health service provider, parent) presents with a pattern of failure to cope with a variety of aspects of his or her job or role. The poor coping results not only from broad skill or knowledge deficits, but from emotional entanglement with a trouble, issue, or person(s) (Conoley & Conoley, 1982).

RET differs from Caplan's mental health consultation in the area of theory, consultative methods, and the different levels at which each type of consultation can be applied.

Mental health consultation relies on psychodynamic assumptions of human behavior. The theory proposes that the loss of professional objectivity of the consultee, evidenced in his or her emotional reaction, results from what Caplan referred to as "theme interference" and the activity of unconscious dynamics including repression.

Ellis (1962) adopted a humanistic-cognitive perspective in explaining emotionally driven professional dysfunctional in terms of an "irrational belief system" which directs the way the consultee thinks, feels, and behaves. Although Ellis rejected the psychodynamic theory of unconscious motivation, he has over the years agreed that specific irrational beliefs operate at a "subconscious" level. That is, individuals may not be immediately aware of his or her beliefs. However, these irrational beliefs are accessible through direct introspection and self-questioning. On a theoretical level, there are parallels between "theme interference" and "irrational beliefs," although their psychodynamics are clearly different.

To reduce theme interference, Caplan (1970) advocated a variety of indirect methods (e.g., use of parables) to be used by the consultant so that the consultee does not feel personally threatened. Caplan strongly cautioned the consultant against explicitly identifying the consultee's unconscious themes. He believes that such a direct confrontation would break down the consultee's defense mechanisms leaving the consultee quite vulnerable. The time-limited nature of the contact between consultant and consultee limits the ability of the consultant to help restore the consultee's ego strength. The reliance on indirect methods makes it unclear whether the consultee will ever get the message that is supposed to help them become aware of the theme interference.

RET's consultation methods are more directive and persuasive. As is discussed later, the RET consultant, while being extremely conscious of the need to build a "consultative alliance" with the consultee, uses many disputing techniques to change the consultee's irrational beliefs that according to RET theory, underlie the consultee's emotional involvements.

A final distinction between mental health and RET consultation is that Caplan reserved the use of his emotional disentangling, theme-reduction procedures for consultee-centered consultation. This is not recommended for client-, program-, or administrative-centered consultation. RET, on the other hand, is seen as an appropriate consultative approach at all levels of consultation to be used whenever individuals are faced with difficult problems and the need to change.

RET THEORY OF CONSULTATION

Rational training can help people function more effectively at work by actively teaching them certain basic principles of interpersonal relations which promote better self-understanding and increase insight into others. It is applicable to all levels of management in business and industry as well as to those individuals who work in the area of "people contact", including labor officials, sales representatives, teachers, clergymen, and officers in the armed forces. (Ellis and Blum, 1967)

The theory of rational-emotive consultation is a derivative of the current theory and practice of RET (e.g., Bernard, 1991a; Ellis & Dryden, 1987; Walen et al., 1980; Walen et al., 1992). The term *rational-emotive consultation* overlaps to some extent with many RET-based prevention and intervention models in mental health and work-effectiveness programs. These are referred to in the RET literature as *rational-emotive education* (Knaus, 1974; Vernon, 1989a, 1989b), *rational parenting* (Joyce, 1992) and *rational effectiveness training* (DiMattia, 1990).

The RET theory of consultation concerns itself with understanding the effectiveness and related mental health of consultees (parents, teachers, custodial caregivers, managers, principals, chief executive officers) whom are responsible for the welfare or functioning of others. RET asserts that when consultees are confronted with activating events, which block them from achieving their goals, it is quite "normal," healthy, and adaptive for them to experience negative emotions such as extreme concern, disappointment, or irritation. For example, when teachers have in class many "noncompliant" children, it is quite natural for him or her to experience extreme annoyance and concern given that their presence prevents the teacher from achieving his or her professional goals, including freedom from distractions to teach all children.

RET advances the argument that most consultees, when faced with negative events, which over a long time frustrate them from achieving their goals, experience inappropriately intense emotional reactions such as rage, panic, and depression. Such emotional reactions are most often inappropriate because they lead to goal-defeating behavior. The teacher, who experiences high levels of anger and a sense of inadequacy when confronted with classroom disruptions, will find it harder to think clearly about how to solve practical problems and to carry out problem-solving strategies.

RET advances a cognitive origin to explain the dysfunctional emotional and behavioral reactions of consultees to difficult problematic or obnoxious events. Rather than arguing that consultees present with deficits in cognitive mediation (consequential thinking, alternative solution thinking) as advanced by interpersonal cognitive problem-solving theorists (e.g., Spivack & Shure, 1974), RET posits the existence of dysfunctional irrational beliefs.

The construct "irrational belief" is central to understanding Ellis' theory. Irrational beliefs and rational beliefs are seen as part of a broad system of what can be considered cognitive personality traits. That is, the belief system exerts a pervasive influence over the thinking, feelings, and behavior of individuals across a variety of situations. Alternatively called *personal paradigm* or *world view* (Bernard & Joyce, 1984), the belief system of individuals is a product of biological, genetic, and social learning influences.

According to Ellis (Ellis & Bernard, 1985) the main irrational beliefs that people tend to hold can be categorized under three major categories, each with many derivatives: (a) "I must do well and win approval, or else I rate as a rotten person;" (b) "Others must treat me considerately and kindly in the way I want them to treatment. If they don't society and the universe should severely, blame, damn and punish them for their inconsiderateness;" (c) "Conditions under which I live must be arranged so that I get practically all that I want, comfortable, quickly and easily, and get virtually nothing that I don't want."

An example of irrational beliefs of teachers derived from Ellis' three main ones, and derivative irrational cognitive processes (see later), are presented in Table 1.1 "The Teacher Irrational Belief Scale" (Bernard, 1991). Above average scores on this scale are associated with high job stress and poor coping skills (time management, classroom management, assertiveness).

TABLE 1.1
The Teacher Irrational Belief Scale (Bernard, 1990)

TEACHER IRRATIONAL BELIEF SCALE

Directions: Indicate the extent to which you agree or disagree with the following statements

Circle 1 for Strongly Disagree (SD)
Circle 2 for Disagree (D)
Circle 3 for Not Sure (NS)
Circle 4 for Agree (A)
Circle 5 for Strongly Agree (SA)

Self-Downing Attitudes

	SD	D	NS	A	SA
1. I think I'm really inadequate when I don't get the approval or respect for what I do.	1	2	3	4	5
2. The prospect of teaching a class I don't have good control over is more than I can take.	1	2	3	4	5
3. I think I'm a failure when I haven't "got through" to a student or class.	1	2	3	4	5
4. I really should be able to solve all my students' problems perfectly.	1	2	3	4	5
5. I should be able to succeed at all the important things I do at school.	1	2	3	4	5
6. To make mistakes or perform poorly as a teacher is for me one of the worst things in the world.	1	2	3	4	5
7. I feel totally hopeless when I don't get all my work done on time.	1	2	3	4	5
8. I can't stand being criticized or thought badly of when I haven't finished something or done it properly.	1	2	3	4	5

Total Score _____
(Average: 25)

(*Continued*)

TABLE 1.1
(*Continued*)

Low Frustration Tolerance Attitudes

	SD	D	NS	A	SA
9. I find it too hard to balance my home and work demands.	1	2	3	4	5
10. I shouldn't have to work so hard.	1	2	3	4	5
11. Schools are really lousy places because they give teachers too much work and not enough time to do it.	1	2	3	4	5
12. It's really bad to have to put in so many hours both inside and outside the classroom.	1	2	3	4	5

Total Score _____
(Average: 11)

Attitudes to School Organization

	SD	D	NS	A	SA
13. One of the things I find totally bad is the lack of communication between teachers and central administration	1	2	3	4	5
14. Teachers should be consulted about decisions	1	2	3	4	5
15. Schools really should attend more to teachers' problems and it is totally unfair when they don't	1	2	3	4	5
16. Without good teacher–administrator communication and support, schools are the very worst places to work.	1	2	3	4	5
17. I can't stand it when I am not consulted about a decision that affects my teaching.	1	2	3	4	5

Total Score _____
(Average: 18)

Authoritarian Attitudes Toward Students

	SD	D	NS	A	SA
18. As a teacher, I should have the power to be able to make my students do what I want.	1	2	3	4	5
19. Students should always be respectful, considerate and behave well.	1	2	3	4	5
20. Students who constantly misbehave are horrible and should be severely punished.	1	2	3	4	5
21. I can't stand it when students misbehave.	1	2	3	4	5
22. It's really awful to have to teach in a class where there are so many problems.	1	2	3	4	5

Total Score _____
(Average: 14)

The ABC's of RET

RET explains dysfunctional emotional upset in terms of a simple ABC model. When consultees are confronted with a negative *a*ctivating event (referred to as "A"), it is quite normal for them to experience a "C," emotional *c*onsequence, appropriate negative emotions. According to RET, appropriate negative emotions are largely caused by an underlying *b*elief system (referred to as "B") characterized by rational thinking (flexible, scientific, sensible, useful). A consultee employing rational beliefs when confronted with many difficult students might think: "I wish very much that I didn't have so many problems in my class. This is very bad for me and other students. Now, how can I go about solving this problem." On the other hand, the consultee who gets upset about disruptive students holds a different set of beliefs. Ellis defined irrational thinking in terms of *absolutistic thinking*. In this process, a person takes something preferential, such as well-behaved students, and converts the preference into a *must* (e.g., "I must have control of my students always. Students should behave well"). According to Ellis, absolutistic thinking is irrational. It does not logically follow that because it would be good for all students to behave well and because many do behave well that, rotten, they all should behave well. It also does not make sense because there is no evidence to support the idea that students who present with underlying emotional, behavioral, or learning disorders should behave well.

According to RET theory, several other cognitive processes derived from absolutistic thinking contribute to inappropriate emotional upset. One belief is *awfulizing,* which means blowing the badness of an event out of proportion ("It is terrible that these students are disruptive"). Another is *I can't stand it,* which means evaluating things that are bad as intolerable ("I can't stand this behavior any longer"). Another is *self-rating,* which involves taking bad events personally by putting oneself down ("Because I don't have control of my class as I should, I'm a failure"). The last is *other-rating,* which involves judging the total worth of another person on the basis of one or more of their characteristics ("Because you are behaving so badly, you are a totally condemnable, no-good person").

RET takes the position that all human being present with self-imposed emotional obstacles that block their solving of practical problems. RET consultative methods are geared toward helping consultees remove these obstacles through cognitive, emotive, and behavioral methods designed to cause change in underlying irrational beliefs.

RET AND THE "CONSULTATIVE ALLIANCE"

When RET consultants work with an individual or with groups, there are several necessary preconditions that need to be in place to ensure that RET will be employed effectively. We believe that these preconditions can be applied across a variety of consultative approaches.

Borodin (1979) described the *therapeutic alliance* as the complex of attachments and shared understandings and activities undertaken by therapists and clients as the former attempt to help the latter with their psychological problems. Borodin emphasized that there are three major aspects of the therapeutic alliance: (a) agreement on the *goals* of psychotherapy, which refer to the goals of what is to be changed; (b) agreement on the *tasks* of psychotherapy, which refer to the activities carried out by both parties in the service of the goals; (c) the *bonds* between client and therapist, which refer to the interpersonal connectedness between therapist and client (see Dryden, 1991, for a detailed discussion of the therapeutic alliance in improving the effectiveness of RET).

We have taken the following speculations of Borodin concerning *effective* psychotherapy and applied them to the consultation process. Borodin argued that effective therapy occurs when therapist and client: (a) mutually agree on the goals of the therapeutic enterprise; (b) understand their own and the other person's therapeutic tasks and agree to carry these out to achieve the client's goals; and (c) have an appropriate bonded working relationship. We propose the elements necessary for a successful therapeutic alliance are also important for a successful consultative alliance. When using RET in individual or group consultation, we recommend that the consultant be aware of the importance of these three dimensions of the consultative alliance.

RET change methods tend to be direct. They teach individuals experiencing difficulties that they partly contribute to their problems by the attitudes and beliefs they have about the problem and their concomitant emotional reactions. Teaching *emotional responsibility,* requires consultees to change their behavior before they can expect their clients to change. The direct confrontation of the consultee's irrational beliefs can be very disruptive to the consultative alliance and to progress. If the consultee experiences the RET consultant as insensitive, nonempathic, or blaming the consultee for his or her problem, the consultative alliance will be at its weakest.

We caution all RET consultants to be sensitive to their own style of introducing RET ideas in consultation and to make sure that the consultee is experiencing his or her intervention constructively. It is important to remember that most consultees enter a consultative relationship looking for solutions to practical problems outside themselves. They do not see themselves as contributing to the problem. Many consultees resist the notion that they are experience emotional involvement that impedes their effectiveness.

Here is a list of suggestions for enhancing the consultative alliance:

1. Tune into the interpersonal style that your consultee most likely and least likely prefers. Be flexible. If the consultee expects formality and structure, keep your jacket on and keep colorful, profane language out. On the other hand, if the consultee dislikes formality, avoid at all costs giving him or

her an ABC lecture and adjust your style to be more informal and laid back.

2. In introducing the consultative process, take the consultee's side. Place yourself in his or her shoes. Experience what the consultee is experiencing.

3. Normalize the consultee's reactions to his or her problems. That is, explain that the reactions being experienced are quite common.

4. Before instituting RET and emotional problem solving, employ *emotional empathy, unconditional positive regard* (especially when you think the consultee is at fault and compromising the welfare of others) and *warmth*.

5. If the consultation is client-centered, assess consultee and others for any information concerning whether the client is a "difficult customer/ person." That is, RET takes the view that certain clients are especially difficult to live with, teach and work for because of their basic temperament plus family background. If there is evidence, communicating to the consultee (e.g., parent, teacher) that he or she has a difficult child and it is no wonder that he or she is experiencing a great deal of emotional stress and practical problems, aids the consultant-consultee bond by reducing consultee guilt.

6. Keep a problem-solving, goal-setting focus. Tell the consultee that the two of you will work together to try to change the behavior of the client or other onerous circumstances or tasks. Emotional self-management (disputing) and behavioral self-management and self-direction by the consultee are to be seen as a means to an end.

7. For the consultee to agree that there is a need to modify his or her own emotional reactions, it is sometimes useful to introduce behavioral interventions first. If between sessions, the consultee finds him or herself less than efficient in applying behavioral skills because of his or her own emotional upset, the consultee may be willing to "own" part of the problem.

8. Attempt to have the consultee label his or her reaction to clients or activating events to see if he or she can label his or her emotions. Socarticly have the consultee assess whether the emotional reaction leads to successful behavior or problem solving. (See Table 1.2).

9. Avoid "knee jerk" and "mad dog disputing." Be cautious and reflective in deciding when to dispute and which irrational beliefs to confront. There is no greater interpersonal sabotage than a RET consultant jumping in during an early part of consultation to dispute an unimportant "should" ("My son should know better than leaving the toothpaste cap off").

TABLE 1.2
Are Your Emotions and Behaviors Helping or Hurting You?

Write down an extremely stressful event that recently happened:

Indicate how you felt and how strongly you felt about it (Using your Stress Thermometer). Tick the feeling and rate its intensity.

_____ angry   _____   _____ down _____
                1   10   1   10

_____ anxiety _____
                1   10

Write down what you did (how did you behave?):

Was your behavior helpful? Did it help solve the problem in the shortterm?

_____   _____
Yes   No

Did your behavior help solve the problem in the longterm?   _____ _____
                                                              Yes   No

Did your extreme feelings help you to think clearly and solve the frustrating event or deal with the upsetting event?   _____   _____
                                                                       Yes   No

In order for you to think clearly so that you can make the best of stressful situations and solve practical problems, you have to first have emotional control. Emotional self-management is one vital key to stress management.

In order to exercise emotional self-management, you need to first become more aware of your habitual, everyday emotional stress reactions situations and to see that they are not helping you get what you want. Once you are motivated to change your emotional and behavioral reactions to situations, you are then ready to modify your thinking.

RET CONSULTATION METHODS

RET consultation methods are in many ways synonymous with those used in RET therapy and derive from RET theory. The major exception, is that RET consultation employs less confrontational methods. Also, with hostile or defensive consultees, RET consultation is less direct.

RET Hypothesis-Driven Assessment

Whether working with individuals or groups, the RET consultant's concern is in assessing the role of emotional distress as an impediment to problem solving, systemic change, or job performance. RET consultative assessment invites the consultant in an interview to discover the extent that the consultee experiences emotional disturbance or behavioral problems. For example, in working with a parent of an underachieving, unmotivated child (Level II), the RET consultant would assess the emotional disturbance the child's parent may experience. The parents may experience anxiety about the future, guilt (feeling down) about the problem, anger toward the child, and frustration about the lack of efficacy changing the child's motivation. Secondary emotional problems such as feelings of guilt about being angry are also assessed (see Walen et al., 1992, for a thorough description of RET assessment and intervention procedures).

The efficacy of RET consultation is partly revealed in its theory, which identifies the likely irrational beliefs of a consultee who experiences inappropriate emotional upset (rage, panic, depression). A RET hypothesis, which requires testing, is that an angry parent of an under-achieving child might think, "He shouldn't be so lazy and he should be more cooperative." Low frustration tolerance might derive from the parental belief that "Parenting shouldn't be so hard and I can't stand it." Guilt derives from unrealistic, self-downing beliefs "I should prevent all bad things from happening to my child and when I can't, I've failed as a parent." Parental ego anxiety concerning child problems is frequently driven by the beliefs that "I must be very successful as a parent and when my child isn't making good progress or is lacking, it's awful."

RET Interventions

RET also empowers the consultant with a set of cognitive, emotive and behavioral methods for disputing irrational consultee beliefs (also see Bernard, 1991; DiGiuseppe, 1991a, 1991b). Cognitive disputing methods involve the consultant engaging in a socratic or didactic questioning process with consultees. This process shows to them that their beliefs are not based on evidence, do not make sense, and are not useful and that they lead to self-defeating behaviors and inappropriate negative emotions. Typical disputing questions include:

1. Where is the evidence? (empirical dispute)
2. Does it make sense to think this way? (logical dispute)
3. Does this belief help you get what you want? (heuristic dispute).

RET cognitive disputational methods can be used to modify automatic thoughts and faulty interpretations of reality (faulty inferences, conclusions) (parent says: "It's all my fault that my child is failing") and underlying irrational evaluations and beliefs ("I should be more successful. It's terrible that my child has this problem."). Typical disputes to counter the irrational beliefs held by special service administrators are presented in Table 1.3.

RET consultation workshops are extremely effective methods for teaching helping parents. The first task in such workshops is to teach *emotional responsibility* (events do not directly cause feelings, it's beliefs and thinking that do). To do this we ask participants to think of an extremely stressful situation that they

TABLE 1.3
Irrational Beliefs Held by Special Service Leaders (McInerney, 1985)

Irrational Idea	Dispute	More Rational Alternative
1. Staff should not have to be encouraged to do their job—the job is reward enough.	Why? What makes them so different from the rest of the human race?	Some staff will probably require encouragement from time to time to do their job.
2. Staff should not need to be told what to do because they are "professionals."	Why? How does being a "professional" qualify one as a mind reader?	Some staff will probably work best in some circumstances with specific direction.
3. Staff should always comply with the organization's accepted procedures and policies.	Is that kind of perfection possible?	It is highly desirable for staff to follow established procedures and policy, but the world won't end if they are less than perfect at it.
4. Staff should never let their personal lives affect their "professional" performance.	What is it about being a special services person that makes one immune to personal stress?	It would be better if staff performed consistently, but at times, they will be affected by other things in their lives.
5. Staff should never question higher authority or be in conflict with it.	How can that be possible? Isn't some disagreement inevitable?	Some staff may question authority or be in conflict with it, but disagreement is not necessarily disastrous.
6. I should always be a successful leader, as well as a special services professional.	Is it possible to be successful all the time?	I would like to be as effective as possible as a leader and will work at it, despite occasional mistakes.
7. I can't stand it when staff don't agree with me or comply with my requests!	What do you mean by "can't stand"? You are standing it and certainly have in the past.	I don't like it when staff disagrees or doesn't comply, but I'll stand it until I come up with a way to do better.

encountered at work (or home). After 30 seconds, we tell the participants that we will pick one of them to come to the front of the room and talk about the problem. This instruction produces varying amounts and types of emotions in different individuals. Some participants experience anxiety about getting picked. Others experience hostility about being told what to do instead of being asked to volunteer. Some participants feel a positive degree of affect such as curiosity. During the 30 seconds, we let the tension build by walking around the room. Just when they think we are about to pick one of them, we say: "I'm not going to pick anyone. I would like each of you to reveal how you felt during the 30 seconds and how strongly you felt it using the stress thermometer" (see Fig. 1.1). The range of individual reactions produced in response to the same set of instructions provides evidence that situations do not cause feelings. If they did, everyone would have experienced the same feels during the 30 seconds. We invite discussion about what caused the different emotional reactions (negative and positive) and move the group to an awareness of beliefs and thinking as causing emotions.

Two popular cognitive methods we have developed for use in RET consultation workshops are the self-acceptance exercise and the catastrophe scale. The self-acceptance exercise helps consultees to manage with feelings of inadequacy (self-downing), to surrender self-rating, and to gain self-acceptance. We ask consultees to complete the self-acceptance circle (see Fig. 1.2). They are told: "Write in the appropriate spaces all those things you like about yourself at work and all those things you dislike about what you do at work. Then, describe your positive and negative characteristics outside work." After about 5 minutes, we ask consultees whether it makes sense to rate their entire self based on one or the other list. We ask whether it is empirically accurate or useful for them to put their

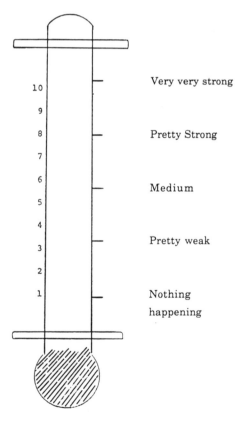

FIG. 1.1. The stress thermometer.

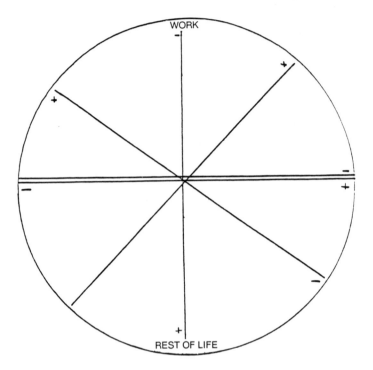

Directions: Write down your positive (+) and negative (-) characteristics

FIG. 1.2. Self-acceptance exercise.

total self down because something bad happened. For example, say: "When you think that you are totally hopeless because your child isn't doing well at school, that means you are saying you are totally hopeless *at everything*. Does this one negative aspect, the fact that your son isn't doing well at school and is unmotivated, take away your other positive characteristics?"

The catastrophe scale (Fig. 1.3) helps consultees to reduce their emotional distress by keeping negative events in perspective. According to RET, emotional distress sometimes derives from consultee's tendency to awfulize. That is, to exaggerate the bad aspects of problems out of perspective by thinking "This is horrible, awful and terrible." In using the catastrophe scale exercise, ask consultees: "Imagine the last time you were very worried, down or angry about a particular problem, person, or situation. At the time you were upset, how bad was it for you on a scale from 0 to 100. One hundred equals the worst thing that could happen, 50 equals medium bad, and 10, a bit bad? Now the scale doesn't go higher than 100!". Give consultees a few moments to consider their rating of the badness of the event that they have in mind, referring to Fig. 1.3 or drawing the catastrophe scale on the board. Then, instruct them: "Now, have a look at this scale of catastrophes. Ninety to 100 are the real catastrophes in the world. Fifty to 90 are the moderately bad things that could happen. Ten to 50 are the less bad things. Less than 10 are the very small, trivial things that can happen." Spend some time with the consultees eliciting things that could happen to them which they would evaluate in the 90–100 category. Write them in (e.g., war, rape, AIDS, permanent paralysis, death of loved ones). Next, have the consultees provide examples of events that they find less bad than catastrophes but still very bad (house burning down, getting fired, a car accident, losing a large sum of money, twisting an ankle). Enter these events on the scale. Then, ask the consultees for an example of an event that would be "a bit bad," something that they would rate as a 10 (e.g., break a plate, break a fingernail). Now, ask: "Go back to the incident, event or situation about which you became very stressed. Where

YOUR CATASTROPHE SCALE

('Putting things into Perspective')

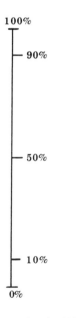

Write down something which occurs at work which leads you to feeling distressed and reduces job performance. _____.

How bad is it? _____%

FIG. 1.3. The catastrophe scale.

would you now put in on this scale compared with other events?" Usually, consultees will place the event lower down the scale of badness then before. (Guard against a consultee placing his or her bad event or situation at the very low part of the scale. This means that it wouldn't really matter). This exercise provides consultees with a clear visual reminder not to blow the negative evaluations of events out of proportion by thinking that they are awful and terrible.

Frequently in consultation workshops, and less often with individuals, the RET consultant formally teaches the consultee(s) the ABCs of RET. Consultees learn a systemic method to analyze and change their cognitive–emotional–behavioral reactions. Consultees will often receive a handout to guide their rational self-analysis. These include the "ins and outs" of disputing (see Table 1.4 "Rational Self-Management Forms") and lists of rational self-statements to aid in the disputing of irrational beliefs (see Table 1.5 "Confidence-Building, Anxiety-Reducing Rational Attitudes").

Other emotive and behavioral methods for changing irrational beliefs are used in group and individual consultation sessions. These include *forceful, evocative use of rational self-statements, rational-emotive imagery, shame-attacking, risk-taking* and *exercises* and *rational prosletyzing* (see Bernard & Wolfe, 1993 for additional concrete RET resources that can be used in consultation). In

TABLE 1.4
Rational Self-Management Form

1. Activating Event (Work Problem) (be specific):

_____

_____

2. Consequences (Negative Behaviors and Stress Emotions):
   My behavior is: _____
   My emotional stress reaction is

_____

3. Beliefs (Irrational thoughts not sensible, false):

_____

_____

_____

4. Goals (How I'd like to behave and feel):
   New Behavior: _____
   New Feeling: _____

5. Rational Beliefs (sensible and true statements):

_____

_____

_____

_____

TABLE 1.5
Confidence-Building, Anxiety-Reducing Rational Attitudes

1. "Just because things are not succeeding today does not mean I'm a "no-hoper" or that I will not succeed in the future."
2. "While it is very desirable to achieve well and be recognized by others, I do not *need* achievement or recognition to survive and be happy."
3. "Mistakes and rejections are inevitable. I will work hard at accepting myself while hating my mistakes and knockbacks."
4. "My performance at work—perfect or otherwise—does not determine my self-worth as a person."
5. "Things are rarely as bad, awful, or catastrophic as I imagine them to be."
6. "I accept who I am."
7. "There are many things about me that I like and do well."
8. "I have done many things at work successfully in the past, I will succeed in the future."
9. "I am intelligent and talented enough to learn what I have to do and how to do it in order to accomplish my goals."
10. "I am confident that everything will turn out okay given that I have my goals, know what to do, and work hard."

rational-emotive imagery consultees take control over their emotional reactions by imaginably reducing the intensity of their emotions in problematic situations. In shame-attaching exercises consultees do things they do not believe they could stand. Risk-taking exercises involve consultees deliberately do something that has a high likelihood of failure. Rational prosletyzing involves convincing others of the irrationality of their beliefs.

For consultees that are defensive, hostile, or resistant, RET consultants employ more indirect methods. In such situations it is best to use *self-disclosure, parables,* references to other persons who have experienced similar problems. These help reveal the role of emotional problems and irrational beliefs in maintaining problems of others.

RESEARCH SUPPORT FOR RET CONSULTATION

As with clinical practice, research in RET consultation has lagged well behind the frequency of its use. Two main types of RET research strategies, *correlational* and *inference,* provide a rationale for RET's use in consultation. Because these studies are discussed in detail in other chapters of this book, we do not attempt to describe them in detail here (see Hajzler & Bernard, 1991).

First, several correlational studies have demonstrated a strong relationship between poor mental health, emotional disturbance (stress), or job ineffectiveness and irrationality in several occupational groups such as teachers (Bernard, 1988), parents (Harrison, 1991), and real estate agents (Gasparis & Bernard, 1991). Bernard's (1991) study of stressed teachers is of particular interest. Bernard designed the Teacher Irrational Belief Scale to examine the relationship of teachers' irrational beliefs and job stress. In the first of two studies with large samples of teachers, Bernard (1988) found teacher irrationality to be correlated between .30 and .50 with different measures of teacher stress. In a second study, Bernard was interested to learn the relative contributions of teachers' irrationality and teachers' coping skills (e.g., time management, assertiveness, classroom management strategies) to teacher stress. Bernard found that teacher irrationality accounted for the main variance in teacher stress. Coping skills accounted for none of the variance in stress after teacher irrationality was accounted for. These findings suggest that stress management programs for teachers should focus on changing teachers' attitudes instead of the current popular focus on teaching coping skills.

Because it has been substantiated that irrationality is associated with problems experienced by consultees at all levels of RET consultation, then a case exists for the next step in RET consultative research. That is controlled outcome studies.

There are several studies reported in this book and conducted over the past decade that suggest that RET is an effective approach when used in consultation. For example, Joyce (1992) found that RET reduced stress in angry parents and improved the parents' perception of child problems. Forman (Sharp & Forman, 1988) included RET in a comprehensive cognitive–behavioral stress management program for teachers. She found that RET was a beneficial stress-reducing intervention. Woods (1987) conducted a stress management workshop using a RET format with staff from a large corporation. Measurement on all the dependent measures after the workshop showed the usefulness of a RET approach in reducing emotional distress within the work place. Duggan (1990) found positive effects of the RET-based "You Can Do It! Student Motivational Program" on improving student general attitude toward their school work. Klarrich, DiGiuseppe, and DiMattia (1987) reported that a RET-based employee assistance program resulted in significant reductions in worker absenteeism and savings to the corporation.

In conclusion, RET consultation methods are being used widely. The efficacy of RET consultation methods have not yet received widespread scientific scrutiny. However, there is continued enthusiasm by RET-oriented consultants for their use. This suggests that RET consultation strategies are bearing fruits for consultees and organizations. We are encouraged that RET consultation can be used to reach the large number of people in need of more support, guidance, and instruction.

REFERENCES

Ash, E., & Bernard, M. E. (1990). *You can do it! Motivational video program (and Leader's Guide)*. Melbourne, Vic: Seven Dimensions Producers.

Bergan, J. R., & Kratochwill, T. R. (1990). *Behavioral consultation and therapy*. New York: Pergamon Press.

Bernard, M. E. (1988). *Teacher stress and irrationality.* Paper presented at the 24th International Congress of Psychology, Sydney, Australia, August.
Bernard, M. E. (1989a). Classroom discipline and the effective self-management of teacher stress. *Primary Education, 20,* 8–11.
Bernard, M. E. (1989b, June). How to stop procrastinating. *Successful Selling,* pp. 12–16.
Bernard, M. E. (1990). *Taking the stress out of teaching.* Melbourne, Vic: Collins-Dove.
Bernard, M. E. (1991a). *Staying rational in an irrational world.* New York: Carol Publishing.
Bernard, M. E. (Ed.). (1991b). *Using rational-emotive therapy effectively: A practitioner's guide.* New York: Plenum Press.
Bernard, M. E., & Hajzler, D. (1987). *You can do it! What every student (and parent) should know about success in school and life.* Melbourne, Vic: Collins-Dove.
Bernard, M. E., & Joyce, M. R. (1984). *Rational-emotive therapy with children and adolescents: Theory, treatment strategies, preventative methods.* New York: Wiley.
Bernard, M. E., Joyce, M. R., & Rosewarne, P. (1983). Helping teachers cope with stress. In A. Ellis & M. E. Bernard (Eds.), *Rational-emotive approaches to the problems of childhood* (pp. 415–466). New York: Plenum Press.
Bernard, M. E., & Wolfe, J. (Eds.). (1993). *The RET resource book for practitioners.* New York: Institute for Rational-Emotive Therapy.
Borodin, E. S. (1979). The generalizability of the psychoanalytic concept of the working alliance. *Psychotherapy: Theory, Research and Practice, 16,* 252–260.
Brown, D., Pryzwansky, W., & Schulte, A. (1987). *Psychological consultation.* Boston: Allyn & Bacon.
Caplan, G. (1970). *The theory and practice of mental health consultation.* New York: Basic Books.
Cayer, M., DiMattia, D., & Wingrove, J. (1988). Conquering evaluation fear. *Personnel Administrator, 24,* 156–158.
Conoley, J., & Conoley, C. W. (1982). *School consultation.* New York: Pergamon.
Curtis, M. J., & Meyers, J. (1985). Best practices in consultation. In A. Thomas & J. Grimes (Eds.), *Best practices in school psychology* (pp. 79–94). Washington, DC: National Association of School Psychologists.
DiGiuseppe, R. D. (1988). Cognitive-behavior therapy with families of conduct-disordered children. In N. Epstein, S. Schebinger, & W. Dryden (Eds.), *Cognitive behavior therapy with families.* New York: Bruner/Mazel.
DiGiuseppe, R. D. (1991a). A rational-emotive model of assessment. In M. E. Bernard (Ed.), *Using rational-emotive therapy effectively: A practitioner's guide* (pp. 151–172). New York: Plenum Press.
DiGiuseppe, R. D. (1991b). Comprehensive cognitive disputing in RET. In M. E. Bernard (Ed.), *Using rational-emotive therapy effectively: A practitioner's guide* (pp. 173–196). New York: Plenum Press.
DiMattia, D. (Producer). (1987). *Mind over myth: Managing difficult situations in the work place* [Audiocassette seminar with workbook]. New York: Institute for Rational-Emotive Therapy.
DiMattia, D. (Producer). (1989). *Self-directed sales success* [Audiocassette]. New York: Institute for Rational-Emotive Therapy.
DiMattia, D. (1990). *Rational effectiveness training: Increasing personal productivity at work.* New York: Institute for Rational-Emotive Therapy.
DiMattia, D. (1991). Using RET effectively in the work place. In M. E. Bernard (Ed.), *Using rational-emotive therapy effectively: A practitioner's guide* (pp. 303–318). New York: Plenum Press.
Dryden, W. (1991). Flexibility in RET: Forming alliances and making compromises. In M. E. Bernard (Ed.), *Using rational-emotive therapy effectively: A practitioner's guide* (pp. 133–150). Plenum Press.
Duggan, E. (1990). *An evaluation of the "You Can Do It! Motivational Program."* Unpublished master's thesis, University of Melbourne, Institute of Education, Australia.

Ellis, A. (1957). *How to live with a neurotic.* North Hollywood, CA: Wilshire Books. (Original work published 1957)

Ellis, A. (1962). *Reason and emotion in psychotherapy.* Secaucus, NJ: Lyle Stuart & Citadel Press.

Ellis, A. (1972). *Executive leadership: A rational approach.* New York: Institute for Rational Living.

Ellis, A., & Bernard, M. E. (1985). *Clinical application of rational-emotive therapy.* New York: Plenum Press.

Ellis, A., & Blum, M. (1967). Rational effectiveness training: A new method of facilitating management and labor relations. *Psychological Reports, 20,* 1267–1284.

Ellis, A., & Dryden, W. (1987). *The practice of rational-emotive therapy.* New York: Springer Press.

Ellis, A., Wolfe, J., & Moseley, S. (1966). *How to raise an emotionally healthy, happy child.* North Hollywood, CA: Wilshire Books.

Forman, S. G. (1990). Rational-emotive therapy: Contributions to teacher stress management. *School Psychology Review, 19,* 315–321.

Forman, S. G., & Forman, B. D. (1980). Rational-emotive staff development. *Psychology in the Schools, 17,* 90–96.

Gasparis, A., & Bernard, M. E. (1991, October). *Work performance: The effect of irrationality, anger, anxiety, skills level, conference and motivation.* Paper presented at the 26th Annual Convention of the Australian Psychological Society.

Gutkin, T. B., & Curtis, M. J. (1990). School-based consultation: Theory, techniques and research. In T. B. Gutkin & C. R. Reynolds (Eds.), *The handbook of school psychology* (2nd ed., pp. 99–118). New York: Wiley.

Hajzler, D., & Bernard, M. E. (1991). A review of rational-emotive outcome studies. *School Psychology Quarterly, 6,* 27–49.

Harrison, W. (1991). *An examination of the correlates of stress in parents.* Manuscript submitted for review.

Hauck, P. (1967). *The rational management of children.* New York: Libra.

Huber, C. H., & Baruth, L. G. (1989). *Rational-emotive family therapy.* New York: Springer Press.

Joyce, M. R. (1990). Rational-emotive parent consultation. *School Psychology Review, 19,* 308–314.

Joyce, M. R. (1992, March). *The effects of a rational-emotive parent education program.* Paper presented at the Annual Conference of the National Association of School Psychologists, Nashville, TN.

Klarrich, S., DiGiuseppe, R., & DiMattia, D. (1987). The cost effectiveness of an employee assistance program using rational-emotive therapy. *Professional Psychology, 18*(2), 140–144.

Knaus, W. (1974). *Rational-emotive education: A manual for elementary school teachers.* New York: Institute for Rational Living.

Kratochwill, T. R., Elliott, S. N., & Rotto, P. C. (1990). Best practices in behavioral consultation. In A. Thomas & J. Grimes (Eds.), *Best practices in school psychology* (Vol. 2, pp. 68–94). Washington, DC: National Association of School Psychologists.

McInerney, J. (1985). Authority management. In C. A. Maher (Ed.), *Professional self-management: Techniques for special service providers* (pp. 86–114). Baltimore, MD. Brooks.

Meyers, J., Parsons, R. D., & Martin, R. (1979). *Mental health consultation in schools.* San Francisco: Jossey-Bass.

Sharp, J. J., & Forman, S. G. (1988). A comparison of two approaches of anxiety management for teachers. *Behavior Therapy, 16,* 370–383.

Vernon, A. (1989a). *Thinking, feeling, behaving: An emotional education curriculum for children.* Champaign, IL: Research Press.

Vernon, A. (1989b). *Thinking, feeling, behaving: An emotional education curriculum for adolescents.* Campaign, IL: Research Press.

Vernon, A. (1990). Rational-emotive education in school consultation. *School Psychology Review, 19*, 322–327.

Walen, S., DiGiuseppe, R., & Wessler, R. (1980). *The practitioner's guide to rational-emotive therapy*. New York: Oxford University Press.

Walen, S., DiGiuseppe, R., & Dryden, W. (1992). *The practitioner's guide to rational-emotive therapy* (2nd ed.). New York: Oxford University Press.

Woods, P. J. (1987). Reductions in type A behavior, anxiety, anger and physical illness as related to changes in irrational beliefs: Results of a demonstration project in industry. *Journal of Rational-Emotive Therapy, 5*, 213–237.

Woulff, N. (1983). Involving the family in the treatment of the child: A model for rational-emotive therapists. In A. Ellis & M. E. Bernard (1983), *Rational-emotive approaches to the problems of childhood* (pp. 367–386). New York: Plenum Press.

Zins, J. E., & Ponti, C. R. (1990). Best practices in school-based consultation. In A. Thomas & J. Grimes (Eds.), *Best practices in school psychology* (Vol. 2, pp. 673–694). Washington, DC: National Association of School Psychologists.

2

Teaching Parents and Teachers RET Through Direct Service to Client

Virginia Waters
Clinical Psychologist, Private Practice

A rational-emotive therapist maintains a dual focus when working with child clients. Not only is the therapist challenged with the goal of teaching the child cognitive, emotional, and practical problem-solving skills, but also with the goal of instructing the significant adults in the child's life with these same skills. The purpose of aiming the rational-emotive therapy (RET) message at the two targets is to maximize the effectiveness of the attitudinal and/or behavioral change providing a readily available source of ongoing reinforcement within the child's natural environment. Therapists and counselors agree that one of the most challenging aspects of working with clients is stimulating them to apply what they have learned in therapy to solving their own problems beyond the therapeutic setting. We have all heard adult as well as child and adolescent clients state that although they understand and agree with the concepts of RET, they find it very difficult to apply the principles in the moment of upset. Consequently, one can see the advantage to a child client of having adults in the real world who can support, encourage, and reinforce the changes they are struggling to make.

All children develop and grow within several different contexts. It is the relationship between the child and these contexts that determines whether the child's growth and interactions will be healthy or disturbed. In order to lay the groundwork for this chapter, I stress the importance of viewing the child as part of a matrix of contexts and outline the way in which a child's development is affected by the system within which he or she develops. The four primary contexts that influence a child's development are personal, familial, social, and global.

The personal context consists of all facets of a child's internal experience and includes physical, cognitive, emotional, temperamental, and behavioral components. These components overlap and interact combining to determine how this particular child is functioning at any given point in development. Some of these factors are primarily determined at conception, such as temperament and eye color, and others are predominantly learned, such as beliefs and behaviors.

Superimposed over the personal context is the familial context that includes all family members both nuclear and extended along with each of their personal contexts. The interaction of the child with each of these familial stimulants further affects and determines the process of development and the quality of functioning. The social context, which includes friends, teachers, school personnel, the community at large, and all of their personal and familial contexts provides an expanding framework. Finally, we add the impact of the child's global context that includes all additional factors such as mass media, ecology, culture, and socioeconomic factors. At any given moment, a child is busy processing input from these four contexts and as a result responds in terms of thoughts, feelings, and behaviors based on this input.

Consequently, disturbance in the child's functioning is usually readily identifiable as cognitive, emotional, or behavioral and can be traced to disharmony or dissonance between the child and any one of the four contexts. A disturbance between a child and his or her personal context can manifest itself in the form of inappropriate feelings. Inappropriate in this instance is used to indicate an emotional reaction that is hurtful, unproductive, and more intense than the situation warrants. This emotional disturbance is usually generated by irrational, unrealistic beliefs, attitudes, and images and results in self- and goal-defeating behaviors. An example of this level of disturbance might be a boy who feels angry much of the time because he thinks his parents, friends, and teachers treat him unfairly. His aggressiveness, expressed verbally, in abusive language and physical attacks is counterproductive to his goal of being liked and accepted. Another example might be the girl who anxiously worries about her school performance, and constantly catastrophizes that she will fail every test, resulting in compulsive and perfectionistic study habits that leave no time for the fun and enjoyment she dearly misses.

Disturbance between the child and his or her familial context occurs when the child's beliefs, feelings, or behaviors are dissonant with those of the family. For example, a child having a temper tantrum because he cannot have just one more cookie might secondarily create a disturbance because his parents believe he should never lose control and that his behavior is awful, terrible, and horrible, thus creating feelings of anger within them. The result then is an interacting problem of the child's primary emotional overreaction that subsequently triggers the parents secondary reaction of anger about their child's anger. One can see that a practitioner working only with the child to reduce angry feelings and reactions will have limited success, unless the parents are also taught how to modify their angry responses.

The social context impacts on the child in a similar manner as that of the familial but with a broader range for it extends to virtually everyone with whom the child comes into contact. So that each person who responds to the child's cognitions, feelings, and behavior influences them in varying degrees. These reactions can be secondary, such as the parent who gets angry at his or her child's temper tantrum. They can even be tertiary, such as the teacher who gets angry at the parent for getting angry at the angry child. It is not necessary to further discuss the global context because that is not the direct purpose of this chapter, but to acknowledge its importance as part of the interacting framework.

The primary goal of RET is to change the attitudes and belief systems responsible for disfunctional emotional and behavioral responses. In therapeutic work with children, the task expands to include changing the attitudes and beliefs of those that impact on the child as well as those of the child. Because the child is evolving within a familial and social framework, it becomes imperative to work with the entire system in order to achieve the therapeutic goals of the child. Consequently, this chapter focuses on how the therapist teaches RET concepts and skills to those who are in the child client's familial and social context while doing therapy with the child. The chapter provides descriptions and explanations of teaching strategies aimed at expanding therapeutic interventions to include parents and teachers. These interventions include both didactic and experiential approaches and are simultaneously focused to have an impact on both the child client and the adult observer.

The multidimensional aspect of RET makes it truly challenging in working with children. The therapist has the option to work with parents and teachers as well as just with the child, thus maximizing the success of therapeutic outcome. There are many fine sources currently available that expound on the clinical applications of RET with children. However, this chapter primarily focuses on how the therapist teaches RET concepts and skills to those who are in the child patient's familial and social contexts.

It provides descriptions and explanations of teaching strategies aimed at expanding therapeutic interventions to include parents and teachers. These interventions include both didactic and experiential approaches and are simultaneously focused to have an impact on both the child client and the adult observer. Although RET with children is traditionally conceptualized as a three-stage process—assessment, treatment, and evaluation—this chapter emphasizes the treatment stage of the process. There are many good resources already currently available that elaborate on assessment and evaluation. This chapter emphasizes the treatment stage of the process in terms of teaching theory and application of RET strategies to parents and teachers while counseling child clients.

THERAPEUTIC TEACHING STRATEGIES
WITHIN THE EDUCATIONAL MODEL

Because RET employs an educational model of disturbance, as opposed to a medical model, it lends itself well to incorporating educational teaching strategies into the therapeutic process. RET practitioners support the idea that most disturbance is the result of maladaptive belief systems functioning in the absence of effective problem-solving strategies. So that the goal of RET is not to find a "cure" as would advocate the adherents of the medical model, but to instruct clients in how to restructure their belief systems while also teaching alternative emotional and practical problem-solving techniques. The process is practical, informative, and active, and welcomes the participation of all who are interested in the growth and development of the child. It is not necessary or even desirable to conduct RET with children behind closed doors, for the more significant people in the child's life who know the principles of RET, the better. There are of course exceptions such as situations in which the child has been abused, or in which the parents are not receptive or are unavailable. However, for the most part, participation of parents or teachers in the therapeutic process enhances and maximizes the benefits for the child.

The RET therapist and client are both expected to be fully active participants in the process. The degree of participation of the adult observer/learner can vary from being totally passive and nonparticipatory to being fully active in the sessions. The degree and type of participation depends on the following variables: (a) the relationship between the child client and the adult; (b) the nature of the problem; (c) the adult's learning style; and (d) the stage of the therapeutic process. The optimal level of participation will likely emerge and be identifiable by the therapist during the course of treatment. The therapist had best keep in mind that the primary goal in these sessions is the treatment of the child and the secondary goal is the instruction of the parent or teacher, or that any dynamic that enhances the child's *skill* acquisition is considered desirable.

Viewing RET as a teaching/learning process opens many possibilities for therapeutic intervention. I describe some of the strategies that can be effectively used to teach RET to child clients and adults, while also giving specific examples of how each strategy can be adapted for use in sessions where the secondary goal is teaching parent and teacher observers.

Teaching Strategies

Modeling

Modeling is a primary learning strategy that involves a learner observing a model exhibiting either a verbal or nonverbal behavior and subsequently assimilating that behavior. Learning can occur through a single exposure or through repeated exposures by the model and practiced responses by the learner. Learning through modeling can either be intentional or unintentional on the learner's part. For example, the young child who learns to swear in the face of frustration by watching his or her parents react this way did not set out intentionally to learn this process. Whereas, a child learning to pitch a softball may intentionally model him or herself on the pitching of a prize-winning player and thereby learn a prize-winning pitching strategy. The rational-emotive therapist is in a prime position to powerfully demonstrate rational emotive theory and techniques through modeling them to both child clients and their parents and teachers. By his or her words and actions, the therapist can reinforce the teaching of RET principles while showing the way these principles translate into behavior. In this way, the rational-emotive practitioner is serving as a model to both the child client and the adult observer. Secondarily, the therapist, in working with the child, can model for the parent a way of relating to the child that is accepting, nonjudgmental, and noncatastrophic.

Modeling lends itself to the demonstration of several key corollaries of RET. These are discussed here.

Acceptance Versus Rating and Judging.   By actively striving to accept the child client unconditionally, the therapist has a dual impact. The message communicated to the child is that although I may not like what you do or say, I can accept you as you are without rating or judging you, and I would encourage you to accept yourself as well. The message that is communicated to the parent is that although you may not like or approve of what your child is doing, I encourage you to accept your child totally while evaluating the individual behavior, and I encourage you to treat yourself with the same respect. Acceptance can be demonstrated by the therapist in both verbal and nonverbal ways. Verbally the therapist can demonstrate acceptance by using nonjudgmental words and phrases and by avoiding using the verb "to be" in reference to the child. For example, if the therapist says to a child "you are (fill in the blank)," then the child is being equated and judged accordingly. A child who is told "you are silly, stupid, bad, worthless, perfect, wrong, etc." is in essence being judged as a totality based on a single attribute or behavior. Consequently, what is being modeled and taught to the child is that if you behave well then you *are* a good person and if you behave badly then you *are* a bad person. Not only is this an inaccurate statement, but it is a damaging one as well. Each individual is a complex compilation of past, present, and future attributes, emotions, cognitions, and behaviors. The totality, due to complexity and flux, cannot be rated, whereas the individual components can be rated in terms of their effectiveness and productiveness. Rating an individual is damaging because the result is often an unproductive feeling such as depression, anxiety, or guilt, and may also result in unproductive behaviors and coping patterns such as procrastination, withdrawal, and violence. By focusing on sorting out and evaluating the individual components of a client, a therapist can convey acceptance of the individual within the context of working on the aspects of his or her beliefs and behaviors that are dysfunctional. Nonverbally, acceptance can be conveyed through tone and volume of voice, facial expression, eye contact, and body language.

Preferring Versus Demanding.   A rational-emotive therapist who models preferring as opposed to demanding indicates to the child and to the observing adult that there are certain behaviors, responses, and reactions that are desirable and goal enhancing and that it is to the benefit of the child to foster and develop these. However, there are no shoulds, oughts, or have tos, and consequently, no demands that must be met. By avoiding the use of demanding words, the therapist reinforces the idea that each individual has a choice of how to behave, feel, and think, and counters the idea that there exists an absolute standard to which all must adhere. For example, if a therapist counseling a child who has a problem constructively expressing anger, says to that child "you must stop hitting your little brother when you are angry and you should never curse at your parents," that therapist is making a demand of the child. This is also inadvertently teaching the child to be demanding of him or herself and also teaching the parent, who is observing the transaction, to be demanding of the child as well as of themselves. The ultimate emotional consequence of an absolutistic demand is unproductive anger and rebellion, for when demands are not met with compliance the result is anger. In addition, most people respond to demands, whether self-imposed or other-imposed, with oppositional behavior or rebellion. So if a teacher says to Andrew, "you *must* sit down and do your work right now," Andrew is as likely as not to respond with "Make me!" However, if the therapist points out to the child that his or her method of expressing anger is unhelpful to him or her and brings negative consequences, the therapist is more likely to engage the child's compliance in searching for ways of reducing the anger and expressing it in a helpful manner. Consequently, the observing parent or teacher is being taught that although it is preferable for this child to behave differently, there is no reason why the child should. Pointing out the preferable alternative to the child, giving a clear explanation of the consequences of noncompliance, and then asking the child to choose, is more likely to result in the preferred outcome.

Concern Versus Catastrophizing.   The therapist, who through words and actions conveys concern, can alleviate anxiety within the child and the parents. Parents are often filled with anxiety over their troubled child and project images of doom and gloom about the future. By focusing the session on problem solving in the present and by avoiding the use of such words as awful, horrible, and terrible in reference to the child and the child's problem, the therapist can reduce unproductive anxiety while emphasizing the importance of teaching the child an effective strategy for dealing with both practical and emotional problems. Conversely, therapists who continue to stress to the child, parents, and teachers, the seriousness and gravity of the child's problem, will generate and accelerate anxiety production, which will subsequently interfere with the readiness of all concerned to acquire problem-solving tools and strategies. Envision the effect on an anorexic client and his or her family of a therapist who constantly reiterates how life threatening this disorder is and how changes *must* be made immediately in order to avert irreversible damage in the future. The effect of such statements is to generate so much anxiety that future progress may be blocked until the anxiety can be reduced. It is difficult, if not impossible, to learn new material and to make significant changes while panicking. Parents can greatly benefit from concern expressed by the therapist. Concern acknowledges that there is a problem without catastrophizing about it or judging it. Concern paves the way for the intervention to follow by putting the problem in a therapeutic context and then prompting all concerned to adopt a problem-solving attitude in terms of its resolution. In short, modeling concern teaches both parents and children an effective approach to changing unproductive behavior, thoughts, and feelings, enabling them to avoid the creation of secondary anxiety that inhibits progress.

Tolerance Versus Intolerance.   In essence, modeling tolerance is giving the verbal and nonverbal message that although I may not like something, I can stand it and accept that it exists. A message of intolerance conveys the idea that not only do I not like this, I can't stand that it exists, and because it exists I must feel angry, depressed, and/or anxious. One of the central tasks of both parenting and teaching involves encouraging children to build greater tolerance to people and events in life that displease them. Tolerance, or the ability to accept unpleasant, obnoxious, or frustrating events without creating emotional upset, is an essential ingredient to success in career and relationships and is a prerequisite to ultimate mastery over tasks of daily living. However, tolerance is often inadequately taught or modeled by parents and teachers for many adults have not acquired this trait themselves. So a father preaching to his son that he should be more tolerant of his teacher's idiosyncrasies, while complaining that he can't stand the way his boss addresses him, is giving mixed messages. The therapist can strive to clearly model an attitude of tolerance by using language that communicates acceptance, by reinforcing and acknowledging tolerance when it is exemplified in the therapeutic session and by striving to demonstrate tolerance in his or her acceptance of his or her clients and their parents and teachers. Although it may be difficult for therapists to convey tolerance for clients who behave in obnoxious ways, it is important to consistently strive to model tolerance. For instance, a therapist may not like that a parent hits his or her child or that the child is abusive to his or her siblings, but to become intolerant of these people and their behaviors is to perpetuate the problem and thus interfere with appropriate intervention.

It's Okay to be Fallible Versus You Must be Perfect.   This last point actually includes all the preceeding ones and serves to summarize the importance of the therapist as model. By accepting his or her own fallibility, the therapist is giving the message that acceptance of oneself and of others should not be contingent upon perfection because perfection is unattainable. The important message here is I can accept you unconditionally and I suggest you accept yourself and others in the same manner. If therapists can communicate the important idea that it is okay to make mistakes and that mistakes can be a springboard to further learning, then parents may become more tolerant of themselves and of their children. Parents often think that they have to be perfect to win their children's love and respect and consequently model this belief for their children. The therapist can offer an alternative belief and demonstrate how acceptance of one's fallibility actually enhances one's productivity by reducing the unproductive feelings that inhibit performance and pleasure.

Didactic

Because RET follows an educational model, it often employs direct didactic teaching methods, especially in teaching the basic tools and strategies of problem analysis and problem solving. The RET therapist whose focus is on the parent and/or teacher of the child client as well as on the child, can choose to employ teaching strategies that are indirectly didactic, directly didactic, or both. An indirect didactic approach involves teaching the parent indirectly while directly working with the child. In observing a therapy session where the focus is on teaching the child RET problem-solving skills, the attentive observer can also learn these same skills. In the direct didactic approach, the therapist is more apt to directly teach to the parent or teacher. This might occur during a session with the child or in a separate session. Teaching the parent or teacher separately might be advisable when the instructional level of the child is either below or above that of the parent, or if the parent is to be included in the process of teaching the child. There are many excellent references to be found that expound upon the didactic presentation of RET materials (Bernard & Joyce, 1984; DiGiuseppe, 1981; Ellis, 1972, 1975; Ellis & Bernard, 1983; Knaus, 1974, 1977; Vernon, 1980; Waters, 1980, 1982).

Role-Play

Role-play is an excellent method of teaching concepts, reinforcing ideas, and practicing newly acquired skills. Therapists have a wide variety of choices of how to incorporate role-play into the instructional structure of the therapy session. These strategies can either involve the parent and or teacher directly as participants in the role-play or indirectly as observers. A big advantage of using role-play with children is that it enables them to learn by doing and as educational research indicates, the more modalities employed the greater the impact of any learned experience. Also, children seem to enjoy being actively involved in the therapeutic process, and as active participants, seem to be more attentive to the process. My experience indicates this is also true for their parents and teachers. There are five primary ways in which role-play can be used in sessions.

Situational Replay.   This technique involves restaging a particular event or situation that was problematic. If this event occurred in the parent or teacher's presence their input can be a valuable part of the process. If there is a discrepancy as to what really happened, the event can be restaged several times to reflect the perceptions of all those present. Subsequently, it can be analyzed in terms of who created what feelings by thinking what thoughts and what were the resulting behaviors. Next, there can be a discussion of what would have been a preferable way of handling that same situation to achieve a more desirable outcome in terms of behavior, feelings, and beliefs (Bedford, 1974). This revised scenario can then be restaged and its effectiveness evaluated. This technique is maximally effective when everyone involved participates and it can provide both the child and the adult observers with a strategy they can then practice on an ongoing basis outside of the therapeutic setting.

Role Reversal.   Role reversal enables the participants to change their perspective on a situation by changing their role. Not only does this provide the participant with the opportunity to view the situation from another's perspective, but it also enables the participant to see him or herself being portrayed as another viewed him or her. So that the scene can be replayed with the parent and child exchanging roles, with both parents exchanging roles with one another, with the therapist playing any of the roles or any combination that would seem effective. When using reverse role-play it is important to include a discussion of feelings, thoughts, and insights gained from playing a different role, and to end with an improved scene in which each character plays themselves as they would like to have played the scene for an improved outcome.

Behavioral Rehearsal.   This technique involves practicing thinking, feeling, and behaving differently in the therapeutic session, so that these changes might be generalized more easily to the world at large. By observing the therapist working with a child, the parent or teacher can then also learn how to reinforce these desirable changes when they occur beyond the therapy session. For example, the child who has test anxiety might rehearse saying calming things to him or herself both prior to the test and during the test to reduce anxiety. The child who has a problem with being physically aggressive when angry might practice counting to 10 when angry, turning away from the person and/or situation that is upsetting him or her, and saying things to him or herself to defuse the anger. The response that the child rehearses is usually quite specific and includes both verbal and nonverbal behavioral elements, thoughts, and feelings. In observing this sequence, the parent or teacher can also learn to reinforce the child for rehearsing at home, reinforce the child when the behavior rehearsed occurs in a natural situation, and support the child by choosing to rehearse an alternative behavioral response that they themselves would like to acquire.

Storytelling.   Storytelling, whether acted out, or just verbalized, serves to engage the child's attentions while focusing on attitude change and skill acquisition. The child can be prompted to tell a story about him or herself about something specific, or about whatever he or she chooses. If the child is reluctant or refuses to begin, the therapist can then make up a story that reflects an area of focus for the child, such as anger, fear, interpersonal difficulty, and so on. Because storytelling is a natural form of expression for children, it often frees them to participate more fully in the therapeutic process. The stories that result can then be acted out within the therapy session. The therapist may also wish to elaborate on the story to further teach or illustrate a therapeutic lesson. For instance, I was once working with a 7-year-old girl who often felt powerless, out of control, and consequently anxious in dealing with all aspects of her life. Early in therapy she proceeded to tell a story about a little dog who went for a walk in the deep, dark woods and got hopelessly lost. She was as unable to finish that story as she was to successfully cope with real-life situations. We explored together what the little dog might have been thinking and feeling. Then we brainstormed helpful self-talk for the dog to say in order to feel calmer, and next we generated as many possible solutions as we could think of to the dog's problem. Finally, the girl eagerly acted out her story and transformed herself from the anxiously lost dog to the calm, resourceful dog who found her way home. This process helped this child internalize these coping skills and eventually generalize them to her life situation. As with the previously described role-play techniques, when used in this manner, storytelling can provide the parent or teacher with an alternative method of communicating and relating to the child. The parent and child can take turns telling stories or can build a story together that they can both act out.

Role-Play With Materials.   Role-play can also employ puppets, toys, art supplies, stuffed animals, and flannel or chalkboard. Virtually any materials that capture the child's interest and imagination can offer the opportunity for therapeutic learning to child clients and adult participants. The use of these materials can also give the therapist the opportunity to observe parent–child interaction patterns and to model appropriate interventions.

Imagery

The use of imagery as a teaching strategy expands the therapeutic arena beyond the boundaries of the office. Imagery enables children to practice better coping skills within the security of the therapeutic office and promotes the generalization of these skills to other settings. The parent or teacher observing the use of imagery can further learn how to work with a particular child to resolve an issue or problem. The therapist may use imagery to elicit the child's beliefs that he or she may be unable to verbalize, to practice cognitive changes, or to generalize changes to other situations.

Young children are often unaware of the cognitions that lead to emotional responses. When asked, "What were you thinking when you had that feeling?" children often respond, "I don't know" or "Nothing." However, when asked what they were seeing or picturing in their minds, they are better able to respond. A 5-year-old boy was brought for counseling because he was extremely frightened whenever his parents left him with a babysitter. He could not tell what thoughts led to the fear, but he was able to say that when he was scared he got a picture in his mind of a house on fire and firemen struggling to put out the blaze. His parents then remembered that several years ago a neighbor's house had caught fire while this child was at home with the sitter. Having made this connection we were then able to proceed to decrease the anxiety by changing the image, as well as by giving him rational, coping statements to say to himself. The parents participated in helping to generate the calming image that served as an alternative to the scarey image and in generating the coping statements.

A third-grade child reported to her teacher that she became so nervous while taking tests that her mind blanked out. In a meeting with both the student and the teacher the girl could not identify any specific self-talk that might have created her anxiety. I used guided imagery in which I first relaxed her and then had her imagine she was in class about to take a very hard test. I asked her what she was thinking and she was able to report several images and phrases. She pictured her paper with a big "0" at the top and her teacher looking disappointed. She also pictured her father looking angry and heard herself saying, "What's the use, I'll fail anyway." With this information, we were able to design a treatment plan that employed both imagery, disputing, role-play, and rational self-talk.

Imagery is also an effective and efficient tool for practicing and rehearsing cognitive and behavioral changes that the child is striving to make. It is often difficult in the moment of a high intensity emotional response for adults as well as children to modify a deeply ingrained response pattern. It is more productive for these alternative responses to be constructed and practiced in a calm, non-threatening environment in which the individual can think clearly. Imagery provides an ideal method of rehearsing these desired changes. The child is more likely to meet with success in changing his or her response style if these changes first occur in an imaged scenario. A sense of success, competency, and hence control can then be developed that may be generalized more easily to the real situation. It is unrealistic to say to a child "All you have to do to overcome social anxiety is think calm thoughts and smile," if the child has never done this in the past. Any teacher will tell you that the key to skill acquisition is a basic understanding of the skill to be learned and then practice, practice, practice. The same holds true for cognitive skills and behavioral patterns being taught within the therapeutic setting.

Imagery practice is also aimed at helping parents and teachers learn their newly acquired cognitive skills and encouraging them to reinforce the practice that the child client will be doing. An example of this can be seen in a 6-year-old first-grade boy who displayed high levels of anxiety and avoidant school behavior. The child said he knew he had to go to school but felt so uncomfortable whenever he got close to the school that he wanted to run away. This reaction began to spread and generalize to times when he thought about school. Consequently, he began to develop many stress-related somatic complaints such as stomachaches, headaches, and abdominal pains. He was actually using imagery very effectively to rehearse feeling anxious. The boy's father, who took him to school in the morning, also began to feel anxious. At the first sign of this child's rising anxiety level the father would start to catastrophize by imaging that the child would get to school and become hysterical and that he would not be able to deal with it. Both father and son were able to use imagery practice to reverse the cycle of negative imagery and began to rehearse a more adaptive response pattern. Both were able to verbalize that they disliked feeling the way they did each morning and both were quite motivated to change. Together we created an alternative scenario for each that involved different reactions. We then had them practice both independently and cooperatively before they attempted to generalize the new patterns to the real situation. They worked well together as a team reinforcing and supporting one another as they rehearsed. It seemed to help both to realize that they had the same problem and they were able to avoid generating secondary guilt and self-downing over having such a problem. The imagery practice continued even as the anxiety levels began to drop to insure that the gains would be maintained. We then practiced generalizing their new calm response to hypothesized situations that might occur in the future so both could see that this method was applicable in a variety of situations.

Reinforcement Theory

An understanding of reinforcement theory is crucial in effecting and facilitating change. The formulation of the corollaries of reinforcement is one of the most significant advances in learning theory in the past 100 years. Very simply, the essence of the theory is that behavior and responses that get attended to, get repeated and those that get ignored get extinguished. Most parents and teachers have heard this and know it to be true, however, continue to respond to undesirable behaviors thereby inadvertently reinforcing them. It is also helpful for children to understand the basics of reinforcement both in terms of their own growth, development, and mastery and in terms of better understanding their relationships with others. So by teaching children cause-and-effect relationships and the impact that consequences have on behavior, the therapist can indirectly teach the observing parent and teacher these same principles. I also work directly with parents and teachers on child management skills by giving them a copy of

Child Management: A Program for Parents and Teachers, which is a programmed text that simply and effectively teaches reinforcement theory as applied to child management.

The following example illustrates the effectiveness of teaching reinforcement theory to children. An 11-year-old girl whom I was seeing in therapy was having problems keeping her 14-year-old sister from coming into her room and taking her things. Neither she nor her mother had been successful in stopping this behavior. After exploring possible reinforcers, the girl mentioned that she did her sister's laundry each week regardless of her behavior. We decided that in this case it would be effective for my client to inform her sister that from now on she would only do her sister's laundry on Saturday if she had stayed out of her room all week. Although the sister protested, this method was successful in achieving the desired goal and the client reported that her sister still went into other family member's rooms but avoided her room. The mother reinforced and supported her daughter in this plan and seeing how successful it was instituted other behavior management programs at home.

Feedback

Both parents and children in therapy benefit from receiving feedback as to how they are progressing toward their goals. It is often very difficult for an individual to objectively assess their progress, in fact they often tend to discourage themselves by thinking they are not making enough progress. Just as a teacher might write comments on a student's paper or offer feedback in the form of a report card, so a therapist can guide a client's progress by providing objective feedback. This is also useful to parents and teachers of child clients who themselves can benefit from feedback as to how well they and the child are doing in meeting their therapeutic goals.

I often find myself reorienting a parent or teacher who complains that a child isn't perfect yet and who misses the tremendous strides the child has made. For instance, the teacher of the previously mentioned boy who was anxious about attending school, complained that he was distractable in group lessons. She was overlooking that for the past 2 weeks this child had no problem entering the classroom, whereas for the prior 2 months he cried each morning. When given feedback as to how well this boy was doing in other areas, she began to reinforce him more for what he was accomplishing and to deemphasize the importance of what he had not yet accomplished. I gave her feedback as to what a terrific job she was doing in the classroom to enable this child to function better.

By observing the therapist give the child feedback, parents and teachers can learn how to more effectively give feedback as well. The beginning of each session is a good time for therapists to review the week and the homework assignment and to give feedback on both. This is also a good time to elicit parent feedback as to how the child is doing and also child feedback as to how the parent is doing. It is helpful if the therapist can first respond to the child in terms of what was good about the past week and then summarize and focus on points that could use some work. Next, in addressing the parents and teachers the therapist can inquire as to what was good about the week and what progress was noted. This encourages parents and teachers to look for progress and to acknowledge it in the child's presence. Likewise, the child may also be asked what progress the parents and teacher have made in responding to him or her. Both children and parents can then give opinions on what areas still require further work. Children can be direct and astute when asked to express their opinions on their parents' behavior. One 8-year-old recently told his parents that he thinks they fight too much and had better work on getting along and solving their differences more constructively like he and his brother were doing.

Homework

Homework is an integral part of any program of skill acquisition. It is essential to assimilate and reinforce learning of new skills and to generalize them to the outside world. Homework can involve information gathering, record keeping, practicing, writing, and reading. Assignments can involve the child alone, the parent or teacher alone, or both working cooperatively. The more imaginative and interesting the assignments the better, for clients will not be motivated to complete homework that is boring and onerous.

Information Gathering.   Information gathering is a good way to actively involve clients in the therapeutic process while sensitizing them to behavioral, cognitive, and emotional stimuli. It is also a good way to encourage an objective, nonjudgmental perspective, for you are requesting that those involved merely gather data, not judge or evaluate it. This sort of assignment might initially involve the child or parent observing and recording behaviors. For example, the child who feels overlooked by the teacher in the classroom might record the number of times the teacher calls on him or her and how many times other children are called on. Parents and children might be given the assignment of recording the number of compliments each receives from the other or the number of times any two family members get into a fight. The information gathered can then provide the basis for reality testing and perceptual checks so that child and parents can determine if the situation is as bad or good as they perceive it to be. This is the first step in RET problem solving.

Information as to frequency of certain self-statements or other cognitions can also be helpful in emphasizing the desirability of cognitive change. One child who was given the assignment of recording negative self-statements in one column and positive self-statements in another commented, "No wonder I'm so depressed all the time, look at how I talk to myself!" A child, with low frustration tolerance, and his teacher, who tended to be demanding of him, were given the following assignment: The boy was asked to record the cognitions that led to and increased frustration and his teacher was asked to record her "should's." When they both surveyed the results it was easy to identify the areas requiring cognitive change.

Frequency and intensity of emotional response can also be recorded and can be used as a baseline if done early in therapy. One girl and her mother were given the assignment of recording the incidence and frequency of the child's angry outbursts. They returned the following week to report they couldn't do the assignment because the child had not had any displays of anger all week. Sometimes the mere process of weekly recording dramatically alters a response. Once the data is gathered than all involved have a clearer idea of what is really happening in terms of the problematic behavior or response. If the child and parent or teacher can work together as cooperating researchers then the stage is set to extend the cooperative effort to include behavioral or cognitive change.

Practice. Practice is an integral part of skill acquisition and is essential to cognitive and behavioral change. Children and their parents or teachers can practice RET skills together for maximum benefit to both. Imagery, problem analysis, role-play, and practical problem solving can all be improved if practiced outside the therapeutic setting. Practice can also include written assignments that might involve using the "ABC" method of problem analysis, disputing an unproductive belief, writing an essay to convince someone that should's lead to upset, or writing a story to illustrate how people upset themselves and how they can calm themselves.

Bibliotherapy. Homework assignments might also include the suggestion of relevant reading materials. Books, pamphlets, and articles on a variety of topics are available for every level from early childhood on up to the adult level. Children and their parents together can read the materials designed for children, whereas parents and teachers can be given supplementary suggested readings suitable for adults. A list of books for children and for parents or teachers appears in the Bibliography at the end of this chapter.

Reteaching

Once a child has learned the basic problem-solving skills, having him or her reteach them to his or her parents or teachers can expedite the assimilation of these skills. One girl who had just learned the anatomy of anger, explained to her angry mother that she was making herself angry by the demands she was making. Having the child reteach the concepts learned in therapy is also a way of evaluating how well the child actually understands what has been taught. In addition, if the parents and teachers are involved in the learning process along with the child they are much more likely to support therapeutic change because they feel a part of the process.

Therapeutic Examples.   The following four case studies illustrate how the previously mentioned strategies can be integrated into a treatment plan that focuses on both the child client and the involved parent or teacher. A cross section of problems and techniques was selected to demonstrate a variety of approaches.

1. *Anxious Child–Anxious Parent:* Molly, a 10-year-old fifth grader, was brought into counseling by her mother who described her as tense, anxious, and clinging. At the first session I met with both Molly and her mother together. Molly's mother did most of the talking with Molly only answering questions that were directed toward her and initiating no spontaneous conversation. Molly's mother described her as constantly fearful and worried. This anxiety had been getting progressively worse over the years and was now interfering with the rest of the family, which was why therapy was being initiated at this time. Molly agreed that she was worried and nervous much of the time, but didn't know why and indicated she was interested in overcoming this problem. The family consisted of Molly, two older brothers, 12 and 15 years old and Molly's father and mother. The initial therapeutic goals agreed upon by Molly are outlined here:

- To teach Molly about anxiety so she can understand where it comes from.
- To identify how Molly creates anxiety and in what circumstances and under what conditions she is most likely to create it.
- To teach Molly how to overcome anxiety by changing her thoughts and behaviors.
- To teach Molly how to prevent herself from creating anxiety in the future.

My initial treatment strategy was to meet with both Molly and her mother at the beginning of each session and then to work with Molly alone for the remainder of the session. However, Molly was so quiet and unresponsive I began to let her mother remain in the sessions to see if this would add or detract from our goals. As it turned out, Molly's mother was a most valuable adjunct to therapy. She revealed to Molly and me that she was also highly anxious and shared some of the same worries and fears as Molly. They were able to see that Molly had learned her pattern of worrying from her mother, who had learned the same pattern from her mother. Consequently, we all agreed that although Molly was the official client, both Molly and her mother would benefit from learning anxiety management techniques and could actually reinforce each other in their applications. By identifying her own anxious thought patterns, Molly's mother helped her to recognize how she created her own anxiety. For example, Molly's mother acknowledged that she constantly catastrophized about the future and was convinced that she would be incompetent to handle whatever came up. Molly admitted that she too was worried about the same thing. In addition, when she saw her mother was worried and fearful she was afraid her mother would get sick and wouldn't be able to care for her.

The more Molly's fear escalated the more fearful her mother became as well. To intervene in this cycle, both were taught the basics of how anxiety is created, maintained, and escalated. In essence, they were taught that anxiety is created when our minds go fast forward into the future, create a catastrophic scenario of what will be there, and then we believe our creation is true and tell ourselves we are unable or incompetent to cope with it. After this didactic explanation, I had Molly's mother explain the same thing to Molly using her own words. Next, I had Molly reexplain it to me using her own words. For homework I asked each of them to explain it to at least one other person. I also had them both keep track of their anxiety levels for a week, rating their level of anxiety on a scale from 1 to 10, three times per day. This data provided a baseline for seeing their progress in anxiety reduction.

In future sessions, they more clearly identified specific beliefs that fed anxiety and outlined ways that these beliefs could be shattered and replaced with more helpful beliefs. Molly and her mother decided they would join forces and call themselves the "Anxiety Busters." If either one was getting into a pattern of anxious thinking that person would first attempt to "bust" the anxiety themselves and if that did not work they would call for help from the other. After a while, Molly and her mother were able to teach these methods to the rest of the family who also decided they wanted to be anxiety busters.

The following are some of the strategies and techniques that were employed by the anxiety busters:

- Keep your thoughts anchored in the present. Future thinking is the enemy.
- Complete the following sentence in as many ways as possible, "Right now I am aware of _____."
- Play the relaxation tape. This was a tape recorded by me which included both physical and mental relaxation exercises.
- Role-play and reverse role-play.
- Practice coping statements (i.e., "Right now I am safe and sound." "I can handle whatever happens in the present.")
- Focus on deep breathing.
- Invite the anxiety to come and even try to increase it. Make yourself twice as anxious as you are right now (paradoxical intention).
- Take a step back and watch the anxiety as it goes up and down.
- Practice making yourself anxious and then calming yourself down using imagery.
- Monitor physical cues that may indicate rising anxiety levels.
- When anxiety begins to rise engage in an incompatable activity, read a joke book, call a friend on the phone, exercise, listen to march music and march around the house.

As anxiety levels began to drop in both Molly and her mother, I recommended that they begin to spend more time with their own friends and less time with each other. They had both begun to withdraw from others prior to coming to counseling because they were more comfortable at home with each other than they were anywhere else. They were encouraged to extend their comfort zone first through imagery practice and then behaviorally. Molly was encouraged to invite friends over after school at least two afternoons a week and this eventually resulted in return invitations being given to Molly. Molly's mother was encouraged to rejoin her bowling team and eventually to return to work part time. Both were also counseled in assertiveness training, because it became apparent when anxiety was lower that both tended to have a passive response style that created problems in interpersonal relationships.

Molly's success in counseling was possible only with her mother working with her both as a model of how to work on her own anxiety and as a support for what Molly was doing. Anxiety reduction freed them both to be more independent and increased confidence by giving them a greater sense of control over their lives.

2. *Angry Acting-Out Child:* At the first session, it was apparent that 8-year-old Jim was angry about being in therapy and was clearly there only because his parents insisted that he come. His parents explained that this indeed was the problem. Jim was angry and oppositional about everything they or any other authority figure did or said. He refused to get up in the morning, he dawdled when getting dressed, he was almost always late to school, and didn't cooperate with the teacher once he was in school. He fought with and dominated his younger brother and had difficulty maintaining friendships. Jim stared at his shoes avoiding eye contact throughout this explanation by his parents. When asked if he agreed or disagreed with what they had said he said he thought his parents were the ones with the problem and he didn't know why he was the one who had to come here. I said that I didn't know yet where the problem was coming from and that one thing we could all work on together was finding out who had the problem and what to do about it. I asked if he would help me do this and he nodded.

The first several sessions were primarily focused on Jim with his parents observing for part of each session. We began by having a general discussion of feelings and where they come from, since I realized Jim felt threatened by the therapeutic process and required some time to "warm up." We progressed to a more specific discussion of anger and its origins. Jim admitted that he felt really angry at his parents because they "bugged" him all the time, constantly told him what to do, and criticized him whatever he did. I admitted that the situation sounded unpleasant to me, and asked if he thought his anger was making it easier or harder to cope with his situation. He said he wanted to make things harder on his parents so they would understand how he felt but that he thought he was really just making things harder on himself. Because it was so uncomfortable being so angry all the time, he agreed that he would like to reduce his anger so that he could find a better way to cope with the situation.

With Jim's parents observing, we worked on reducing his anger in the following ways:

a. Taught him to identify angry feelings before he expressed them by tuning in and rating his feeling tone on a scale from 1 to 10 several times a day.

b. Identified and disputed care beliefs that created and fed the anger such as, "My parents shouldn't treat me this way," and "I can't stand not getting what I want."

c. Helped Jim formulate anger-reducing coping statements such as "I may not like the way my parents treat me but there's no rule against it," and "I can stand not getting what I want even if I dislike it."

d. Had him gather information on:
   • The number of orders received each day from his parents.
   • The number of criticisms.
   • The number of compliments.

e. Practiced anger-reducing through role-play and imagery involving Jim and both of his parents.

f. Had Jim teach his parents how they created and how they could reduce their own anger.

As Jim learned better control over his angry feelings and responses we integrated his parents more directly into the therapeutic process. They both admitted to Jim that they were perhaps too demanding of him and when presented with the data that he had gathered as to the numbers of demanding and critical statements versus supportive statements they were surprised to see so few of the latter. They read *Child Management* and further realized they had been reinforcing Jim for his angry oppositional behavior by attending to it. It was suggested that they begin to look for opportunities to reinforce Jim for constructive behaviors. We used role-play to practice improved communication and giving feedback in a helpful rather than hurtful manner.

Jim felt increasingly in charge of his feelings and behaviors and consequently felt more in control of his life—he was able to respond to frustration and aggravation more constructively and was even able to teach his little brother to raise his frustration tolerance level as well. Jim's parents were able to recognize his efforts to change and supported his efforts with praise. They continued to work on giving up their unrealistic demands that he be perfect and were able to engage in practical problem solving when difficult issues arose requiring negotiation.

3. *Depression:* Lucy was a 4-year-old girl who was the only child of parents seeking a divorce. Lucy was living with her mother and visited her father on weekends. Lucy's mother brought her to counseling because she seemed to

change when her father moved out of the house. She became quieter, more withdrawn, hyperemotional, and had sleep disturbances. She became anxious and clingy when it was time to go to school and had lost interest in playing with her friends. Lucy's mother said she couldn't really understand what had brought about this dramatic change because Lucy still got to see her father on weekends and hadn't really seen him that much during the week prior to the separation. I initially met with Lucy together with her mother, suggesting to the mother that she might passively observe our interaction. Lucy was initially quiet and reserved but articulately answered all questions asked of her. When asked what she was told about coming to my office she responded that her Mommy had told her that I was a special kind of doctor who helped people with hurt feelings. When asked if she had hurt feelings, she responded that she sometimes did. I then went on to explain to Lucy and her mother that I did indeed help people with hurt feelings learn how to change them to helpful feelings. I explained that I often worked with children to teach them about where their feelings come from and how they can solve their problems and change things in their life which were troubling them. When asked what she would like to change in her life, Lucy responded that she would like her Daddy to come home to live. I explained that I couldn't change the situation between her parents but I could perhaps help her to feel better about it.

We further explored both Lucy's feelings and thoughts to determine more specifically to what her behavioral changes could be attributed. Using several different techniques such as storytelling, role-play, bibliotherapy, and imagery we were able to determine that Lucy was primarily depressed at the loss of the familiarity of the family unit. She was also experiencing anxiety and anger to a lesser degree.

I chose initially to work on alleviating the depression, which was the most debilitating of the emotional reactions, with the thought that Lucy might also be less anxious or angry if she were less depressed because she would then be able to experience pleasure once again. I chose to let Lucy's mother continue to observe our sessions so that she could learn how to respond and work with Lucy outside of the therapeutic session. I suspected that Lucy's mother might be modeling depression that Lucy was copying. So subsequently I wanted to give the mother the opportunity to learn something about her own depression and to see an alternative way of relating to her child.

I worked with Lucy using a combination of didactic and experiential techniques. I find that even the youngest of clients can learn the basics of RET if presented in a way they can understand. After first assessing that Lucy understood what I meant by feelings. I explained to Lucy that feelings come from what we think inside our heads. "It's like we have a big television set inside our heads with pictures and with sounds, sometimes we only see the pictures, sometimes we only hear the words or sounds, but much of the time we have both pictures and sounds. Think about watching your favorite television show, what sorts of feelings do you have—happy, excited, surprised, tickled? Now think about a time when you watched a show you didn't like—maybe it was too scary, or too boring, or too sad. What could you do if you had uncomfortable or hurtful feelings from watching a particular show? That's right—you could leave the room. What else could you do? Turn the TV off or change the channel! So when people have certain thoughts or ideas, it's like tuning in to a TV channel. If these thoughts and ideas are helpful, they can stay tuned. If they are hurtful, they can change the channel. I'd like you to try and pay attention to what you are feeling and see if you can tune in to the channel and find out what station your mind is on. That will be very helpful to you for I can then teach you how to change your channel if it's hurtful to you."

Lucy then practiced by first choosing her own channel and then seeing what feeling came as a result. Next we played a game in which I suggested a feeling and had Lucy tell me what was playing on the channel to create that feeling. I further suggested that Lucy explain the game to her mother and that the two of them play the TV feeling game at home. This enabled both mother and daughter to get a clear sense of the thinking–feeling connection, one of the primary building blocks of rational-emotive theory.

To take this a step further and to elicit some of the cognitions contributing to Lucy's depression, I encouraged her to make up stories that went along with certain feelings such as happy, scared, excited, mad, and sad. These stories offered insight into Lucy's thought process and provided her mother with another tool for understanding and working with Lucy outside of therapy. I encouraged Lucy and her mother to spend time together telling stories or acting them out using dolls, stuffed animals, and puppets. Lucy's stories frequently included young forest animals such as bunnies and bears, which were either neglected or abandoned by their parents. These young animals were then placed in grave danger from their natural enemies such as wolves and hunters.

We used these stories to help Lucy understand the origin of her depression and to give her coping strategies for overcoming it. Lucy, her mother, and I role-played her stories with each of us playing different parts in different stories. I modeled coping strategies for Lucy when I played the role of the abandoned animal.

First, I demonstrated helpful self-talk such as "I may be alone but I can learn to take care of myself" and "If I stay calm, I'll be in better shape to care for myself." I also demonstrated practical problem-solving skills in terms of how the animals if they remained calm could think about how to best handle the situation.

We also used reality testing to point out how very unlikely it was for baby animals to be totally abandoned by their parents. Even if one parent left home, the other parent would be around to take care of the baby.

By handling the depression indirectly we were able to determine causation and design a course of treatment that could be directly administered. Lucy's mother was taught how to elicit images and cognitions from Lucy and use them in storytelling and role-play to help her resolve her distress and gain reassurance. This technique proved to be useful for both Lucy and her mother in reducing depression and anxiety, opening communication, and promoting coping skills.

4. *Attention Deficit Hyperactivity Disorder in the Classroom:* Tom was a bright, outgoing first grader, who had been diagnosed by his pediatrician as having attention deficit hyperactivity disorder (ADHD), a condition characterized by distractability, impulsivity, emotional intensity, and hyperactivity. He had been placed in Mrs. Brown's first-grade class. Mrs. Brown was a highly structured teacher who prided herself on having a class where every student was "on task" at all times. Classwork was divided into seat work on which the children were expected to work independently, and group work, in which she stood in front of the class and taught a lesson. A resounding clash occurred between Tom's style of classroom functioning that was active, verbal, and disorganized and Mrs. Brown's style of classroom management. Tom was referred for counseling and was perceived by Mrs. Brown as being disruptive, manipulative, and immature. After observing Tom in the classroom, I could see that the problem was not his alone. I could also see that Mrs. Brown would not be directly amenable to acknowledging or working on her problems. I suggested that I work with Tom directly at school and requested that Mrs. Brown observe our sessions hoping to work with her indirectly.

Initially, Tom was delighted to work with me. He liked the individual attention and openly stated that he liked getting out of the classroom. He was indeed distractable and had difficulty staying on task. Rather than get angry and punitive toward him when he digressed, I gave him a signal (finger on nose) to remind him he was getting off the topic and gave him the chance to reorient himself.

I was hoping to demonstrate to Mrs. Brown that Tom could be helped to attend better with encouragement and a gentle reminder, whereas her method of scolding and criticizing him first added to his agitation and made it more difficult for him to attend.

Tom and I discussed where feelings came from and the nature of helpful and hurtful feelings. I asked him to keep track of his feelings in the classroom for 1 week using faces to indicate happy, mad, sad, and scared feelings. He was eager and enthusiastic about this assignment and we worked on a chart together where he could record these feelings. When he brought the chart back the next week, he had done a good job of recording for each day and it was apparent that he felt mad, sad, and scared much more often than he felt happy. I then asked him when he thought he could concentrate best? When he was happy, mad, sad, or scared? He replied that he could think best when he was happy but not *too* excited because when these other bad feelings were around he just couldn't get his mind off how awful he felt and as a result he tried to do things in the classroom to cheer himself up, like talk to other kids during seat work time. We then zeroed in on situations where he typically had disruptive or hurtful feelings and I taught him the ABC problem-solving format. He learned to identify the thoughts that made him mad, sad, and scared, and practiced coming up with alternative thoughts that would create feelings more conducive to concentrating and getting his work done.

In observing this process, Mrs. Brown was better able to understand the context of Tom's behavior and was also, able to see her part in exacerbating it. By demanding that he perfectly fit into her model classroom, she was applying pressure which resulted in greater disruption and distractability. By giving up her demands of him, Mrs. Brown lessened Tom's emotional static enabling him to focus his attention better. After observing their effectiveness, Mrs. Brown also became more open to using reinforcers for good behavior in place of scolding and criticizing undesirable behavior, and as a result the tension level of the whole classroom was drastically reduced.

BIBLIOGRAPHY

Bedford, S. (1974). *Instant replay.* New York: Institute for Rational Living.

Berger, T. (1971). *I have feelings.* New York: Human Sciences Press.

Ellis, A., & Harper, R. A. (1975). *A new guide to rational living.* North Hollywood, CA: Wilshire Books.

Ellis, A., Moseley, S., & Wolfe, J. L. (1966). *How to raise an emotionally healthy happy child.* New York: Crown and Hollywood: Wilshire Books.

Garcia, E. J., & Pellegrini, N. (1974). *Homer the homely hound dog.* New York: Institute for Rational Living.

Gardner, R. A. (1973). *The talking feeling doing game.* Cresskill, NJ: Creative Therapeutics.

Gerald, M., & Eyman, W. (1981). *Thinking straight and talking sense.* New York: Institute for Rational Living.

Hauck, P. A. (1967). *The rational management of children.* New York: Libra.

Knaus, W. J. (1974). *Rational emotive education: A manual for elementary school teachers.* New York: Institute for Rational Living.

Tosi, D. J. (1974). *Youth: Toward personal growth, a rational emotive approach.* Columbus, OH: Charles E. Merrill.

Vernon, A. (1980). *Help yourself to a healthier you.* Washington, DC: University Press of American.

Waters, V. (1979). *Color vs. rational.* New York: Institute for Rational Living.

Waters, V. (1980). *Rational stories for children.* New York: Institute for Rational Emotive Therapy.

Young, H. S. (1977). *A rational counseling primer.* New York: Institute for Rational Living.

3 Problem-Centered Consultee–Client Consultation

John F. McInerney
Cape May, New Jersey

Consultation with adults, whether parents, teachers, or other child-care workers, about the emotional and behavioral problems experienced by children is a significant form of mental health service delivery in applied settings. Whether consultation occurs in the clinic, school, or private office, it represents a major source of assistance to adults in their attempt to respond to the identified difficulties of children and adolescents. Consultation is an indirect form of treatment for emotionally and behaviorally disturbed children. The potential effectiveness and efficiency of this approach, when compared to the magnitude of the problems experienced by children and the scarcity of resources for sometimes less efficient individual treatment, provides more than adequate justification for special professional attention to consultation as a potentially powerful resource. Considering that young children and some adolescents are occasionally unable or often unwilling to participate in individual treatment, the case for consultation as a major resource for addressing childhood and adolescent problems is further strengthened.

Consultation often involves working with parents. In a generic sense, many forms of family therapy, parent counseling, and parent training groups are a response to parents' perception of a need to learn how to better help their child with emotional and behavioral problems. Parent education as well as much of what occurs in parent–teacher conferences in schools are indirect attempts to intervene in the problems experienced by children and adolescents. Whether consultation is informal or structured, the consultant in effect attempts to re-educate or persuade the consultee to change their thoughts, feelings, and actions regarding the child or adolescent. This goal of changing feelings and behavior in response to the child and his or her problems is seen as the means whereby significant others can directly reduce the problems and promote improved adjust-ment. A basic premise of this approach is that although parents or other adults in the child's life may not have caused the child's disturbance in any direct way, they can influence it. Consultation aims at teaching more effective ways of influencing the child.

This chapter reviews a specific method of consultation based on rational-emotive psychology and the clinical practice of rational-emotive therapy (RET). Rational-emotive consultation (REC) is outlined in terms of both the process of consultation and the method that might be beneficially employed in effectively and efficiently assisting parents or other adults in intervening in child problems. In addition, in a later section, four relatively frequent categories of presenting concerns regarding children and teenagers as often described by their parents and teachers are outlined. Throughout this chapter, discussion and examples often focus on parent consultation as conducted on a one-to-one basis between consul-tant and consultee rather than that which might be done in a group setting. The term *parent* in this chapter may be used interchangeably with teacher or other child-care worker unless otherwise specified.

RATIONAL-EMOTIVE CONSULTATION: GENERAL ISSUES

The following section reviews the general principles of rational-emotive consul-tation in terms of its basic assumptions, the development of rapport, and the establishment of a credible, persuasive consultation relationship, assessment of consultee and client problems, and disputing consultee irrational beliefs. A brief overview of some often encountered consultee irrational beliefs that interfere with effective child management and problem solving are provided. Finally, some suggestions concerning consultation follow-up are presented.

Basic Assumptions

Rational-emotive consultation is based on the principles and methods of rational-emotive therapy as described by Ellis (1962, 1977; Ellis & Whiteley, 1979; Walen, DiGiuseppe, & Wessler, 1980). It shares RET's view of human distur-bance and sees the purpose of consultation as twofold. Consultation is first aimed at identifying and changing the consultee's self-defeating thoughts, feelings, and actions about the child problem so that more effective interaction with the child may take place. Second, REC aims at indirect service for the child by assisting parents, teachers, or significant others in implementing and then persisting in a series of steps aimed at improved, rational management of the child.

Like RET, REC views human disturbance as largely resulting from irrational beliefs. These irrational beliefs create and maintain emotional disturbance and self-defeating patterns of behavior, whether in the consultee or the child or adolescent client. Both adults working with children and children themselves behave in self-defeating ways as a result of misinformation or irrational thinking about themselves, other people and/or the long-term consequences of their behavioral attempts to cope. REC then, not only attempts to address emotional roadblocks and self-defeating patterns of behavior significant others have regarding child management, but also endeavors to promote through direct re-education more rational, effective and empirically valid methods of child management. REC intervenes in the behavioral, emotional, and/or academic difficulties of youngsters through improving the rational problem-solving skills and rational child management abilities of those adults working with them.

The process and methods of REC are consistent with those characteristic of RET. Consultation is viewed as a directive, re-educational process. The consultant is seen as a special kind of teacher with expertise in both the teaching of rational self-management for adults and in the rational management of developmental and situational emotional or behavioral problems in children and adolescents. Consultation is focused by the consultant on here and now concerns as they are presented by the consultee and deduced from reports of the identified child's emotional and behavioral characteristics. Although some direct and indirect assessment of the target youngster is often indicated and is discussed here, formalized assessment is not seen as required. In REC, the focus remains largely on present and future behavioral concerns, rather than on definitive diagnosis or the collection of extensive historical information to determine the cause of the child's behavioral or emotional symptoms.

The directive and focused nature of REC lends itself to short-term and problem-focused consultation that is clearly suited to many clinic, school, and general private practice settings. As with RET in general, the directive and focused nature of this approach requires considerable thought, interaction, and persistence on the part of the consultant. It requires that the consultant assess the presenting problem as described by the consultee as well as assess the consultee with regard to emotional roadblocks and cognitive misconceptions interfering with a more effective management of the child's difficulties. It also requires that the consultant be relatively efficient and effective in assessing the resources available to the consultee both personally and through the setting in which consultation occurs that might be focused on the identified child's difficulties. It is often critical to accurately assess these resources so that realistic expectations regarding the time, effort, and persistence that might well be involved in effectively addressing child difficulties can be made explicit. Although short-term consultation can be both effective and efficient, in the author's experience it fails to have the desired impact on children's problems, not so much due to conceptual or professional inadequacy as to insufficient time and persistence applied by consultee to the process. In this respect it is important for the rational-emotive consultant to have an accurate and realistic appraisal of his or her resources for follow-up on consultation. In some settings where resources for sufficient consultation are unavailable, effective consultation will in all likelihood not be achieved.

Relationship Building

The process of effective consultation involves a relationship between a consultant and one or more consultees who interact with a goal of assisting an identified child or adolescent client eliminate or better manage an emotional or behavioral problem. In RET we do not see special power stemming from characteristics of the therapeutic relationship. We do, however, recognize that the establishment of an effective relationship between the therapist and client is an important first step in the change process. Likewise in REC, the relationship established between the consultant and consultee may be critical to the success of consultation and therefore, some attention to the establishment of this relationship on the part of the consultant is clearly appropriate. Because of the nature of the consultation enterprise, which may involve only a few encounters between consultant and consultee, it may be of additional importance that an optimally effective relationship be established from the outset.

The process of REC requires that the consultant, with the participation and agreement of the consultee, endeavors to identify and help change consultee thoughts, feelings, or actions that are interfering with effective child management. Once the consultee gains greater self-control, REC hypothesizes that they will be better able to solve the problems of the child. In the light of this understanding, the consultant should consider what relationship qualities are most likely to promote this form of persuasive relationship (Frank, 1961) in which the consultant attempts to modify consultee's self-defeating thinking.

The social psychology of interpersonal influence has demonstrated that people are more likely to change their opinion in the direction of someone they consider to be an expert (Wessler & Wessler, 1980). Often, by definition, the consultant is an expert and perceived as such by the consultee. In addition, it is often useful for the consultant to briefly describe his or her particular expertise with regard to the client's problems. Sometimes this expert power is imbedded in one's professional role or title. In some other situations it may need to be established with some simple statements of fact concerning the consultant's experience, professional training and/or knowledge regarding problems at hand. It is often useful in this regard if the consultant has some direct observational knowledge of the child or adolescent who is the source of concern to the consultee.

Related to the issue of expertise in the establishment of an effective relationship for consultation should be the issue of the consultant's credibility. Again, the social psychology of influence suggest that individuals whose opinions are viewed as *credible* are more likely to be influential. Credibility, however, is a somewhat complex matter, in that it involves not only one's defined role as an expert but also the consultant's communication of this expertise in a way that the consultee views as "making sense." For the consultant, it is often easier to be right than to be persuasive. For example, defining one's expertise by quoting numerous scientific studies regarding the behavior modification of unruly 5-year-olds may or may not persuade the parents of an overactive 5-year-old that the consultant is indeed someone to whom it is worth listening. In many cases, credibility may be more effectively and efficiently established by simply demonstrating a genuine concern about the consultee's problems with the identified client and establishing in a nonthreatening and nondogmatic way one's experience as a consultant in addressing these problematic issues. Credibility is also a quality of the consulting relationship that probably evolves best when the consultant demonstrates a genuine interest in what the consultees have to say and further demonstrates a willingness to collaborate with them in applying the consultant's knowledge and experience to these problems.

Although a consultant needs to pay attention to expertise and credibility, neither of these alone might be sufficient to persuade the consultee to try some recommended alternative solutions to the problems presented by the child or adolescent client. A further factor is the establishment of a nonjudgmental point of view with regard to both the consultee's efforts to address the client's problems and the child or adolescent client's problems in themselves. Regardless of the irrationality of awfulizing about being judged, if the consultee perceives the consultant as judging them and the child or as judging them as the result of the child's problems then some significant roadblocks in the consulting relationship have developed. It is probably better at the very least to avoid judgmental or critical appraisal of the consultee's work with the client or the nature of the client's problems themselves until a relationship is more firmly established, or better still, to avoid these types of statements entirely.

Most of use who have worked to any extent with parents or who might be parents ourselves are aware of the often commented upon phenomenon that "I can criticize my child but nobody else better." In this regard, even when the consultee may be quite critical or judgmental of the child it may be ill advised to join in this criticism. It may be better to assist the consultee in reframing their criticisms or judgments in more rational and, therefore more manageable terms. This would further assist in the development of a more effective consulting relationship in that it is an additional way of demonstrating the consultant's genuine interest in helping address both the consultee's difficulties with the child and serve the child client as well.

Part of establishing an effective consulting relationship is the establishment of *reasonable expectations* on the part of the consultee regarding both the consultation process and it's outcome. Reasonable expectations for time and effort are best established quite directly. Once an appreciation of the consultee's concerns has emerged, direct statements about what may be involved in making the changes necessary for a more positive outcome are worth pointing out. No matter how expert, credible, or genuinely interested the consultant may be, without reasonable expectations of what may be involved in making long-lasting changes, the consultee may not complete the consultation process. In order to determine what might be reasonable regarding expectations from the consultation process, it is worth asking the consultee how long the child's problem has been a concern. In a general way, particularly with parent consultees it can be useful to address the expectation issue by explaining that the problems they are most concerned about did not develop overnight and probably will not change overnight either. A child or adult learns to approach certain situations on a trial-by-trial basis over the course of many trials. They will learn new solutions to the problem situation, but almost never on a one trial basis.

Sometimes in working with consultees who are directly and intimately involved with the client's problems, such as would be the case with parent consultations, it is often useful to further the establishment of the consulting relationship by encouraging or affirming the consultee's own sense of power and expertise regarding the problem.

When working with parents, for example, it has often been my experience that they know a great deal about parenting in general and are really quite expert regarding the parenting of their troubled or troublesome child. Parents, however, incorrectly believe that because their child has particular problems or is disturbing to others, they have somehow failed and, therefore, are at a total loss as to how to contribute useful information or experience to the consultation process. One way to address this problem is to in effect re-empower the consultee with regard to his or her knowledge of child management in general and the management of this child in particular. This might be done by indicating to the consultee that there are many areas in his or her life with the child in which he or she competently and successfully performs his or her role. It can be useful either from experience with the consultee or from direct questions, to obtain information about these areas of success. I have found it worth stating to many parent and teacher groups that they "already know" how to perform their particular role with other children as well as the identified client. Simply asking consultees if, in their opinion, being consistent with the child is important is one way to establish this. The vast majority of adults will readily agree that consistency is most important in child management. If you then ask them if they are consistent with the child in question, they will quite often see the irony in the situation and readily admit they are not. This establishes a point worth making. Namely that, what one knows and what one characteristically does may not be the same thing. Following this line of reasoning, the consultant might well make the point that the consultee does indeed already know, or has at least a number of good ideas about how to better manage the identified client but that for a variety of reasons that will be discovered through the consulting process, these good ideas are not always put into action and/or are not immediately successful even when occasionally applied. In particular, the role of consultee negative emotions in blocking their use of child management skills already in their repertoire can be gently introduced.

For REC to proceed effectively, it is important for the consultant to communicate the fact that the consultee's thoughts, feelings, and actions regarding the client problem are of critical importance to the success of the consultation process. This establishes one of the major methods of REC in process; namely, that the consultant and consultee will share ideas about the child's problem in such a way as to empower the consultee to apply more of what they know to be effective toward more systematically and persistently addressing these problems. It also alerts the consultee to one of REC's basic assumptions; namely, that before a child will change, the adult has to change. Consultation from the rational-emotive perspective is not simply an "ask the expert" exercise. So often in our offices, clinics, and schools we have all experienced the situation in which we have provided a consultee with the technically "correct" answer to dealing with a child problem that they have disregarded, discredited, or simply not chosen to apply because they have not been fully persuaded that the proposed solution has merit in the particular case in point or because they have not felt that their concern and depth of emotion about the problem has been fully acknowledged or "understood." Sometimes the consultant's direction is disregarded because the consultee has not been given a realistic appreciation of the time that might be involved in addressing the problem at hand. In other cases, it may be that the consultant's advice, although technically correct just adds to the consultee's sense of being overwhelmed, of being incompetent, and/or of being incapable of, or unable to manage the problem. Clearly, all of these outcomes interfere with successful consultation.

With attention to establishing a persuasive relationship with the consultee in which credibility, genuine concern, and understanding of the emotional impact the problem has on the consultee, consultation toward shared problem solving proceeds most effectively.

Assessment

Although extensive assessment is neither necessary nor sufficient for effective REC, some assessment of the target child's behavioral and emotional difficulties is indicated. Clinical assessment data might be obtained in any one of or several of the following ways. In some consultation settings, such as schools and clinics, reports or ratings of the child's behavior and emotional problems are available and these records can be reviewed either before or at the initial meeting with the consultee. Parents can be asked to briefly fill out a standard behavioral rating checklist and/or developmental history regarding the child prior to the first meeting with the professional consultant. Direct observation, clinical interview, or psychological testing of the child by the consultant might also be an assessment option. Finally, some time and effort should be spent in a discussion of the consultee's perceptions of the identified child and his or her difficulties. This can be obtained through a clinical interview process in which direct questions are put to the consultee requesting a description of the child's behavior, temperament, reaction to frustration, and often quite importantly, the child's reaction to the consultee's interaction with and intervention into the child's problems.

Often it is useful to help the consultee focus on the one or two major presenting concerns regarding the child's behavioral, emotional, or academic problems. This permits the consultant to conduct a structured clinical interview, focused initially on these issues so that some appraisal of the child's difficulties can be obtained for later reference when specific problem-solving interventions are planned and prescribed.

In the same context, it is important to assess the consultee's emotional and behavioral reaction to the identified client's disturbing affect or behavior. It is important to know what is typically done and what has been tried in the past as well as the consultee's thoughts and feelings about these efforts.

Once a tentative picture of the child's disturbed feelings, behavioral deficits, or self-defeating actions emerges through clinical assessment and the consultee's emotional and behavioral responses to these presenting complaints have been appraised, it is probably wise for the consultant to share these appraisals with the consultee. Even when the parent's involvement in the child's problem is at present quite negative and unhelpful, this information can be presented in an honest but nonjudgmental way. The purpose of consultation is to improve parenting not to condemn it or help parents feel guilty about their parenting. At this point, feedback from the consultee can save valuable time and effort that might be misdirected in the event that the consultant and consultee have not developed a shared understanding of the child's problem. It is probably most useful to keep these definitions of the child's problems and the consultee's reactions to them framed as general observations rather than all inclusive diagnostic statements. Providing the consultant and consultee have evolved a shared understanding of the problems, the consultation process may proceed toward the goal of helping the consultee respond more effectively to the client and thereby indirectly intervening in the client's emotional and behavioral disturbance.

Disputing Consultee Irrational Beliefs

Disputing in consultation is aimed at identified or inferred irrational beliefs held by the consultee regarding the nature of the identified client's problem or the consultee's management of it. In addition, irrational beliefs regarding emotionality in general and perfectionistic ideas regarding child and personal self-management are also likely. The disputational methods of RET as described by Walen et al. (1980), Wessler and Wessler (1980), Bard (1980), Dryden (1984), and Ellis (1962, 1977) can be used when such irrational and self-defeating beliefs are identified or inferred.

As described in the literature just cited, disputation can be didactic and employ essentially the consultant's counterexplanation of an irrational belief, or a more socratic approach may be taken whereby the consultant poses a series of questions that allows the consultee to inductively reason and discover the self-defeating nature of the irrational belief. Disputation can be both philosophic or pragmatic. A philosophic dispute aims at what Ellis referred to as "the elegant solution" whereby the client comes deductively to a more rational belief, whereas a pragmatic dispute aims at demonstrating the dysfunctional consequences of the irrational belief and it's attendant excessive negative emotions, thereby providing evidence of an advantage for the consultee to change the belief. We have no clear-cut evidence that one form or method of disputation is superior to another in terms of its outcome.

Largely, the disputational process is a matter of the consultant's experience and preference as well as the consultee's involvement, verbal ability, and other characteristics. It may be, however, that given the fairly short-term and highly goal-directed nature of REC that the methods most frequently used will be of the more didactic, educational, concrete, and pragmatic variety. Although there are a wide number of potential irrational beliefs that when held by a consultee would present emotional and behavioral roadblocks to both the consultation process and the improved management of the problems of the identified client-child, several more common ones with suggested disputes are reviewed in the following sections.

WORKING ON CONSULTEE EMOTIONAL DISTRESS

In the following section, a variety of frequently presenting consultee emotional problems are presented. RET/REC techniques for teaching rational self-management are highlighted.

General Emotional Upset About Child Problems

A fairly general and frequently occurring emotional roadblock to the consultation process might be the degree of emotional distress or disturbance experienced by the consultee about the identified child's difficulties. Certainly, most of us who have served as consultants to parents concerned with the problems of their disturbed or disturbing youngster have heard statements like "I just don't know what to do with Jimmy. Nothing I do seems to work." When you respond to this statement by questioning the consultee's degree of emotional upset, you will often be met with a statement such as "Of course I'm upset, I'm very upset. If he doesn't stop behaving this way he will be thrown out of school and never learn anything." When you question this and ask in effect, "Is your upset about Jimmy's problem helping you manage him better?" the consultee may respond with a statement such as "You don't understand, you would be upset too, if this happened to your child. Of course I have to be upset, or nothing will ever change." Clearly, there are a number of misconceptions and irrational beliefs inherent in this briefly described dialogue. Chief among these is the notion that feeling strongly about a problem requires that one be emotionally quite disturbed about it. Certainly, some of us irrationally believe that the only time that we can act to change difficult problems is when we are very, very upset. From a psychological point of view, however, we know that virtually all forms of human performance are adversely affected by high degrees of emotional disturbance. In fact, being emotionally upset is a major roadblock to rational problem solving and by implication a major roadblock to rational child management (Hauck, 1967; McInerney, 1983). When a consultee presents a high degree of emotional disturbance about the problem, which usually becomes apparent quite early in consultation, it is appropriate and may well be necessary for further progress for these beliefs to be challenged straight away.

In disputing parents' beliefs about having to be upset about their child's problems, it is often useful to use pragmatic and didactic methods first. For example, one might question the consultee's degree of upset further, and in specific and concrete ways inquire as to whether being upset has helped in any way manage the child's disturbed or disturbing behavior. For example, one might ask a parent quite upset about the youngster's refusal to do homework assignments if becoming angry and yelling and screaming has been successful in getting the youngster to do homework. Clearly, sometimes the answers you get to these questions will be surprising. It may be that yelling and screaming does get junior to do his homework. In which case it would be wise to inquire further how the consultee feels after having yelled and screamed and indeed after having had to yell and scream each night, week after week in order for the youngster to do the homework. With this kind of questioning it is often logical to point out that even when disturbed and upset emotions work, they do not work very well or only work well at tremendous cost. Once the consultee is able to acknowledge this point of view, other issues may arise such as how the youngster might be made to behave better without all this emotional disturbance on the part of the adult. This of course, provides a classic therapeutic opening for a very specific and didactic discussion of rational self-management and specific rational parenting suggestions.

It is worth pointing out to the consultee in following up on the previous discussion, that firm rather than angry and active rather than overwhelmed child management is probably most effective in the long run with a wide variety of child and adolescent emotional and behavioral problems. In effect, didactically presenting these discriminations, that is between firm and angry, active and overwhelmed, you are disputing the consultee's irrational belief that one must or should be upset when the child behaves in a disturbed or objectionable way. This is a fundamental discrimination to make because almost all behavioral methods of child management require firm, persistent action in order to lead to a beneficial outcome rather than angry or hostile and inconsistent responses on the part of the adult. In teaching these discriminations, the consultant is beginning to present a model of rational child management that involves rational self-talk on the part of the adult and planned and firm but moderate action.

Anger and Blame

Anger comes from the demand that what is, not be. In effect, it is a demand that the child not be who they are and act the way they have been acting. The consultant can readily agree with an assessment of the disadvantages of the behavior in question while strongly choosing to disagree with the demand that the child not be what he or she is, namely a youngster with disturbing behavior. Almost certainly, the child is not disturbed or disturbing in every circumstance, but in certain key areas where there are easily identified disadvantages to this behavior the child does quite often behave this way. Demanding that that simple fact not be so can only lead to anger, frustration, and hostility on the part of the adults charged with managing this youngster. Clearly, that anger serves no useful purpose in the long run although it may have some limited short-term advantages. It would be far better if the consultee were able to rationally accept this objectionable and disadvantageous behavior as a fact while not approving of it, so that high levels of anger that interfere with the child management might be reduced.

Anger–Guilt–Self-Blame

In other circumstances, when questioning the consultee's emotional reaction to the problem behavior of the child it might become apparent that not only is the consultee generally angry about the problem but he or she is also feeling guilty that he or she has lost his or her temper. This is a related drawback to high levels of anger, which is referred to as the anger–guilt cycle. After being angry we turn our demandingness against ourselves and say, "I never should have lost my temper and now I should do something to make up for it." Much of the inconsistency we see in child management, particularly when anger characterizes the initial reaction to a child's disturbed or disturbing behavior, results from secondary guilt in which the adult inappropriately attempts to compensate for this guilt by rewarding the child. Although this reward may not be deliberate but rather be in the form of extra adult attention, it has the effect of increasing not decreasing the probability of future problem behaviors.

When the anger–guilt cycle is in evidence, discussion about the guilt-driven overcompensation for the previous anger can be useful in pointing out to the adult the self-defeating nature of the cycle. Some children do indeed learn that it is OK for mom or teacher to be mad at them because when they get over it they are nicer than ever. This message is often misperceived by adults as a temporary improvement in the child's behavior. But when one looks at it with a broader perspective, no real change has occurred. Discussion about the futility of guilt or self-blame is also in order. There is no evidence that an adult who loses his or her temper with his or her child is an awful, horrible, or worthless person who must be punished by guilt in order to change. Certainly, from all we understand about it, anger is not a particularly useful way to manage a youngster, but losing one's temper merely proves one's human fallibility rather than one's abject worthlessness. Pointing this out forcefully can be a readily helpful dispute for the guilt side of this anger–guilt cycle. Both anger and guilt need to be addressed in order to clear the way for more consistent and persistent management of the identified client child's difficulties.

Blaming Others

Sometimes it is apparent that the consultee believes irrationally that someone, virtually anyone other than the child or themselves, should and must be blamed for the child's problems. This is a situation that occurs fairly frequently in school settings. It also occurs in clinic settings with consultations about school problems. Essentially it stems from a number of identifiable or inferred irrational beliefs on the part of the consultee. The major one being that "people should be blamed and punished for their mistakes." If you are a parent who blames and damns yourself for your mistakes and views your child as an extension of yourself, then a very emotionally painful situation may prevail. A common and often identified defense is to project this blame on to someone else. For example "Jimmy wouldn't behave badly if his teacher last year had taught him properly" or "Johnny would not behave badly if the other children in his class did not tease him," and so on. Although it would be therapeutic to philosophically attempt to dispute the underlying belief that "everyone should be blamed for their mistakes," in most consulting settings, that will be a difficult undertaking. It might be better to attempt to address this issue pragmatically from the point of view of questioning the value of blaming someone else and becoming quite upset about that rather than accepting responsibility for the problem and working hard to do something about it. That type of pragmatic dispute presented firmly but with some sensitivity to the consultee's inferred fear of accepting responsibility for the situation can be effective. In some cases it may lead to further disputation of the related irrational belief that they should be severely blamed and censured themselves for their child's failure or disturbance.

It is often useful to discuss with the "blame-prone" consultee in a very direct way the idea that even children have free will and imperfectly choose some of their own mistakes. Adults, even teachers, parents, or others simply do not have godlike powers and will never have the ability to totally control a child, even their own. Children will make choices and respond to their environment in ways that are uniquely their own. And, in some ways the adults in this child's life will be relatively powerless to do much about it. The adult can do some things about it but really cannot rationally hold themselves responsible for everything a child does or the child stops being human and becomes a less than human robot.

Worry and Ego Anxiety

The consultee's anxiety about the child's problems can present a significant roadblock to changes in child management or problem solving. In extreme form, anxiety might result in an overreaction to minor problems or a disorganized and ineffective response to major ones. Anxiety or "worry" comes from beliefs about predictions of future catastrophe. Essentially, some present sign or behavioral indication is seen as "proof" that some awful problem will result in the future that will have "dangerous" or disasterous consequences for the child or parent. The former type of anxiety is often referred to as *anticipatory anxiety* and the latter as *ego anxiety*. In both instances, two related irrational beliefs are operating; the future can be known with 100% certainty and awful or horrible events must be worried over in order to prevent them.

When anticipatory anxiety is identified as a consultee problem it can be addressed directly by disputing the mistaken belief that the future can be perfectly predicted and also that future problems will always be catastrophic. We do not have special powers to predict the future and all future "problems" are not disasters. In any event, future problems are not prevented by anxiously anticipating them and exaggerating how awful they might be. Rather, one is better off thinking rationally and realistically about the future and acting out of concern rather than anxiety. High levels of anxiety interfere with almost all human performance. It is not a fact that awful future events can be prevented by worrying about them. In some cases it can be argued that worry makes some parenting and child management problems worse because a worried and disorganized adult will have a great deal of trouble being firm and consistent.

Ego anxiety is a somewhat more subtle problem to identify in that it involves the consultee's anticipation of personal failure and lost sense of worth or esteem. For example, if a parent fears that his or her failure to manage his or her child adequately is a sign of his or her own worthlessness, the parent will be anxious and desperate in his or her attempts to control the child. In situations where parent or teacher self-worth appear to be at stake, discussion can be directed at these issues. Adult control of any child is imperfect. No matter how "good" one might be as a parent, children make some of their own choices and create their own problems. In any event, the adult would be better off not measuring his or her worth by his or her child's success or failure relative to some relative standard. A philosophy of self-acceptance rather than contingent self-worth would make more sense and can be directly encouraged. This more rational philosophy will also provide an important form of primary prevention for parental exhaustion, discouragement, and reactive depression due to "failures" as a parent and person.

Low Frustration Tolerance–Discomfort Anxiety

A related form of anxiety is often referred to as *discomfort anxiety* which leads to low frustration tolerance (LFT). Discomfort anxiety is the fear of emotional discomfort as the result of its inferred "unbearable" characteristics. I a sense, discomfort anxiety is anxiety about future anxiety. For example, "If my child is not changed now I will never be able to stand him in the future." Implied in this kind of thinking is the idea that anxiety, emotional discomfort, or practical frustrations are literally "dangerous." Often one will hear parents in consultation say "I couldn't stand it if. . . ." Discomfort is only discomfort, not a progressive deadly disease. Helping children change their habits of thinking, feeling, and acting is by definition frustrating because adult power over children is limited. Discomfort and frustration are therefore unavoidable and are only made much worse by the irrational demand that they not exist in the first place.

Discomfort anxiety is not the only source of low frustration tolerance in adults (or children). LFT can also result from impulsivity or demandingness from other sources. The "I can't stand it! . . . It must not be, . . ." can be more rationally framed as "I don't like it but will have to put up with it while I work to change it."

Frustration tolerance is a very necessary survival skill in any work with disturbed or disturbing children. The consultant can, where needed, directly shape improved frustration tolerance by direct self-instructional strategies, framing more realistic expectations about the child, and supporting the consultee in seeking support from others in expressing and appropriately venting some of their inevitable frustration. Likewise in situations where frustration is objectively significant and/or unavoidable, the consultee can be instructed in basic stress management strategies so that he or she can better recognize personal limits and develop less self-defeating ways of coping with frustration. Consultees might be encouraged to reward themselves for managing frustration without anger; to use various forms of distraction such as exercise or relaxation when frustration builds up; and, to seek the support of peers and other significant adults to help the consultee work on improving his or her LFT.

Other Intra- and Interpersonal Problems

In addition to the constellation of disturbing thoughts and emotions, consultees might bring any number of other emotional roadblocks to the consultation process. These might include a degree of anger at their partner, namely the client's other parent who may or may not be present and participating in the consultation. This problem can be dealt with by identifying it and asking the consultee whether he or she would like some help with it. Also, one might ask the consultee or both parties if they are both participating whether these differences and the resulting anger will interfere with implementing the consultant's recommendations. The simple fact that the consultees are asked this question may sensitize him or her to the possible conflict and/or may lead the consultee to settle his or her differences or set them aside in the interest of following the consultant's recommendations. In any event, sometimes problems such as these and other intrapersonal emotional disturbance experienced by the consultee may require treatment in its own right. The frequency, amplitude, and duration of disturbance on the part of the consultee should be used to direct the consultant with regard to recommendations for other treatment. Even with another treatment is indicated, however, there is no a priori requirement that the consultation be discontinued or deferred. Although emotional disturbance either interpersonally or intrapersonally certainly complicates the consultant's job and may realistically affect the outcome, they are not a specific reason to invalidate the consultant's efforts.

REC, as the process has been defined, is different than individual RET with a client who happens to be a parent who might be worried about his or her child. The focus of REC goes beyond helping the adult. In REC, the defined purpose of consultation is to provide indirect service to the child. Although this may be a distinction that is not always clear, in REC it is the consultant's role to direct consultation toward not only reducing parental anxiety but *specifically* improving child adjustment. By definition of the consultant–consultee relationship, the child is the identified client and the ultimate target of intervention. It may be that in some cases (e.g., a couple with serious relationship problems, or an alcoholic parent) direct treatment of the adult is indicated before effective child-focused consultation can take place. Recommendations for such treatment are an important part of consultation when they are indicated.

PRACTICAL PROBLEM SOLVING

In the process of REC, consultation is clearly incomplete if only the consultee's identified or inferred irrational beliefs and/or emotional disturbance about the client's problems are addressed. In addition to identifying and attempting to remove attitudinal and emotional roadblocks to effective change, the consultant also needs to help the consultee with practical problem solving by making specific recommendations. In my experience, the more specific and simple these recommendations can be made, the better. The consultant enters this phase of consultation with the goal of specific advice giving. Clearly, the advice provided needs to be appropriate to the identified client's problems as described by the consultee and assessed by the consultant.

No matter how appropriate and persuasive the consulting relationship is nor how effectively the consultant has disputed some of the consultee's irrational beliefs and thereby minimized emotional roadblocks to effective consultation, if the advice given is inappropriate, incomplete, or poorly communicated, the major purpose of consultation has not been achieved. For example, if the consultee were concerned about repeated temper tantrums on the part of a youngster and after adequate involvement with the consultant agrees to manage his or her own angry thoughts and emotions in response to the temper tantrums in a different way but the consultant failed to recommend age-appropriate effective behavioral responses for the management of this temper tantrum, then consultation will not succeed in providing indirect service to the child-client. This, of course requires that the consultant truly be somewhat of an expert on the behavioral management of the common problems presented by the identified client, children, or youths. It also requires that the consultant be enough of an expert to explain what may well at first glance appear to be relatively complex behavior modification principles in simple, straightforward, and concrete ways so that they may be implemented by the consultee.

Certainly, the specific recommendations that can be made are many and varied depending on the problems under consideration. First and foremost, a recommendation needs to be made in such a way that it can be realistically implemented by the consultee. Regardless of what the literature on behavior modification might say, few parents or teachers are capable of or interested in conducting an experiment such as that which might be presented in the *Journal of Applied Behavioral Analysis*. Certainly they are capable of being oriented toward the need for specificity, consistency, and adequate records but probably have neither the time nor realistically the inclination to develop complicated schedules of reinforcement or elaborate single subject experimental designs. In this regard, it is important for the consultant to stay with relatively simple and specific interventions that can be clearly described to the consultee. In addition, the importance of simple record keeping regarding the intervention and its outcome should be stressed. Without some degree of record keeping it is impossible to determine whether the intervention has even been implemented let alone whether it has been successful or not.

I have found it quite useful when making recommendations to consultees, to take some time and care in explaining in a concrete way the concept of behavioral consequences. Almost all adults are familiar with the notion that rewards and punishments influence behavior. This notion of rewards and punishments, which may be referred to as consequences, can be used to present to the consultee the all important concept of "contingent consequences." Behavior that tends to result in a contingent reward tends to be repeated, whereas behavior that tends to result in a contingent withdrawal of a reward or a punishment tends to be decreased in frequency. This simplified version of the law of effect without the necessity of an elaborate discussion of the differences between positive and negative reinforcement does need to be clearly understood by the consultee so that a specific intervention may be undertaken. Rewards and/or punishments that are noncontingent, that is occur regardless of the child's behavior are self-defeating. This is a critical concept to get across because many cases clearly indicate that histories of noncontingent reward and punishment lead to a clearly disturbed emotion and behavior on the part of children and teenagers. It is important to appraise the consultee of the nature of rewards and punishments so that this concept of reinforcement is practically understood. In many cases, what an adult may perceive as a punishment, for example, a verbal reprimand, may be perceived by an oppositional child or teenager as a kind of reward. This may be particularly the case if the child or teenager has decided that aggravating his or her parent or teacher is so invigorating that the child finds it reinforcing. It is worth spending time with the consultee in describing generally useful concepts of contingency management and rewards as well as penalties that may be age appropriate for the youngster in question.

Another useful concept to briefly describe is the notion of "response cost contingencies." Essentially, this effective method of behavior management involves penalizing a child for an unacceptable response by withdrawing a reward or imposing a sanction. In many cases, older children or teenagers who will not work for rewards will make an effort to change in order to avoid penalties. The importance of consistency in any contingency management plan should also be stipulated to the consultee. It is a widely known but often ignored fact that, contingencies that are consistent are generally more effective. Certainly, although this is more work for the adult involved, it is most likely to result in a beneficial outcome for the management plan.

At this phase of consultation, after a general model of behavioral intervention has been presented and explained it is important for the consultant to begin to collaboratively design a specific intervention plan. It is important to stress the necessity of keeping records. The simpler the record keeping the better, although I prefer a record that not only includes the adult's intervention and the child's reaction to it but also some indication of the adult's emotions and responses to the child's behavior and his or her self-talk as well. Part of the intervention plan might also stress the idea of giving the plan fair trial, that is putting it into effect and persisting in its application for long enough to be able to tell whether the intervention has succeeded. It may well be true that a major cause of failure in behavioral intervention is a lack of persistence rather than an inappropriate plan. It is sometimes quite useful to schedule follow-up consultation sessions after the intervention has had enough time for a fair trial. It might be appropriate in many cases to permit the consultee to contact the consultant if the consultee runs into any problems or develops new questions, but it is probably efficient to delay the next consulting session until the intervention has been tried and some data about its success has been generated.

FOLLOW-UP

Follow-up is a very critical element in effective REC. Follow-up should take into account a reasonable opportunity for the consultee to implement the recommendations and can then begin with a review of the results of the intervention as recorded in the agreed upon manner. It is usually appropriate to begin a follow-up session with a kind of question such as "How did you do with implementing what we discussed last time?" This might also be followed with a request to see the data or records of how the intervention went. As in RET in general, it is pointless to prescribe homework for a client to work on in between sessions if you are not going to check it and make it a part of the ongoing treatment. Likewise in REC, follow-up consultation sessions need to have some continuity and begin by reviewing the interventions that were prescribed in previous sessions. Often the consultee will have discovered a new problem that he or she may wish to discuss, yet, without this continuity and without some review of the basic teaching that went on in earlier sessions, the consultation model loses some of its educational power. In reviewing the results of an intervention, it is worth looking at not only what went wrong or in effect what did not work, but also attention needs to be paid to that which did work, in short what went right. It is almost always appropriate to strongly provide verbal reinforcement and support for the consultee's effort at the intervention. Progress, not perfection, is the goal. Therefore, effort should be recognized, praised, and enhanced regardless of how successful and unsuccessful the prescribed intervention may have been.

Specific following up on whatever prior discussion occurred concerning the consultee's personal plan for the rational management of dysfunctional thoughts and feelings in reaction to the child's problem is also indicated. Here again, reinforcing efforts toward more rational emotional self-management with praise and encouragement is indicated. It is also important, where possible, to help the consultee draw the conclusion that with moderate emotional reaction to the client's presenting difficulties on the part of the consultee, implementation of the consultant's intervention recommendations occurs more easily and efficiently. The data collected by the consultee on the effects of the intervention can be used to reinforce this finding that improved rational management does more successfully address the child's behavioral and emotional disturbance in ways that previous patterns of adult to child interaction were unable to do.

In many cases, the consulting relationship will involve more than a few consulting sessions. Regardless of the number, it is important that the consultant and the consultee agree that follow-up will occur. The goal of REC is to not only make expert recommendations but to see that they are effectively and persistently implemented. That is why an important emphasis is placed on removing emotional and behavioral roadblocks to this implementation. Planned and specific follow-up over time is probably the best way to see that the longer range goal of consultation, that is namely some improvement in the identified client's emotional and behavioral difficulties, is achieved. Without sufficient follow-up and persistence, consultation is merely the exchange among adults of information on the one hand and advice on the other. Follow-up on initial consultation sessions connects this advice giving with specific effects on the behavioral and emotional responses of the child or adolescent client. With follow-up, adjustments in the prescribed intervention can be made based on a careful consideration of the intervention's outcome. In addition, and maybe most importantly, the frequent frustration, discouragement, and/or newer emotional challenges experienced by the consultee as they work at changing can be addressed as they develop. Many forms of recommended intervention initially meet with success. Those that result in long-range changes, however, are probably those that are followed up upon persistently and adjusted according to the feedback of experience obtained by the collaboration of the consultant and consultee.

COMMON PRESENTING CONCERNS AND SAMPLE CONSULTATION STRATEGIES

In the following sections, four common patterns of childhood and adolescent emotional and behavioral disturbances are described. These categories are not seen as mutually exclusive or independent diagnostic entities. They do describe, however, relatively consistent categories of child emotional and behavioral difficulties often presented by adults working with these children.

From the point of view of cognitive therapy in general and RET in particular, childhood and adolescent disturbance can be described as resulting from what Hauck (1983) referred to as neurotic emotional problems and/or manipulative behavior problems. Bernard and Joyce (1984), DiGiuseppe and Bernard (1983), and DiGiuseppe (1981, 1982, 1988, 1989) have all described this disturbance as resulting from both the child's irrational and therefore disturbance-producing beliefs and also the child's disturbing habits of behavior that are often directed at obtaining certain social reinforcement from the significant adults in the child's life. It can be said that the problems of children as presented by adult consultees might be practically separated into those involving child emotional disturbance, disturbing behavior, and/or combinations of both because they are not mutually exclusive.

Overanxious–Apprehensive Child

Overanxious or apprehensive children are typically described by the consultee as approaching tasks with evident fear. Such children may also have developed a variety of defenses against this fear or anxiety that result in under performance, avoidance of new or challenging situations, and a degree of social isolation. Many of these children may meet the diagnostic specifications of "overanxious disorder" (*DSM III-R,* APA, 1988, p. 63). These children might be described as evidencing symptoms of anxiety with general tension, a variety of nervous habits, various phobias, poor sleep patterns, and frequent psychosomatic complaints. Despite cognitive ability, such children may perform poorly in school as the result of their apprehensive approach to learning tasks and performance anxiety that interferes with achievement on standardized tests. In younger children, developmentally inappropriate evidence of continued separation anxiety may be present. In adolescence, anxious overconcern about performance and social acceptance is quite common.

Children's fears appear to fall into three broad categories: fear of rejection (disapproval anxiety), fear of failure (performance anxiety), and fear of fear (discomfort anxiety). These fears or apprehensions might take the form of an exaggerated expectation of danger from external events, anxious preoccupation with loss or abandonment, and/or preoccupation with exaggerated perceptions of threats to self-worth through failure, rejection, or being seen as inadequate and fearful.

Fear and anxiety may be seen as essentially adaptive responses when objective danger is present but as self-defeating responses when the perception of threat or danger is exaggerated or inappropriately generalized. All individuals experience fear or apprehension from time to time. In this regard, it is impossible to avoid this experience. Overgeneralization of this sense of danger, however, results in both emotional distress and sometimes chronic tension but also behavioral avoidance of incorrectly labeled dangerous situations or individuals.

The rational-emotive treatment of children with these clinical difficulties has been described by Grieger and Boyd (1983), Bernard and Joyce (1984), and Waters (1980). As in the treatment of adult anxiety problems (Ellis, 1982), treatment involves both the identification and modification of irrational fear-producing beliefs and behavioral changes oriented toward approaching feared situations and thereby demonstrating improved self-confidence. Ellis (1978, 1980), Ellis, Wolfe, and Mosley (1978), Hauck (1967, 1983), and Waters (1980, 1982) described why children develop anxiety, the role of parents in this development, and specific irrational beliefs that lead to parent–child anxiety problems. Children and adolescents who rigidly demand that any situation be free of all risk of disapproval, rejection, or self-defined failure require considerable encouragement on the part of adults in order to face fearful situations. The parent of an overanxious child may appear to the consultant as an individual both bewildered and frustrated by the child's anxious emotionality and avoidant behavior. Often, these adults, despite their confusion and frustration will be essentially sympathetic to the child's anxiety and may indeed share the child's anxious view of the world. In particular, they may exaggerate the dangerousness in a variety of situations and may have historically been over protective or in other ways inadvertently reinforced the child's fear. Sometimes, the consultant will note that the parents have sent a double message to the child to the effect that independence and high levels of achievement are guarantees of approval, while reinforcing in the child the idea that they are not capable of independence or coping with rejection and, therefore, need to be protected. Some adults themselves may also model a fear of failure and rejection that only serves to reinforce the child's fear. In contrast, although with the same resulting effect, the consultant may detect in some adults an exaggerated competitive attitude which, although not overtly stigmatizing failure, over values the potential payoffs of winning over others.

The consultant working with the parents of an overanxious child would do well to help the parents examine their own beliefs about the "dangerousness" of people, places, and things, as well as help them reassess their emotions and belief about failure and rejection. In a related fashion, the consultant should also assess parents' beliefs about their own discomfort that results from fear and anxiety. An exaggerated sense of discomfort and anxiety on the part of an adult may lead to reinforcing the child's overanxious attitudes and behavior. The consultant may assist the consultee in identifying and reexamining these beliefs in a number of ways. A description of the rational-emotive explanation of fear and anxiety may be particularly helpful. It is also useful to examine with the consultee the problems that result from "self-rating." If rejection or self-defined failure are psychological disasters and result in diminished self-worth, it is logical to worry excessively about these disasters and seek at all cost to avoid them. If, however, rejection, failure, or any number of other disappointments or frustrations in life are unavoidable but do not result in diminished potential for future pleasure or achievement, then they need not be feared excessively or avoided.

Once the consultant has offered the parents a more rational understanding of the psychological nature of anxiety, the consultant should explain to the parents the importance of presenting a more fear-tolerant outlook to the apprehensive or overanxious child. This might be done through direct discussion with the child or it might be done through self-disclosure regarding the parents' fears and ways in which they have rationally managed them. Personal stories and anecdotes might be particularly helpful. It is probably not helpful to encourage or model "fearlessness," because it is unlikely that an apprehensive child will credibly identify with this and it is questionable as to whether a fearless attitude is necessary or realistic. The consultee needs to be encouraged to more openly discuss anxiety and fear with the child or teenager. This would allow the young person to better identify his or her emotional discomfort, label it appropriately, and manage it with less resort to avoidance. It is also a good idea for the consultee to tell the child that facing fears is hard work and takes time. Realistic expectations are useful antidotes to magical thinking and the self-downing many children experience when their anxiety does not automatically disappear in response to their initial efforts to face it.

In collaboration with the consultant, the consultee can be encouraged to examine the specific contingencies of reinforcement operating with respect to the child's apprehensive, overanxious, or avoidant approach to things. It may be that avoidance as a method of anxiety reduction works too well for the child. The child's avoidance may be reinforced by adult attention or other social reinforcers. It also provides the child with considerable control over adult attention and reassurance. Parents can be encouraged to socially reinforce with attention and encouragement, the child's effort in successive approximation toward a goal rather than nonperformance.

The adult, due to his or her own discomfort with the child's anxiety, may be overprotective. This emotional condition is called *projected discomfort anxiety.* In large part, it results from erroneous parent assumptions regarding the child's inability to cope with anxiety or emotional discomfort (e.g., "My child can't stand anxiety or emotional discomfort. It will cause psychological damage."). Less overtly it also reflects parental beliefs about their own ability to cope with the emotional discomfort that might result from actions to help the child overcome avoidance. Parents may fear losing their child's love or fear being overwhelmed with discomfort and frustration if their efforts with their child do not achieve immediate results. In both instances, the result is that the parents covertly or overtly support the child's anxious avoidant behavior.

Because of parents' own poor frustration tolerance or exaggerated attitude about competition, they may punish or negatively reinforce imperfections and inadvertently shape a child's impossible expectation or demand for constant approval and perfect performance. Parental disapproval of a child's imperfect efforts at approaching difficult tasks may encourage the child to conclude it is better not to try than to try and fail. It also can reinforce the child's exaggerated view of the emotional discomfort, which now includes parental disapproval, that results from less than perfect efforts.

Assisting a child in overcoming an apprehensive or overanxious approach to life may require that parents learn to positively reinforce approximations of behavior counter to the apprehension and avoidance. With young children this might involve positively reinforcing small efforts on their part to face their fears. It might also involve positively reinforcing approximations of independent behavior within limits at which the child or adolescent can succeed without overwhelming discomfort. Although care needs to be taken so that the child does not develop dependence on immediate and high levels of reinforcement or encouragement, praise and reward will probably work best with an apprehensive and avoidant youngster. This is also a way of behaviorally disputing the child's belief in his or her own inability to cope. The consultant would do well to specify this behavioral program as much as possible with the consultee. In addition, ways in which general tension may be reduced, through exercise, relaxation, and shared entertainment, noncontingently may also be encouraged.

Impulsive Children

The impulsive child is often described as one who is unable to focus attention or to concentrate except for short periods of time. Such children may also be motorically overactive. The degree of impulsivity may be seen as existing on a continuum from mild to severe. Such children present as particularly difficult in most classroom settings because their poor attention and concentration makes it difficult to keep up with the class and because their impulsive, disorganized, and poorly regulated behavior is often disruptive to others. Consequently, they are often underachievers despite evident cognitive potential. In addition, they may have developed a variety of defenses against their underachievement that might involve a variety of attention-seeking behaviors that in adolescence often expresses itself as an exaggerated attachment to the social approval of their peers. Because their history of impulsivity and poor concentration may result in further academic failure and high levels of negative adult attention, children who might initially be best described as impulsive often later develop oppositional, negativistic, or aggressive attitudes toward authority that further exacerbate their adjustment difficulties.

Children such as those just described may meet the diagnostic criteria for "attention deficit disorder" (APA, 1988, p. 50). Theories regarding the organic versus the psychosocial genesis of impulsivity not withstanding, it would appear that impulsivity might most productively be considered a disorder of temperament as well as a skill deficit with respect to attending as well as tolerated frustration (Bernard & Joyce, 1984; Chess & Thomas, 1984). Cognitive behavioral approaches including teaching rational self-talk to impulsive children have been described by Michenbaum (1977), Kendall and Braswell (1985), and Kendall and Fishler (1983). In all of these approaches, a self-control training model (Mahoney & Thoresen, 1974), is utilized to help children develop self-regulation. In addition, Knaus (1983) has described rational-emotive approaches toward developing improved frustration tolerance because impulsivity and this difficulty often go hand in hand.

Impulsive children often present significant challenges to the adults in their lives. Parents or teachers of impulsive children may often seek consultation because of their frustration, anger, and sense of inadequacy in the face of this "difficult" child. Often they will describe the youngster in question as "hyperactive" and provide a history of difficult, impulsive, and poorly organized behavior evident from earliest childhood. Because impulsive children are often disorganized, distractable, and overreactive to stimulation they more than other children, may trigger angry adult reactions. These adult reactions may be particularly exaggerated and problematic when the child's temperament is very different from the adult's highly organized, structured, and responsible approach (DiGiuseppe, 1988). Certainly, a parent whose personal style and preference is to "discuss" problems with his or her impulsive child so that he or she "understands" how to behave in the future will inevitably be frustrated by the ineffectiveness of this approach. Likewise, a parent who maintains unreasonably high or rigid standards of conduct for an impulsive child will experience problems. Adults, who for reasons of their own, have low frustration tolerant philosophies or who are intolerant of emotional discomfort will certainly experience emotional distress when challenged with managing an impulsive youngster.

Very often, the consultee will present his or her concerns about the impulsive, overreactive child in terms reflecting his or her sense of inadequacy in responding to the youngster. Often one will hear statements like "I tried everything, but he just won't listen." This statement is of course important in that children who are impulsive have significant difficulty in attending and "listening." Such a statement reflects a mismatch between the parent's preferred style of interaction with the child and the child's temperament. Likewise, a parent who lacks frustration tolerance might present with a statement such as, "I can't stand it when she won't sit still." This can reveal more about the parent's frustration tolerance than the child's activity level. In addition, because impulsive children often make poor social judgments, parents and other adults working with them may present with primary concerns about the child's failure to learn from punishment. This may be further complicated by their mistaken belief that the best way to teach children to behave by their rules is to harshly punish them when they do not. Often the impulsive child has difficulty learning from his or her mistakes because little thought or reflection went into making them in the first place. Teaching an impulsive child to slow down and think by punishing his or her mistakes rather than more correctly reinforcing their efforts to slow down may accentuate mismatch between the adult's approach and the child's needs, creating further conflict.

In order to manage an impulsive child more successfully, the adult consultee will need to re-examine some of his or her beliefs about how children "should" behave and also how successful parental or adult intervention or discipline needs to be. The consultant may assist in this by describing in cognitive behavioral terms the impulsive child's primary difficulty that is their possibly inherited temperamental tendency toward overreaction, disorganization, and limited attention span. All attempts at adult intervention need to take these characteristics into consideration. Clearly, a parent who believes that a child *should* "listen" will repeatedly have this rule violated when a highly impulsive child is incapable of doing so. The anger and frustration that results may lead to further roadblocks to management in the form of extreme discouragement, a rejection of adult responsibilities for managing the child, and/or repeated yet ineffective punishment. Similarly, the parent who "can't stand" the child's restlessness and distractability, particularly when that child has relatively limited control over it, at least to begin with, might benefit from rethinking this attitude. Clearly, there is no evidence that impulsive children cannot be tolerated. Parents and teachers tolerate them with varying degrees of success all the time. Because a statement intolerant of the child leads only to anger, it serves no purpose. Adults working with impulsive children would benefit from the description of a more rational philosophy toward tolerating the child's frustrating and difficult behavior. In order to be able to better manage it, at times the best way for the consultant to best help the consultee overcome some of these self-defeating attitudes is to model more rational self-talk for them in difficult situations. This may involve something as basic as redirecting the consultees to consciously and rationally tell themselves "although I dislike this behavior, I can stand it," rather than automatically awfulizing about it and making demands that it not be the way it is.

Many consultees respond favorably to the idea that both firmness and warmth may be most effective in managing impulsive children. Firmness suggests that the parent or adult is in charge rather than the impulsive child. It also implies that limits are set and enforced. The warmth dimension implies that discipline is nonpunitive and that the child or teenager as a whole has the adult's love and acceptance, whereas a particular impulsive behavior may be disapproved of. It may be an important distinction with impulsive children, particularly those who have been impulsive all their lives and have relatively little control over it without considerable effort on their part and those of their adult caretakers to help them learn self-control strategies. When the consultee is able to calmly and nonpunitively set limits, the impulsive child may be better able or at least more likely to respond favorably.

Behavioral intervention for children with an impulsive approach to things might best be described as involving the use of positive reinforcement to develop responses incompatible with impulsivity. Because impulsive or attention deficit children are overreactive to their environment, simple, concrete methods of management are more likely to be successful than highly vocal, unstructured, or disorganized methods. It is probably most helpful in attempting to assist impulsive children to not concentrate on their academic achievement as a focus for behavioral training. For impulsive children who may be underachievers, reinforcement should be provided for doing rather than doing well. At a more basic level, doing "slowly and carefully" might be positively reinforced rather than accomplishing assignments or getting correct answers. A variety of games, even simple ones like checkers, can be used for self-control training. In a modification of checkers, children could be reinforced for taking 10 seconds between each move rather than making 10 moves in a second. Because restructuring something as fundamental as impulsivity may be a lengthy and time-consuming procedure, care should be taken not to overreinforce the youngster. Token economy type tasks may be quite appropriate here with points or markers exchanged for some specific or tangible reinforcement. Quite often with younger children, praise alone is a positive reinforcement for their efforts to slow down and think before they act. Clearly, punishing impulsive behavior may be ineffective. When an impulsive child behavior requires a negative consequence, a response cost contingency in which something that is a positive reinforcer is taken from the child as a penalty for an impulsive act is more appropriate and potentially effective. Although punishment may temporarily inhibit impulsive behavior, its side effects render it less effective in the long run.

Oppositional–Negativistic Children

The negativistic or oppositional youngster is one who is typically described as being antagonistic to adult authority. He or she may refuse to follow simple classroom or family rules because they are "unfair." A typical response for such youngsters to frustrating or demanding situations is a passive–aggressive with-drawal from them. Various forms of avoidance might be seen in response to a difficult task ranging from a feigned helplessness to blatant procrastination and various forms of creative excuse making. Certainly, some oppositional and nega-tivistic youngsters do become angry and act out their anger when pressed to comply with adult demands. This anger, however, is most often expressed ver-bally or indirectly through running away rather than through interpersonal ag-gression. In adolescents, oppositional youngsters seem to strongly identify with peer values and adamantly oppose adult standards and requirements in their attempt at achieving independence. Both in the family and the classroom, the negativistic or oppositional child is often socially appealing and seen as quite capable. For teachers in particular, this can be most frustrating in that the nega-tivistic youngster may ask for and accept extra help or special consideration and would certainly appear to have the cognitive potential to perform. Despite this apparent interest in achievement, these children will often avoid the respon-sibilities of academic performance by not completing assignments, losing com-pleted assignments, and not preparing for tests.

The youngsters described here may generally meet the diagnostic criteria of "oppositional disorder" (APA, 1988, p. 56). In terms of diagnostic specifica-tions, these youngsters are seen as capable of age-appropriate social judgment in that they know right from wrong, yet for reasons of their own, they passive–aggressively reject authority through noncompliance and manipulation. They do not generally violate major societal norms but are often quite emotionally dis-turbed intrapersonally (e.g., angry, depressed) and clearly quite disturbing to adults responsible for their management. Particularly in adolescents, a long-standing pattern of oppositional behavior may result in additional adjustment difficulties, including peer-influenced substance abuse, rejection of family rules, and run away attempts. In some cases, oppositionality in adolescents may also be accompanied by symptoms of depression that are clearly a major concern given this type of youngster's overall style and apparent willingness to "cut off their nose to spite their face."

In addition, oppositional or negativistic youngsters may be those who have failed to develop a self-accepting attitude toward themselves and/or confidence in their ability to achieve and cope. In many ways this is much like adult depression in that the passive–aggressive or oppositional youngsters may at a different level see themselves as essentially helpless and worthless. In a peculiar way, despite the negative and clearly self-defeating consequences of their opposi-tionality, they seem reinforced by it. In adolescents in particular, this form of oppositionality may reflect attempts at establishing independence. Therefore, adult negative attention is reinforcing in that it defines their independence in their own eyes as well as those of their important peer group. There is then a pay off for saying no even when objectively the consequences of saying no are disadvan-tageous. Not only does the oppositional and negativistic youngster often avoid the demands of many situations, but the youngster may also develop a sense of self-esteem from opposing perceived injustice and always being ready to "stick up for themselves." Unfortunately, such youngsters rarely can see beyond their own emotional needs and despite the fact that their rejection of adult authority and direction is self-defeating they would appear to be looking for acceptance and tolerance rather than the disapproval and punishment that their negativistic behavior most frequently creates.

In a basic way, oppositional and negativistic children and teenagers seem to be saying "it's my life and I'll run it my way." Clearly, this is a challenge directed at any adult with responsibility for their management. Whether oppositional youngsters are rebelling against a history of objectively unfair or inconsistent adult treatment or have never learned a frustration tolerant attitude and irrationally think that they always have to have it their way, the disturbing effect this oppositional behavior has on adults is the same. The consultant may assist the consultee in identifying and modifying beliefs about childrearing in general as well as the particular child in question which may be poorly matched to the problems created by oppositionality. On the philosophical level, it may be useful to explain that regardless of how we may feel about it, the child or teenager's life is indeed his or her own. The youngster will make choices that will have consequences independent of whether the adults involved would prefer those choices or whether those choices are truly in the youngsters' best interest. If the adult irrationally believes that he or she must have control and power over his or her children and that children must never differ with adult authority, conflict is inevitable. If parents have strongly reinforced in the child the kind of "rugged individualism" that encourages and supports the youngster even in inappropriate attempts at independence, then conflict with authority outside the family may be quite likely. In consulting with parents of oppositional children, it is important to ascertain both parents' attitude about "independence." Because independence may be a stereotypically masculine value, fathers' beliefs about this, particularly with respect to their sons, may shed some light on how some youngsters may view themselves as more independent and autonomous when they oppose authority.

Managing an oppositional youngster requires frustration tolerant attitudes on the part of the adult. Persistence rather than power will probably pay off. In addition, parents or other adults who have difficulty tolerating conflict may inadvertently reinforce negativism through their avoidance of conflict by ignoring the youngster's refusal to comply with simple rules and procedures. In both regards, adults involved with children described as negativistic or oppositional may need to recognize the meaning of this behavior to the youngster and the persistence it may require in addressing it. Angrily overreacting to the oppositionality may reinforce it. Passively avoiding confrontation by tolerating the youngster's rejection of rules will only result in more negative consequences for the youngster. Making excuses for the youngster in the face of conflict with other authorities in school or the community will only further reinforce this pattern.

The consultant should analyze with the consultee the long-range consequences of permitting oppositional behavior to go completely unchecked. It would also be a good idea to encourage the adults charged with managing these children to recognize that they are the adults so that they can avoid unnecessary conflict while sanctioning with logical consequences the disregard of important rules.

Behavioral parenting strategies that might best apply to oppositional and negativistic behavior involve a recognition of a lack of absolute control over the youngster's choices. Despite the absence of complete control and regardless of what choices the youngster makes, both short- and long-term consequences result. Although difficult for many parents to do unless they are vigorously talking sense to themselves, it may be appropriate to allow natural consequences to take their course when a youngster refuses to comply. For example, if a youngster refuses to do a homework assignment, it may be appropriate to permit the youngster to take the consequences of that choice in school. In addition, in a similar way, community authorities in extreme cases, may be useful in underscoring other forms of logical consequences for problems such as truancy, curfew violations, and underage alcohol use. Above all, it is important that the oppositional youngster not be permitted to charm, manipulate, or in any way effectively avoid all consequences resulting from his or her oppositional behavior. Response cost contingencies are probably the most effective behavioral methods with oppositional youngsters. A calmly but firmly administered penalty as a cost for failure to comply with simple rules may be far more powerful than discussions, lectures, or interminable groundings. Penalties should be reasonable and time limited. They seem best administered in the absence of anger and recrimination. With younger children, in addition to response cost contingencies for noncompliance, some effort should be made to use positive reinforcement to strengthen cooperative behavior. Although this may be initially less successful, simple verbal approval for cooperation might well further strengthen the value of using negative consequences for oppositionality.

Having reasonable expectations regarding the success of behavioral interventions with negativistic or oppositional youngsters is important and should be reinforced by the consultant. Generally, oppositional behavior in some ways "pays off" for the youngster. It can reasonably be expected that these payoffs would not be immediately eliminated. Beginning to help the youngster to think in terms of the logic of consequences in the long run, however, is an important accomplishment no matter how long it takes. Often, the shear frustration of repeatedly addressing this problem leads some adults to give up before a reasonably fair trial has been undertaken. As stated in many other areas of this chapter, progress rather than perfection is what to look for. There is little to be gained from a gratuitous test of wills, however, and if the adult is able to readjust his or her view of what is at stake, some oppositional difficulties can be honestly renegotiated. This requires, however, that both the adult and youngster agree to abide by the results of the negotiation. Although a formal contract is not necessary in all cases, some stipulation of what will happen if the negotiated rules or procedures are not followed by either party should be addressed.

Some rules are clearly nonnegotiable. For example, it would be a mistake for an adult to permit a teenager to use drugs occasionally as some form of negotiated agreement. Despite this, however, a vast number of rules both in the family and in the school can be discussed and reevaluated in the light of shared understanding of their importance and the short- and long-term consequences of noncompliance. The consultant can suggest to the consultee some areas where negotiation might be appropriate as well as some response cost strategies that can be brought to bear if negotiations fail to respond. Warm, firm limit setting and the youngster's perception that limits will be set no matter how much he or she opposes them may well provide the best atmosphere for some collaborative negotiation. A final point worth making is that negotiation best occurs before a problem rather than after it. Negotiating rules as well as penalties for future behaviors along with a calm and rational approach to managing continued difficulties may provide the best hope for managing oppositional youngsters.

Hostile–Aggressive Children

The youngster who presents as angry and hostile might best be described as one who resents authority and attacks in order to defend him or herself from what is viewed as unfair demands. Youngsters whose aggression and anger present significant problems no doubt have low frustration tolerance and may have a history of impulsivity. In addition, they are less well socialized and may be more immature in their development of social conscience than oppositional or negativistic youngsters. In many ways, angry or aggressive children seem to view the family, classroom, and community as conspiring to devalue their person. Often, histories of psychological and physical abuse can be identified in the most poorly socialized and highly aggressive of such youngsters. It is most likely that they have experienced significant punishment in the past but punishment that was administered in an aggressive, inconsistent, and often depersonalizing way.

Depending on the frequency, amplitude, and duration of these youngsters' aggressive responses, they might meet the diagnostic specifications for "conduct disorder–unsocialized, aggressive type" (APA, 1988, p. 53). In some cases, however, their aggressiveness is more situation specific and expressive of a deficit in self-control or strong exposure to angry and aggressive models in the family or peer group. Aggressive youngsters might be seen as falling into essentially two categories. Some are intensely hostile and direct their hostility and aggressiveness toward authority. This may reflect an intense anger at inconsistent or punitive earlier experiences with authority figures. On the other hand, some youngsters' aggressiveness may be more or less exclusively directed toward peers. This form of aggression may stem from an exaggerated fear of rejection by peers or perceived need to prove one's "toughness" in the face of peer competition. In either case, hostility and aggression create significant management difficulties for adults working with these youngsters. Often, aggressive youngsters in addition to having a low tolerance for frustration will also have poor histories of positive reinforcement for appropriate social behavior.

In the rational-emotive treatment of youngsters with conduct disorders (DiGiuseppe, 1983, 1988, 1989), the problems presented by aggressive and angry youngsters are identified and the emotional and practical difficulties experienced by adults charged with managing them are recognized. As with the oppositional and negativistic youngster, managing an aggressive or hostile youngster can be most frustrating and difficult. In consultation, the consultant would do well to assist the consultee in reexamining his or her attitudes about frustration tolerance. Clearly, to manage an angry and hostile youngster in an angry and hostile way due to one's own difficulties with frustration tolerance is a script for failure. In addition, the very combative nature of aggressive children can cause even the most tolerant of adults to defensively overreact to this aggression. The consultee should be asked to explore how personally he or she takes the child's hostility. Even if the anger and hostility is intended personally by the child, some degree of rational distance from it may be necessary in order to manage it better. Angry and disturbed youngsters behave rather consistently in angry and disturbed ways. Accepting this fact while working hard to change it might provide the adult with sufficient leverage to set limits and enforce them in a nonangry or aggressive fashion. With angry youngsters, it is relatively natural to be caught up in the anger. Certainly, hostile and aggressive behavior is intended to intimidate, yet counterintimidation is usually not very productive in the long run. Even with youngsters whose anger problems are episodic and situationally specific, a firm but controlled rather than angry response would appear to yield the best long-term results. In many cases, aggressive children justify their aggression by blaming someone else for it. It is probably best for the adults involved not to give them that someone to blame.

From a behavioral point of view, once the adults involved have been able to master to some extent their own angry response to an aggressive youngster, response cost contingencies would appear most powerful. This is not to suggest that positive reinforcement for more cooperative and prosocial behavior is less important but rather that the aggressive behavior is more immediate and problematic. Time-out procedures in response to anger episodes can be effective. They provide a cooling off period in which even the angriest youngster will eventually spend some negative emotions.

Attempts to involve one's self in the youngster's rationalization for his or her angry outburst by trying to find and assign blame for the fight or argument are generally pointless. It is better to focus on what the youngster did in acting out rather than why he or she did it. No matter how provoked, an aggressive or violent act is inappropriate. There are both immediate and long-term consequences for this kind of inappropriate and aggressive behavior. A fair but not harsh penalty may be most appropriate for these anger outbursts. Once the youngster has had time to regain some emotional control, he or she can be expected to do something to make up for the outburst. This could be an unpleasant task or other penalty such as being denied a reward that was anticipated. If the youngster can be engaged in some problem solving regarding his or her aggressive outburst, self-control strategies such as those used with impulsive youngsters might be taught using direct positive reinforcement. Positive reinforcement for engaging in behaviors incompatible with an angry or aggressive outburst might also be appropriate.

Aggressive youngsters can be taught to solve interpersonal conflicts nonaggressively, but this often requires that a great deal of shaping and reinforcing prosocial behavior be undertaken. In working with the aggressive youngster, it would appear that what the adult does, rather than what he or she says, in response to the hostility and aggression may be most important. Preparing a plan about how anger in a particular youngster will be handled by the adult can be a very useful and important function of consultation. Armed with this plan, the consultee will be better prepared to manage his or her own emotional reaction to the youngster's anger and disturbance. If a plan, such as the described combination of time-out and response cost, has been worked out in sufficient detail and possibly even rehearsed by the consultee, then consultation has resulted in something useful.

No anger problem, however, is modified in a single trial and therefore with hostile and aggressive youngsters more than with many others, the consultant should take care to reinforce reasonable expectations as to time and effort on the consultee's part before dramatic results are to be anticipated. The major value of having a plan to manage this form of aggression is that even if it is not immediately effective, we know that it is better than an angry or aggressive response that is clearly ineffective.

SUMMARY AND CONCLUSIONS

This chapter has outlined the process of REC as an efficient and effective model of intervention in the mental health problems of children and youth. Its focus is primarily on using a consultative relationship with the adults working with disturbed or disruptive young people with a variety of problems to help these adults, be they parents or teachers, overcome their own attitudinal and emotional roadblocks to improved child management and to then follow through on implementing them. It differs from psychotherapy with adults distressed about their children in that the focus of intervention is the child's disturbance not the adult's distress. Despite the personal and potential clinical significance of adult disturbance, the consultant–consultee contract is a specific and limited one, namely, intervention that can and will make a difference in the child's adjustment. Within this focused contract, the methods of RET are employed to identify and correct adult thoughts, feelings, and behavior as they relate to children's adjustment problems. Because of the focused nature of REC and its derivation from the theory and practice of RET, it can be applied in a wide variety of settings where time and professional resources may be limited. The potential for beneficial application of REC is viewed as considerable. It can be used as a model for organizing effective intervention in many of the most commonly presenting patterns of childhood adjustment problems.

REFERENCES

American Psychiatric Association. (1988). *Diagnostic and statistical manual of mental disorders* (3rd ed., rev.). Washington, DC: Author.

Bard, J. (1980). *Rational-emotive therapy in practice.* Champaign, IL: Research Press.

Bernard, M. E., & Joyce, M. R. (1984). *Rational emotive therapy with children and adolescents: Theory, treatment strategies, preventative methods.* New York: Wiley-Interscience.

Chess, S., & Thomas, A. (1984). *Origins and evolution of behavior disorders: From infancy to early adult life.* New York: Brunner/Mazel.

DiGiuseppe, R. (1981). Cognitive therapy with children. In G. Emery, S. Hollon, & R. Bedrosian (Eds.), *New directions in cognitive therapy* (pp. 50–67). New York: Guilford.

DiGiuseppe, R. (1982). Problems of children and their parents. In R. Grieger & I. Z. Grieger (Eds.), *Cognition and emotional disturbance* (pp. 212–226). New York: Human Sciences Press.

DiGiuseppe, R. (1983). Rational-emotive therapy with conduct disorders. In A. Ellis & M. E. Bernard (Eds.), *Rational-emotive approaches to the problems of childhood* (pp. 111–132). New York: Plenum.

DiGiuseppe, R. (1988). A cognitive behavioral approach to the treatment of conduct disorder children and adolescents. In N. Epstein, S. Schlesinger, & W. Dryden (Eds.), *Cognitive-behavioral therapy with families* (pp. 183–214). New York: Brunner/Mazel.

DiGiuseppe, R. (1989). Cognitive therapy with children. In A. Freeman, K. M. Simon, L. E. Beutler, & H. Arkowitz (Eds.), *Comprehensive handbook of cognitive therapy* (pp. 515–533). New York: Plenum.

DiGiuseppe, R., & Bernard, M. E. (1983). Principles of assessment and methods of treatment with children. In A. Ellis & M. E. Bernard (Eds.), *Rational-emotive approaches to the problems of childhood* (pp. 45–88). New York: Plenum.

Dryden, W. (1984). *Rational-emotive therapy: Fundamentals and innovations.* Beckenham, Kent: Croom-Helm.

Ellis, A. (1962). *Reason and emotion in psychotherapy.* New York: Lyle Stuart.

Ellis, A. (1977). The basic clinical theory of rational-emotive therapy. In A. Ellis & R. Grieger (Eds.), *Handbook of rational-emotive therapy* (pp. 3–34). New York: Springer.

Ellis, A. (1978). Rational-emotive guidance. In E. L. Arnold (Ed.), *Helping parents help their children* (pp. 91–101). New York: Brunner/Mazel.

Ellis, A. (1980). Discomfort anxiety: A new cognitive-behavioral construct. *Rational Living, 15,* 25–30.

Ellis, A. (1982). Psychoneurosis and anxiety problems. In R. Grieger (Ed.), *Cognition and emotional disturbance* (pp. 17–45). New York: Human Sciences Press.

Ellis, A., & Whiteley, J. M. (Eds.). (1979). *Theoretical and empirical foundations of rational-emotive therapy.* Monterey, CA: Brooks/Cole.

Ellis, A., Wolfe, J. L., & Moseley, S. (1978). *How to raise an emotionally healthy, happy child.* Hollywood, CA: Wilshire.

Frank, J. D. (1961). *Persuasion and healing.* Baltimore, MD: John Hopkins Press.

Grieger, R. M., & Boyd, J. D. (1983). Childhood anxiety, fears and phobias: A cognitive behavioral psychosituational approach. In A. Ellis & M. E. Bernard (Eds.), *Rational-emotive approaches to the problems of childhood* (pp. 211–240). New York: Plenum.

Hauck, P. A. (1967). *The rational management of children.* New York: Libra Publishers.

Hauck, P. A. (1983). Working with parents. In A. Ellis & M. E. Bernard (Eds.), *Rational-emotive approaches to the problems of childhood* (pp. 333–366). New York: Plenum.

Kendall, P. C., & Braswell, L. (1985). *Cognitive behavioral therapy for impulsive children.* New York: Guilford.

Kendall, P. C., & Fishler, G. L. (1983). Teaching rational self-talk to impulsive children. In A. Ellis & M. E. Bernard (Eds.), *Rational-emotive approaches to the problems of childhood* (pp. 159–188). New York: Plenum.

Knaus, W. (1983). Children and low frustration tolerance. In A. Ellis & M. E. Bernard (Eds.), *Rational-emotive approaches to the problems of childhood* (pp. 139–158). New York: Plenum.

Mahoney, M. T., & Thoresen, C. E. (1974). *Self-control: Power to the person.* Belmont, CA: Brooks/Cole.

McInerney, J. F. (1983). Working with parents and teachers of exceptional children. In A. Ellis & M. E. Bernard (Eds.), *Rational-emotive approaches to the problems of childhood* (pp. 387–414). New York: Plenum.

Michenbaum, D. (1977). *Cognitive behavior modification.* New York: Plenum.

Walen, S. R., DiGiuseppe, R., & Wessler, R. L. (1980). *A practitioner's guide to rational-emotive therapy.* New York: Oxford University Press.

Waters, V. (1980). *Rational stories for children: Rational parenting series.* New York: Institute for Rational Living.

Waters, V. (1982). Therapies for children: Rational-emotive therapy. In C. R. Reynolds & T. B. Gutkin (Eds.), *Handbook of school psychology* (pp. 570–579). New York: Wiley.

Wessler, R. A., & Wessler, R. L. (1980). *The principles and practices of rational-emotive therapy.* San Francisco: Jossey-Bass.

4 Rational-Emotive Parent Consultation

Marie Joyce
Australian Catholic University

School psychologists who work with parents will be interested in the applications of rational-emotive therapy (RET) with parents. The approach used in this chapter to describe parent consultation parallels the mental health consultation model developed by Meyers, Parsons, and Martin (1979) to describe consultation with teachers. Meyers et al. described the model in four levels:

Level 1: Direct service to the child. This has traditionally been the predominant form of psychological services involving a psychologist working directly with the child.

Level 2: Indirect service to the child in which the consultee who is a person responsible for the child (parent, teacher) implements an intervention resulting from the consultation process.

Level 3: Direct service to the parent (or teacher), focusing on helping parents improve their own functioning and especially overcoming emotional difficulties in relation to parenting, which indirectly promotes the child's welfare.

Level 4: Service to the organization (family, school). Help is provided to the child by reorganizing some aspect of family life. This is the most indirect form of consultation.

RET consultation with parents focuses only on Levels 2 and 3. Levels 1 and 4 are not relevant to this discussion.

This chapter examines the two types of RET parent consultation and describe ways in which RET can be implemented with individual parents or groups of parents from either clinical or nonclinical populations. The theory of rational-emotive parent consultation is presented and illustrations are provided for parent–child problems. Before the various ways a school psychologist can employ rational-emotive parent consultation are described, the theory of rational-emotive parenting is presented. (I use these RET consultative approaches most frequently in the delivery of services to parents in my practice as a school psychologist.)

RET AS PARENT CONSULTATION

RET parent consultation can be applied at one of two levels:

1. *Indirect service to the child* is when the parent is the consultee and the child is the client. This aims to increase parents' ability to solve their children's practical problems (e.g., behavioral, emotional, learning) and to achieve the goals of parenting as a consequence of parents acquiring emotional self-control skills. This first level, which parallels Meyers' Level 2 (indirect service to the child), identifies the child as the client and main beneficiary of RET parent consultation. Although parents themselves will, as a consequence of learning rational-emotive self-control skills, experience an improvement in mental health through a lessening of emotional stress, this outcome facilitates the parents' solving of child problems and fosters the social, emotional, and educational development of the children.

2. *Parent mental health consultation* is when the parent is the client. This level, which parallels Meyers' Level 3 (mental health consultation), recognizes the improvement of parent mental health as an end in itself. Within this context, the client who is the recipient of RET parent consultation is the parent. (The child is seen, indirectly, as benefiting from a reduction in parent stress.) If, therefore, there is a need in the parent population for stress management programs, the consultant could consider the present RET approach as a useful one.

In assessing and remediating parenting problems, RET employs a dual analysis of parents' emotional problems and of parents' practical problems. This distinction is crucial to understanding how RET is applied to parenting issues. Practical problems of parents refer to problems parents encounter with their children (e.g., emotional, behavioral, developmental) and are often resolved by parents through the learning and application of specific parenting skills (e.g., discipline skills, communication, tutoring). Emotional problems of parents occur when parents experience disturbed negative emotions about a practical problem they have with their children. These disturbed emotions (e.g., rage, anxiety, guilt) are seen in RET as not only exacerbating parent stress, but also as making it much harder for parents to solve their practical problems. For example, a parent may experience feelings of high anxiety when the child's developmental rate is apparently slower than other children's, or feelings of inadequacy, depression, or anger when his or her discipline methods are failing. RET parent consultation differs from behavioral consultation in targeting parent emotions for change.

RET proposes that high intensity negative emotions of parents (a) derive from irrational beliefs about themselves and their parenting; and (b) are inappropriate and self-defeating, primarily because they produce emotional distress in the parent, undermining mental health; (c) interfere with effective practical problem solving; (d) can occasion further emotional problems in their child (e.g., anxiety, guilt, resentment, self-pity or anger); and (e) can lead to a deterioration in the parent–child relationship.

RET AND PARENTING

History

RET has concerned itself with issues of parenting over several decades. In the late 1960s, Ellis, Moseley, and Wolfe (1966), in their book *How to Raise an Emotionally Healthy, Happy Child,* presented rational-emotive ideas to help parents understand common child problems and ways these problems might be alleviated. The problems dealt with included fears, anxiety, hostility, sex and conduct problems, and lack of self-discipline. Ellis et al. focused on the importance of the parent's emotional state while interacting with the child. For example, they recommended to parents who are helping their child overcome fears: "Calmness in dealing with a child's fears is one of the prime requisites for helping him to overcome them" (p. 65). In teaching parents about a child's lack of self-discipline, they suggested:

> In most cases where a child refuses to accept any discipline . . . it is his parents, rather, who won't accept any wrestling with him and who weakly refuse to take the consequences of forcing him to discipline himself. This is often an outcome of their own feelings of inadequacy, their fears and guilt at acting "hostilely" toward a child. (p. 129)

A number of other RET writers have addressed the problems of parents. Hauck (1967), in his book *The Rational Management of Children,* analyzed some of the irrational attitudes commonly held by parents in relation to their children and detailed some of the common "parenting styles" and the consequences of these for the children. Grieger and Boyd (1983) described six disturbed parenting styles associated with anxiety, fears, and phobias in children. The parenting styles described by Hauck and by Grieger and Boyd are discussed here in relation to child mental health.

Several RET theorists have been concerned with the application of RET to parents of particular populations of children. For example, DiGiuseppe (1983, 1988) dealt with the parents of conduct disorder children and McInerney (1983) addressed problems encountered by parents of handicapped children. Other published RET literature on parenting includes Barrish and Barrish's work (1985) on the RET treatment of parental anger, and Woulff (1983), who integrated RET with family therapy.

Parenting Styles

RET hypothesizes (e.g., Bernard & Joyce, 1984) that the child's parents create the most important environmental conditions by their parenting style. Parents not only teach behavioral patterns but also contribute to parent–child interactions emotional elements that react with the child's inborn tendency to think irrationally and self-centeredly. Such tendencies can be modified or reinforced by parental attitudes and practices. Children with "difficult" temperaments (Chess, Thomas, & Birch, 1965) are particularly at risk when exposed to the styles of parenting discussed here. RET has made a contribution to understanding some of the maladaptive habits parents (and children) manifest and how they can be overcome.

Hauck (1967) presented a RET rationale of parenting styles in which he discussed two dimensions of parenting: kindness and firmness. He identified the "kind and firm" approach as being consistent with RET and the philosophy of rational parenting. It involves the parent frequently discussing behavior with the child, helping the child build up tolerance for the inevitable frustrations of life by setting limits, and thinking well of the child, even when he or she is misbehaving. Each of the other three styles of parenting Hauck presented ("kind and not firm," "unkind and firm," and "unkind and not firm"), is shown to have destructive effects. Kind and not firm parents are loving but indulgent toward their child and are likely to produce "the spoiled brats, the weak and dependent, and the emotionally infantile" (Hauck, 1967, p. 43). Unkind and not firm parents are cold, critical, and inconsistent toward their child, leading to confusion and inconsistency in the child, because whatever he or she does seems to be wrong. Thus, RET hypothesizes a link between lack of firmness by the parent with poor self-discipline in the child.

A further link is proposed between parental unkindness and child's low self-esteem and so the unkind and not firm regime is seriously lacking in both aspects. The unkind but firm style has the beneficial feature of helping to develop habits of responsibility and self-discipline, but at a high cost to the mental health of the children who frequently suffer anxiety and depression associated with blame and guilt.

In an account of parenting styles associated with anxiety, fears, and phobias in childhood, RET practitioners Grieger and Boyd (1983) identified six disturbed styles:

1. the *criticism trap,* the most common style, is characterized by excessive criticism, nagging, blaming, correcting, ridiculing, and putting down the child;
2. *the perfectionism trap,* in which parents place excessive pressure on the child to always achieve highly and do well; when the child performs poorly they criticize and get angry, and when the child performs well they let the child know that he or she could have done better;
3. in *the scared rabbit trap* parents communicate excessive fear of danger and discomfort with uncertainty;
4. the *false positive trap* and
5. the *guilt trap* are styles that provide excessive and indiscriminate positive affection for the child, with little or no limit setting; and
6. the *inconsistency trap* is characterized by parents either dealing with the child according to their mood, or criticizing the child strongly and frequently but without setting rules.

All of these styles are associated with irrational beliefs and disturbed negative emotions in the parent and with undesirable consequences for the child's mental health.

Irrationality and Emotional Distress

From a RET perspective, psychological stress in parents is manifested in intense and enduring levels of parent emotionality including excessive anger, guilt, anxiety, and self-downing. A RET view of parent emotional stress focuses on parents' beliefs especially about themselves and their parenting, and about their child and their child's behavior. Recent research (e.g., Joyce, 1989) has found irrational beliefs about parenting to be correlated with emotional stress in parents. Examples of irrational beliefs that RET hypothesizes to underlie parent extreme emotional upset are as follows:

Parental Anger

1. There are bad and wicked people in the world, and the only way to make bad people into good people is by being very severe with them, beating them, and telling them how worthless they are (Hauck, 1983).
2. Children should always and unequivocally do well (e.g., be motivated, achieve, etc.) and behave correctly (e.g., be kind, considerate, interested) (Grieger & Boyd, 1983).

3. A child and his or her behavior are the same, and thus children who act badly or err are bad (Grieger & Boyd, 1983).

Parental Depression and Self-Downing

1. If you are not loved and approved of by important people in your life, you are worthless. Rejection is painful and almost devastating and you cannot avoid being upset when rejected (Hauck, 1983).
2. If my child misbehaves frequently it is awful and I am a failure as a parent (Bernard & Joyce, 1984).
3. My self-worth is tied to how I do as a parent, so I had better not make mistakes (Grieger & Boyd, 1983).
4. I am worthless because my child has so many problems (Woulff, 1983).

Parental Ego Anxiety

1. I must have the love and approval of my child at all times (Bernard & Joyce, 1984).
2. My child must do well in everything (Bernard & Joyce, 1984).

Parental Generalized Anxiety

1. I must worry about my child at all times and help him or her overcome problems (Grieger & Boyd, 1983).

Parental Low Frustration Tolerance

1. Difficult issues in life are best handled if they are avoided as long as possible (Hauck, 1983).
2. If something is frustrating, it must be avoided at all costs (Grieger & Boyd, 1983).
3. I cannot stand my child's behavior (DiGiuseppe, 1983).
4. My child shouldn't be so difficult to help (Woulff, 1983).

Parental Guilt

1. I am the sole cause of my child's problems (DiGiuseppe, 1983).
2. If I make a mistake, it will always affect my child (McMullin, Assafi, & Chapman, 1978).
3. It is awful for my child to suffer and I must therefore prevent it at all costs (Grieger & Boyd, 1983).
4. I must never do the wrong thing with my child. If I do, I am a failure (Bernard & Joyce, 1991).

These examples provide a selection of the irrational ideas that RET practitioners work on in order to help parents eradicate them from their thinking.

Research

Research evidence from the four studies encountered in the literature (Berger, 1983; Bruner, 1979; El-Din, 1982; Hultgren, 1977) that have employed RET with parents is inconclusive. Changes in parent irrationality were found in both the Bruner and Berger studies, but not in Hultgren's. Berger failed to obtain changes in parent emotionality, whereas El-Din found changes in child behavior as a consequence of RET. Lack of detailed descriptions of and comparability between independent treatments and dependent measures employed makes findings difficult to interpret and summarize.

The Rational Parenting Program described later in this chapter was evaluated by Joyce (1989) with a sample of 48 nonclinical parents. The study examined the effect of the Rational Parenting Program on four groups of dependent variables: parent irrationality, parent emotionality, parent perceptions of child problems, and the perception of participants' parenting by their spouses. Parent emotions studied were trait anxiety, state anxiety, self-downing, anger, guilt, discomfort, and well-being. Validation evidence was established for the Belief Scale (Berger, 1983), which was used to measure parent irrational beliefs, by means of factor analysis of the scale on a separate sample.

Results of the study showed that the program was effective in reducing parent irrationality, both overall and for each subscale of the revised scale. Significant changes in the Low Frustration Tolerance subscale were the strongest followed by changes in Self-Worth and Demandingness. In the area of emotionality, results showed the Rational Parenting Program was effective in significantly reducing guilt in experimental group subjects and, for those parents with moderate to high entering levels of anger and state anxiety, the program was effective in reducing levels of those negative emotions. No differences in intervention effects were found for two experienced leaders. Further analysis of effects, for experimental subjects only, found that changes in parent irrationality were correlated with changes in emotions, namely guilt, self-downing, and trait anxiety, these being associated with cognitive changes in Self-Worth and Low Frustration Tolerance. Exploratory findings from a 10-month follow-up showed that both the changes in irrationality and the changes in emotions were maintained. Of particular interest in this follow-up was the finding that reduction of perceived child behavior problems in the long term is associated with long-term changes in parents' beliefs about their own self-worth. It appears that parents who lessened their global self-rating then experienced fewer child behavior problems. This supports the RET view that the detrimental effect of irrational beliefs of parents can be alleviated by education in rational parenting and that child behavior problems as perceived by the parent can be reduced in this way.

INDIRECT SERVICE TO THE CHILD

This type of consultation is usually done with an individual parent or with two parents. When it has been assessed that parental emotional problems are contributing to or exacerbating their child's problems—or when the practitioner detects that it is the parent who owns the problem and that the child's presenting problem is developmentally "normal"—RET is an appropriate treatment of choice for use by a school psychologist. The central treatment goal when using RET parent counseling techniques with an individual parent or parents is helping them to reduce their emotional problems about their parenting and their child. The main RET technique employed involves identifying and disputing their irrational beliefs. All of the disputational methods employed in RET can be adapted to parent problems—cognitive disputation, emotional disputation, and behavioral disputation (Walen, DiGiuseppe, & Wessler, 1980). Cognitive disputation is most often done by teaching the ABC model (Ellis, 1962) in concrete examples relevant to the current problems. For example, the child's aggressive verbal behavior may be the Antecedent (the "A") or activating event for the parents' intense angry feelings and behavior, which includes yelling and threatening the child and blaming the child for his or her faults. These feelings and behavior are the Consequence or "C." The ABC model stresses the role of the parent's rational and irrational beliefs (the "B") in bringing about the "C," namely the particular feelings the parent experiences about the event "A." Irrational beliefs that parents hold will most likely combine "shoulds"/"demands" ("she shouldn't behave like this; she should behave properly"), ("she must do what I want and stop all this nonsense"), "awfulizing" ("it's awful for a child to treat her parent this way"), and low frustration tolerance ("I can't stand being treated this way!") and global rating ("she's a rotten little kid for acting this way"). Parents can be helped to see the link between their irrational ideas and their (ineffective) ways of feeling and responding. They can learn to dispute these by being asked and learning to ask themselves challenging questions: Where is the evidence for that idea? Is that a logical thought? Is the thought really true? Is holding the belief helping me or hurting me? Is it helping or hurting my child?

There are a number of steps in teaching the ABCs of RET to parents.

1. Parents learn emotional awareness of focusing on emotions and learning to accept them. They learn that emotions vary in intensity and can be appropriate or inappropriate.
2. The ability to discriminate among emotions and to label them is developed through building an emotional vocabulary.

3. Parents are taught to think consequentially about emotions and their effects. This can help to motivate them to change the way they feel, by changing some of the beliefs and thoughts that underlie their disturbed emotions.

4. The ABC model is taught as a structure for helping parents to identify their irrational beliefs.

5. Parents learn to use disputation methods to enable them to change their beliefs.

6. A variety of homework exercises provide opportunities for parents to engage in problem identification and assessment, and later to practice disputation.

The following are some suggested homework exercises for parents working on emotional problem solving.

For *angry* parents:

1. Monitor angry feelings daily using the Feeling Thermometer or an anger scale of 0–100.

2. Record angry episodes and do an ABC analysis for each.

3. Listen to a tape of their previous RET session.

4. Practice Rational Emotive Imagery (REI) for their recurrent "As."

5. Make a list of possible reasons why the child is the way he or she is.

6. Write down their thoughts on any occasions when they managed to reduce their anger.

For *self-downing* parents:

1. Write a list of their positive characteristics as parents on a card and read it twice a day.

2. Use thought-stopping to interrupt self-downing self-talk.

3. Write out ABC sheets for times when they feel most down (e.g., say, over 7 on the Feeling Thermometer).

4. Say aloud to the spouse or another adult rational self-statements such as "Even though my child's problem is continuing, I don't have to put myself down."

5. Have their spouse make rational self-acceptance statements to the parent and reinforce efforts to overcome downing. For example, a spouse could say: "I can see that you are really working hard to accept yourself more. Well done! It was great when you came through that bad patch this morning and kept on trying."

For *anxious* parents:

1. Daily rehearsal of anti-awfulizing thoughts (written down for them by the practitioner).
2. Make a list of possible events worse than the worrying ones.
3. *Answer* the "what if . . ." questions that underlie the anxiety.
4. Practice saying aloud to the child calming down thoughts when the child is anxious.

It will be clear that these procedures are a mixture of concrete and more sophisticated methods. It is my experience that although parents can function at an abstract philosophical level when functioning at their best, much of the time (and perhaps especially when they are emotionally stressed), they can benefit from very simple concrete disputational methods.

Case Illustration

The following case illustrates RET parent consultation in which parent emotional states played a part in maintaining the child's problem and provided an obstacle to alleviating the problem.

John (aged 12 years) had been the victim of a sexual assault by a trusted babysitter 6 years previously. His parents came for consultation because of the following concerns:

1. John had never discussed the experience with anyone and the parents believed that it may be having an ongoing bad effect on his mental health.
2. John was soiling frequently at home and refusing to clean himself up immediately.
3. John had outbursts of anger in the family—in conflicts with father, mother, and younger brother—with occasional destruction of property.
4. John was having difficulties with his schoolwork.

The goals of the initial session with the parents were to assess the nature of the child's problems, the desirability of direct intervention with the child, and the nature of the parents' role in the child's problem. Regarding the parents, assessment revealed that the mother was experiencing high levels of anxiety in relation to John's problems and frequently felt completely "fed up." John's father was less involved with the day-to-day details of his sons's life but on occasion became very angry with John and engaged in verbal battles with him. Both parents also felt very guilty about the assault to which John had been subjected and this was intensified by John having said to the mother several times that she was to blame for what happened (because she left the children in this person's care).

During the consultation, the therapist asked each parent about his or her negative feelings and helped the parents focus on and express how these feelings were affecting their own well-being, and their ongoing relationship with their son. They were helped to understand that these feelings, although not the cause of the problems, were contributing to "bad scenes" at home and poor handling of the child when he was experiencing his problems.

The common antecedents that occasioned the mother's guilt were: John's soiling, his blaming of her, her own thoughts about the assault, and memories of previous mistakes and accidents, including a fall the child experienced when in her care. The irrational beliefs the mother held were: "These bad things should not have happened. I am to blame for them happening and because of that I don't deserve any respect" (guilt and self-downing); "It's horrible and awful to have a child with a soiling problem. When he soils and won't clean it up it's unbearable. I can't stand it" (awfulizing and low frustration tolerance); "I must worry all the time about his school difficulties. They probably mean his future will be a disaster. He won't get a job" (anxiety).

Parental strengths included an overriding warm and loving attitude to their children, a lively sense of humor, and a commitment to work toward their child's well-being. The father was firm in his discipline and supportive of his son, but had a tendency toward anger when the child's behavior was extreme, so there were occasional angry confrontations between father and son. The father's irrational beliefs included similar guilt-producing ones to the mother's, and additional beliefs that his son should not and must not behave in certain ways (i.e., lose his temper).

As the father was less available for attendance at sessions than the mother, the therapist worked with him at the first session, disputing his irrational demandingness toward his son and teaching him directly that continuing to get angry was getting in the way of helping John overcome his problems. Rational self-talk was modeled: "John is behaving this way at present. That is all he has learnt so far," "If I get angry it'll only make things worse," "Even if I'm angry before I know it, I can then calm myself down to improve the situation."

The mother attended six fortnightly sessions and worked on challenging her irrational beliefs. Examples of the challenges employed with the mother include: "Can a parent prevent every bad possibility for her child?" "Can a parent accept herself as a person, even when a mistake has been made in parenting?" "Given her knowledge at the time could she have prevented the assault?"

Because of the severity of the child's problems, John was also seen separately for weekly RET sessions for some months. Contact was maintained with the mother by telephone after her sessions were finished to help her maintain her efforts and also to check John's reports about his behavior at home. Improvements were made in all problem areas: Parents became calmer and dealt consistently with difficult situations; John overcame his angry outbursts and his soiling problem (he aimed for and achieved what he called "zero weeks"); and his schoolwork improved.

MENTAL HEALTH CONSULTATION FOR PARENTS

In my experience, in school settings individual parents infrequently approach a school psychologist requesting mental health consultation to reduce their stress. When working on child problems, parent stress-related mental health problems sometimes emerge and individual mental health consultations may follow. The more usual form of mental health consultation with parents, however, is in groups and this type of rational-emotive consultation is almost synonomous with rational parent education.

RET consultation with parents in groups is not only a cost-effective method but is positively evaluated by parents as relevant and helpful. Groups can be run in schools or community centers in either day or evening settings, and parents can attend together, in different groups, or singly. Recruitment for groups run by school psychologists is generally done through school newsletters. Sometimes an introductory lecture is provided to give parents preliminary ideas and information about the groups.

Rational-emotive consultation with parents in groups is based on the principles of Rational-Emotive Education (REE) (Knaus, 1974). Rational parenting is distinguished from other approaches to parent education. These include behavioral programs that teach child behavior management (Forehand & McMahon, 1981; Patterson, 1971); Parent Effectiveness Training (PET; Gordon, 1976, 1980), which is derived from reflective counseling approaches and teaches communication skills; and Systematic Training for Effective Parenting (STEP; Dinkmeyer & McKay, 1982, 1983), which draws on Adlerian principles. These parent education programs have sometimes been employed with clinical populations (e.g., behavioral) and more often with nonclinical (PET and STEP) groups. Although the rational-emotive education of parents is frequently integrated with therapeutic techniques in the clinical consultations, as described earlier in this chapter, the interest in this section is in its use with groups of nonclinical parents.

Rational-emotive parent education has been developed for use with groups of parents in order to reduce their everyday stress (as an end in itself) as well as to improve their parenting skills so that their children manifest fewer problems and enhanced adjustment (Joyce, 1989). Thus, the main focus of this program is a mental health consultation but there is some overlap with indirect service to the child. The 9-week program of $1\frac{1}{2}$-hour weekly sessions teaches rational-emotive ideas to parents in four main areas: (a) management of their own emotional stress, (b) child discipline, (c) problem solving for child problems, and (d) the development of rational personality traits in children. These areas are dealt with in nine sessions:

1. Parents have feelings too!
2. Emotional stress in bringing up children.
3. Rational discipline.

4. Rational self-acceptance for you and your child.
5. Rational coping in a crisis.
6. Understanding children's emotions.
7. Children's problems—Rational problem solving I.
8. Children's problems—Rational problem solving II.
9. Teaching rational attitudes to children.

Parents learn first to label feelings and monitor their intensity by the use of the Feeling Thermometer (Bernard & Joyce, 1984). They also learn that their disturbed negative emotions can interfere with their functioning as parents. Emotional responsibility, that is, taking charge of their own emotions rather than blaming other people or events for how they feel, is taught by means of the ABC model applied to parenting examples, enabling them to explore their irrational parent beliefs and to challenge and change these. This is the first step in achieving the goals of rational-emotive parent education, which aims to teach parents to think more rationally, so that they will feel better (less distressed), be more effective problem solvers in everyday difficulties, and provide healthier models for their children in dealing with difficult, disappointing, or frustrating events.

in learning rational discipline, parents focus on any troublesome negative emotions that they may customarily feel when disciplining their child, especially in situations where the child is not readily compliant. For example, they explore the maladaptive role of anger, worry, and self-downing in discipline situations and practice disputing their underlying irrational beliefs before implementing their discipline strategies.

Two sessions are devoted to rational problem solving of specific problems each parent wants to discuss. These frequently include such common difficulties as social shyness, bedtime problems, sibling rivalry, aggressive behavior, homework problems, temper tantrums, and emotional difficulties such as jealousy. In these sessions, parents learn to apply what they have learned in understanding the role of their own beliefs and emotions, and so work out ways to calm themselves first, then help calm the child if necessary, and finally proceed to practical problem solving to alleviate the problem.

The fourth area, the development of rational personality traits, enables parents to begin exploration of ways they can model and reinforce in their children habits of rational thinking that will encourage the child to deal with life in ways that are flexible, nondemanding, nonexaggerating, and tolerant of themselves and others when mistakes are made, or people "do them in."

An illustration of a session may clarify how the program works. Take, for example, Session 5, "Rational coping in a crisis." Rational-emotive goals for this session are to (a) discuss with parents common antecedent events associated with anxiety in the parent (e.g., school failure, chronic illness in the child) and the emotional and behavioral consequences that frequently occur when the parent is

TABLE 4.1
Session 5: Rational Coping in an (Anxiety) Crisis
(or, "Can Parents Worry TOO MUCH?")

Common "As" That Occasion Worry in Parents

School problems—	child fails in exams
	child doesn't do homework
	child is slow at learning to read
	child is unhappy at school
	child is in trouble at school for misbehavior
	child refuses to go to school
Social problems—	child does not have many friends
	child is very shy
	child frequently gets into fights
	child steals or shoplifts
Home problems—	grandparents interfere
	spouses differ in approach to problems
Other child problems—	immature behavior persists (e.g., thumbsucking, bedwetting, etc.)
	child has nightmares
	child shows fear
	child has chronic or recurrent illness

Common "Cs" Associated With Anxiety

worry	shake
upset	feel sick
stew	get headaches
ruminate	pains in stomach
cry	digestive upsets
feel tense	"churning"

Common "Bs" That Lead to Anxiety

1. I must succeed as a parent at all times. If I fall short of my standards or fail, that would be awful and prove I am a failure.
2. Having this problem is AWFUL, HORRIBLE, and a CATASTROPHE. I shouldn't have it.
3. Because my child has this problem now, that means he or she will probably always have it. What if he or she never . . . has friends, learns to swim . . .
4. My children cause my worry and unhappiness. They must change for me to feel better.
5. I must worry and stew about the uncertainties of the future.

very anxious (see Table 4.1, "Can Parents Worry TOO MUCH?"); (b) help parents identify common irrational beliefs underlying anxiety, and practice identifying their own irrational ideas; (c) generate disputes for those beliefs. Table 4.2, "The ABCs of Calm Parenting," is an example of the ABC model applied to this area of parenting problems. Parents complete the sheet in the session as a

TABLE 4.2
The ABCs of Calm Parenting

A (the Antecedent)	B (my Beliefs)	C (the Consequence)	D (Disputation)
I *worry* most when:	What I think and say to myself:	What happens after: I feel worried __ I stew 10 I feel tense My head hurts I churn	Changing our self-thought My rational thoughts at this event could be:

basis for discussion and especially for generating a homework exercise tailored to their individual habits of (irrational) thought.

SUMMARY

Meyers et al.'s (1979) consultation model has been found useful in describing two types of rational-emotive parent consultation. Preliminary research findings on the use of RET with parents indicate that parent irrational beliefs are associated with parent emotional stress and that RET interventions can reduce this emotional stress and help parents become more effective problem solvers with their children. The scientific basis for employing RET with parents is yet to be firmly established. Schools would appear to be ideal settings in which the empirical utility of rational parenting programs can be assessed by school psychologists.

REFERENCES

Barrish, H. H., & Barrish, I. J. (1985). *Managing parental anger: the coping parent series.* Shawnee Mission, KS: Overland Press.

Berger, A. (1983). The role of irrational cognitions in the phenomenology of anger and guilt in parents of disturbed children. *Dissertation Abstracts International, 44,* 1.

Bernard, M. E., & Joyce, M. R. (1984). *Rational-emotive therapy children and adolescents.* New York: Wiley.

Bernard, M. E., & Joyce, M. R. (1991). RET with children and adolescents. In M. E. Bernard (Ed.), *Using rational-emotive therapy effectively: A practitioner's guide* (pp. 319–347). New York: Plenum Press.

Bruner, G. G. (1979). The effect of rational-emotive/Adlerian study groups on the locus of control, rationality of beliefs and behaviour of participating mothers and their target children. *Dissertation Abstracts International, 40,* 5-A, 2476.

Chess, S., Thomas, A., & Birch, H. G. (1965). *Your child is a person.* Middlesex: Penguin.

DiGiuseppe, R. A. (1983). Rational-emotive therapy and conduct disorders. In A. Ellis & M. E. Bernard (Eds.), *Rational-emotive approaches to the problems of childhood* (pp. 111–136). New York: Plenum Press.

DiGiuseppe, R. A. (1988). A cognitive-behavioural systems approach to the treatment of conduct disorder children and adolescents. In M. E. Bernard & R. A. DiGiuseppe (Eds.), *Inside rational-emotive therapy*. New York: Academic Press.

Dinkmeyer, D., & McKay, G. D. (1982). *The parent's handbook. Systematic training for effective parenting*. Circle Pines, MN: American Guidance Service.

Dinkmeyer, D., & McKay, G. D. (1983). *The parent's guide. Systematic training for effective parenting of teens*.

El-Din, M. K. (1982). Impact of leisure counselling of parents of mentally retarded children on the leisure functioning of those children: A study using rational-emotive imagery. *Dissertation Abstracts International, 43*, 9.

Ellis, A. (1962). *Reason and emotion in psychotherapy*. Secaucus, NJ: Citadel Press.

Ellis, A., Moseley, S., & Wolfe, J. (1966). *How to raise an emotionally healthy, happy child*. Hollywood, CA: Wilshire Books.

Forehand, R. L., & McMahon, R. J. (1981). *Helping the non-compliant child*. New York: Guilford.

Gordon, T. (1976). *PET in action*. New York: Wyden Press.

Gordon, T. (1980). Parent effectiveness training: A preventive program and its effects on families. In M. Fine (Ed.), *Handbook on parent education*. New York: Academic Press.

Grieger, R. M., & Boyd, J. D. (1983). Childhood anxieties, fears and phobias: a cognitive-behavioural-psychosituational approach. In A. Ellis & M. E. Bernard (Eds.), *Rational-emotive approaches to the problems of childhood*. New York: Plenum Press.

Hauck, P. (1967). *The rational management of children*. New York: Libra.

Hauck, P. (1983). Working with parents. In A. Ellis & M. E. Bernard (Eds.), *Rational-emotive approaches to the problems of childhood*. New York: Plenum Press.

Hultgren, A. V. (1977). A rational child management approach to parent education. *Dissertation Abstracts International, 37*, 9-A, 5607.

Joyce, M. R. (1989). *An evaluation of the effectiveness of a rational-emotive parent education programme*. Unpublished doctoral dissertation, University of Melbourne, Australia.

Knaus, W. J. (1974). *Rational-emotive education: A manual for elementary school teachers*. New York: Institute for Rational Living.

McInerney, J. F. (1983). Working with parents and teachers of exceptional children. In A. Ellis & M. E. Bernard (Eds.), *Rational-emotive approaches to the problems of childhood*. New York: Plenum Press.

McMullin, R. E., Assafi, I., & Chapman, S. (1978). *Cognitive restructuring for families*. Lakewood, CO: Counseling Research Institute.

Meyers, J., Parsons, R. D., & Martin, R. (1979). *Mental health consultation in the schools*. San Francisco: Jossey-Bass.

Patterson, G. R. (1971). Behavioural intervention procedures in the classroom and the home. In A. E. Bergin & S. L. Garfield (Eds.), *Handbook of psychotherapy and behaviour change: an empirical analysis*. New York: Wiley.

Walen, S., DiGiuseppe, R., & Wessler, R. (1980). *A practitioner's guide to rational-emotive therapy*. New York: Oxford University Press.

Woulff, N. (1983). Involving the family in the treatment of the child: a model for rational-emotive therapists. In A. Ellis & M. E. Bernard (Eds.), *Rational-emotive approaches to the problems of childhood*. New York: Plenum Press.

5 Teacher Stress Management: A Rational-Emotive Therapy Approach

Susan G. Forman
Rutgers, The State University of New Jersey

In recent years, stress-related concepts and constructs have received a great deal of attention in psychological literature because of the relationship of stress to emotional, cognitive, behavioral, and physiological problems. Stressful life events, personal characteristics, and social/environmental conditions have been areas of focus for those investigating the causes of stress. Occupational settings have been identified as potential sources of stress because they provide a context in which performance and relationship demands are made (Elliott & Eisdorfer, 1982). A number of occupational groups have been studied in relation to job stress. Some studies have shown that those in human service fields experience a higher incidence of stress-related problems than those in other occupations (Greenberg, 1984). Among these types of professionals, teachers have received considerable attention in the literature as an occupational group that has significantly high stress levels resulting in negative effects on individuals, as well as the teaching profession and educational system.

The first studies of incidence of teacher stress appeared in the 1930s. Nationwide surveys conducted by the National Education Association (NEA) during this decade and in subsequent ones have consistently indicated that a significant number of teachers have experienced stress at moderate or considerable levels (Coates & Thoresen, 1986). Surveys done in the 1970s by state teacher associations and unions indicated that more than 50% of teachers identified stress as a significant problem resulting in physical or mental symptoms (Cichon, 1978; New York State Teachers Association, 1979). Truch (1980), in summarizing the results of numerous teacher stress surveys, reported that up to 90% of teachers reported experiencing job-related stress, and 95% indicated the need for stress management courses. Recent surveys have indicated that a large percentage of teachers would not choose the profession if they had the choice to make over again and do not plan to continue to teach in the future ("Poll probes," 1980; Vance & Schlechty, 1982).

DEFINITION OF STRESS

Numerous definitions and conceptualizations of stress have been presented in the literature. The most comprehensive and widely accepted of these views stress as a process that involves an interaction between an individual and the environment. This approach, developed by Lazarus (1966), includes a stimulus or stressor, intervening variables, and a response as the components of stress. Stressors are viewed as having the potential for differential effects across individuals. The individual's perception of the environmental demand as a threat and the response capability of the individual to cope with the environmental demand determines the effects of a stressor. This interactional approach to stress emphasizes the active role of the individual in mediating potential stressors in the environment.

Occupational Stress

Occupational or job stress is stress that is related to the work environment. Beehr and Newman (1978) defined *job stress* as a situation in which job-related factors interact with a worker to change his or her psychological or physiological condition. Kahn (1981) further described a cognitive–mediational model of job stress in which an organizational environment in combination with an individual's personal characteristics and interpersonal situation will lead to a psychological perception of the environment. These perceptions lead to emotional, physiological, or behavioral responses that may result in changes in physical or mental health, depending on the person's coping skills.

Teacher Stress

Congruent with the interactional approach to stress, Kyriacou and Sutcliffe (1978) defined *teacher stress,* a specific type of job stress, as a response to negative affect, usually accompanied by potentially harmful physiological changes, resulting from aspects of the teacher's job, and mediated by the perception that job demands are a threat and by coping mechanisms used to reduce the threat. Moracco and McFadden (1981) highlighted the role of cognitive–mediational factors in teacher stress by emphasizing the importance of teacher perceptions of potential stressors in the work environment and the role of coping skills in successfully managing these stressors. Potential stressors become actual stressors in the work environment if a teacher perceives them as a threat to well-being or self-esteem. The teacher's coping skills will determine how successfully the stress is managed. Similarly, Leach (1984) indicated that the discrepancy between perceived work demand and ability can result in physiological and biochemical changes that are stress reactions. Kyriacou (1987) further emphasized the role of cognitive–mediational factors in teacher stress by stating that teachers' perceptions of their circumstances and the degree of control perceived are widely acknowledged as crucial factors in teacher stress.

EXTERNAL STRESSORS

In a comprehensive review of the literature on sources of teacher stress, Turk, Meeks, and Turk (1982) found that seven problem areas were consistently identified in the 49 studies they examined: (a) poor school environment, (b) pupil misbehavior, (c) poor working conditions, (d) personal concerns of the teacher, (e) relationships with parents, (f) time pressures, and (g) inadequacy of training.

Poor school environment was identified most frequently as a contributor to teacher stress, being cited in 49% of the 49 studies reviewed. This category included such problem areas as relationships with administrators, conflicts with parents, conflicts with colleagues, poor communication with colleagues, poor public opinion of schools, student apathy, job insecurity, and role conflict.

The second major contributor to teacher stress was pupil misbehavior. Teacher concerns focused on maintaining discipline, dealing with disruptive students, and maintaining a positive teacher–pupil relationship.

Poor working conditions were also a frequently cited source of teacher stress. Two consistently identified problems in this area were large classes and inadequate salaries. In addition, poor facilities and excessive nonteaching duties have also been reported.

Personal concerns of teachers included concerns about their students liking them, unrealistic expectations of their professional abilities, and discomfort with feelings of hostility or annoyance toward administrators, staff, and students. Less frequently reported in the literature were anxiety about parental opinions or problems and dealing with parents, time pressures due to excessive workloads, and inadequacy of training resulting in difficulty in organizing activities, generating student interest, and dealing with individual differences.

In an earlier review of studies on sources of teacher stress, Coates and Thoresen (1976) found differences in concerns and sources of anxiety for beginning teachers and experienced teachers. Beginning teachers' concerns and anxieties focused on (a) ability to maintain classroom discipline, (b) gaining approval from students, (c) their knowledge of subject matter, (d) what to do if they make mistakes or run out of materials, and (e) how to relate personally to other faculty, the school system, or parents. In contrast to these concerns, which are largely anticipatory and self-focused, concerns of experienced teachers were related to actual task demands and job characteristics. These included (a) time demands,

(b) difficulties with pupils, (c) large class enrollment, (d) financial constraints, and (e) lack of educational resources. Other studies have found role-related stress, the degree of fit between a teacher's role expectations and the actual experiences of that role to be related to teacher stress (Pettegrew & Wolf, 1982).

COGNITIVE-MEDIATIONAL FACTORS: IRRATIONAL BELIEFS

Ellis (1978), in writing on the rational-emotive therapy (RET) perspective of stress, stated that "stressful conditions vary significantly in relation to the perceptions and cognitions of those who react to these conditions" (p. 210). He provided elaboration on this issue indicating that although some situations may be intrinsically stressful, in most situations, people create their own negative feelings by having certain beliefs about the situation. Their disturbed stress reactions follow directly from their beliefs. Although the activating situation significantly contributes to what an individual may think and believe, it does not cause it. Bernard, Joyce, and Rosewarne (1983) similarly contend that "most psychosocial stress derives from the manner in which the individual thinks about and appraises a situation" (p. 418). Empirical studies provide supporting evidence for these contentions by showing that cognition-related personality characteristics such as external locus of control (Harris, Halpin, & Halpin, 1985), tendency toward worry, high conscientiousness, and high standards (Kyriacou & Pratt, 1985) have a relationship to high teacher stress.

A number of authors have written about specific irrational beliefs commonly held by teachers that may contribute to work-related stress (Bernard & Joyce, 1984; Bernard et al., 1983; Forman & Forman, 1978; McInerney, 1983). Bernard and Joyce provided a listing of 16 major irrational beliefs of teachers. These include the following:

1. I must have constant approval from students, other teachers, administrators, and parents.
2. Events in my classroom should always go exactly the way I want them to.
3. Schools should be fair.
4. Students should not be frustrated.
5. People who misbehave deserve severe punishment.
6. There should be no discomfort or frustration at school.
7. Teachers always need a great deal of help from others to solve school-related problems.
8. Those who don't do well at school are worthless.
9. Students with a history of academic or behavioral problems will always have problems.

10. Students or other teachers can make me feel bad.
11. I can't stand to see children who have had unhappy home lives.
12. I must be in total control of my class at all times.
13. I must find the perfect solution to all problems.
14. When children have problems, it's their parents' fault.
15. I must be a perfect teacher and never make mistakes.
16. It's easier to avoid problems at school than to face them.

Bernard (1988) reported on two studies involving the Teacher Irrational Belief Scales (TIBS), which consists of 30-items that require teachers to indicate, on a 5-point scale, the extent to which they agree or disagree with irrational attitudes. Items were developed to assess four irrational thinking processes relative to four teaching problem areas. The irrational thinking processes included: demanding/absolutistic thinking, "awfulizing" or the tendency to blow things out of proportion, low frustration tolerance, and global rating. Teaching problem areas included classroom management, student learning/emotional problems, time and workload pressures, and problems with school administration. A principal components analysis yielded four factors: self-downing, authoritarianism, demands for consideration, and low frustration tolerance. Experienced teachers were found to be less irrational than teachers with little experience. In addition, teachers high in irrationality were found to experience more stress than those who were less irrational. Self-downing and low frustration tolerance were found to be most strongly associated with high stress levels. The relationship between teacher stress, teacher irrationality, and self-reported coping skills (i.e., classroom discipline skills, time management skills, relaxation skills, communication skills, assertion skills, emotional control skills, and overall teaching skills) was also examined. The results suggested that teacher irrationality was more strongly associated with teacher stress than self-appraised coping skills. Bernard (1988) hypothesized that high levels of irrationality may prevent teachers from employing and/or developing coping skills that could be used to deal with external stressors.

THE RET CONCEPTION OF TEACHER STRESS

The RET conceptualization of the causes of emotional stress for teachers (anxiety, anger, depression) includes the teaching environment and the individual teacher. There is little question that certain teaching environments contain many more demanding and threatening stressors than others. Teachers who work in schools where they are exposed to actual physical intimidation are more at risk for stress than those who work in safer teaching environments. Certain schools, because of the characteristics of the student population, teaching staff, and administrative structure, have a higher incidence of classroom management problems, poorly motivated students, high staff conflict, and nonsupportive administrators who operate in noncommunicative and nonconsultative ways. Research has shown that these stressors are associated with higher levels of stress within a teaching staff (e.g., Kyriacou, 1987).

RET also places a great deal of emphasis on the attitudes of teachers toward stressors they encounter in teaching. Irrational teacher beliefs are hypothesized to operate in a proactive fashion to exacerbate stressors that exist in the teaching environment. Teachers who bring with them high needs for achievement and approval, and who put themselves down when faced with not achieving their goals (e.g., lack of student achievement, "sea of blank faces") and/or being criticized (or not recognized) by fellow teachers or administrators, are more likely to experience emotional stress than teachers who hold fewer irrational teacher beliefs. Teachers who hold authoritarian-demanding attitudes toward students and student discipline are likely to experience excessive stress in the face of disruptive students. Teachers who have low frustration tolerance and believe that "teaching is *too* hard" and that "teaching *shouldn't* be so hard" are likely to become extremely stressed by time and workload pressures. These hypotheses have recently been supported by Bernard (1988). Proponents of RET contend that certain teachers, given their personalities, are likely to bring irrational attitudes to their teaching environment and that these attitudes will lead them to experience teaching demands and threats as more emotionally stressful than those teachers who confront he same teaching stressors from a more rational perspective. In addition, teachers will tend to think more irrationally, the more they have experienced strong, negative emotional arousal, and strong emotional arousal frequently occurs as a consequence of teaching over a prolonged period of time in a teaching environment with lack of support and reinforcement, and many teaching stressors.

An example of the role of teacher irrationality in teacher stress has been described by Bernard (1989):

> Consider a typical classroom, 7E, with a typical disruptive student, Billie Bloggs. He comes into class late, doesn't have all his books, hasn't done his homework, makes silly comments throughout the period, gets out of his seat to belt Alex who sits two seats in front of him, throws spit balls when his teacher turns his back, and when he can, reads *Playboy*. The situation is objectively demanding because Billie Bloggs' teacher has not only to get through the lesson with his other students, but has also to figure out how to motivate and control Billie Bloggs. The degree of stress in this situation is, however, largely under the influence of Billie Bloggs' teacher. . . .
>
> Two of Billie's teachers might react quite differently to Billie. Mr. Jones rationally thinks to himself: "I would prefer for Billie to behave himself and for me to have control over his behavior. It is a hassle for me to teach this class with Billie in

it. I don't like it, but, no doubt, I can put up with it. I wonder how I am going to motivate Billie or, at least reduce his disruptive influence." As a consequence of these rational attitudes toward Billie, Mr. Jones would feel somewhat uncomfortable and stressed, but not "off the wall" and, equally important, he would be in a position to solve his and Billie's problems.

Mrs. Smith, a teacher of similar age, intelligence, background and experience, creates a different problem for herself about Billie Bloggs' behavior. Mrs. Smith thinks about Billie in a quite different and stress-creating fashion. "Billie *should always* behave himself in my class and I *should* be able to have perfect control over my students at all times. This is really *awful* that Billie is misbehaving. *I can't stand it* when Billie acts this way. Billie is really *rotten and really deserves to be punished. . . .*"

Why are Mrs. Smith's attitudes irrational? Briefly, while it would be desirable if Billie acted better, there is no law of the universe that says he *must*. By *demanding* good behavior (rather than desiring it), Mrs. Smith is setting herself for excess stress whenever she is faced with misbehavior in the class. Mrs. Smith also exaggerates the problem by thinking, "This is awful," which really means that it is 100 percent bad or worse. An objective rating of Billie's behavior would put it in the moderate range (40–50 percent of life's catastrophes). Mrs. Smith's idea "I can't stand Billie's behavior" is central to almost all self-created stress. This idea is irrational because while it is certainly unpleasant to have to teach a class with Billie Bloggs in it, she, patently, can stand it even though she doesn't like it (it hasn't killed her, she's never fainted, her eyeballs haven't popped out). And finally, she is overly stressing herself by the thought that because Billie is misbehaving, he is totally rotten and hopeless. By *globally rating* Billie's value as a person from one instance of his behavior, Mrs. Smith is irrationally equating self-worth with behavior, and, as a consequence, is more angry and frustrated than need be. (pp. 8–9)

Following are additional illustrations of the RET conceptualization of stress. These provide teacher stress examples of Ellis' (1962) three-stage model of emotions, which includes an activating event, beliefs about the event, and the emotional consequence that results from thoughts and beliefs about the event.

Situation 1.   Almost the entire class fails a test (24 out of 28).

Thoughts

Teacher A	Teacher B
1. I must be a terrible teacher.	1. Those stupid kids.
2. I'm so dumb and incompetent.	2. I shouldn't have to work with dumb kids like that.
3. It's my fault that they didn't learn the material.	3. They never learn anything.
4. I'm just useless.	4. All they do is take up space.

5. The principal will find out and I'll probably be fired.

6. I might as well quit.

5. It's their own fault they failed the test.

6. They never do anything but play around.

7. It's impossible to do anything with kids like this.

Feelings: Depressed, Anxious   Angry

Teacher C

1. 24 out of 28 failed—that's not good.

2. I guess I better look at what's going on here.

3. All my other classes did well, I thought I taught the material well and went over it several times.

4. Maybe the material was too hard for them.

5. Maybe these kids aren't as bright as the others I've had.

6. Maybe the test was too hard.

7. Well instead of guessing, I could try to get some feedback from the class.

8. It is possible they need some help on developing study skills.

9. I could also talk to their previous teacher to get some information about them.

10. This isn't going to be easy.

11. Oh well, if all the kids were exactly the same I guess this job wouldn't be interesting.

Feelings: Concerned, Calm

Situation 2. It's the second week of school. Johnny just hit Mark in the face and threw a book across the room. He has been out of his seat, running around the room and hasn't completed any of his work (Forman, 1983, p. 281).

Thoughts

Teacher A	Teacher B

Teacher A

1. This is terrible.
2. I'll never be able to control this kid.
3. He's gonna destroy the entire class.
4. The other teachers are gonna hear about this and they'll think I'm incompetent.
5. They'll probably all be talking about me in the teachers' room.
6. The principal will probably fire me soon.
7. I'm so useless.
8. I can't do anything right.

Feelings: Depressed, Anxious

Teacher B

1. This is awful.
2. What a little monster.
3. Kids like that shouldn't be allowed in school.
4. I shouldn't have to deal with this.
5. His parents should do something about him.
6. By this time he should know how to behave.
7. He's a hopeless case.

Angry

Teacher C

1. Looks like I have a problem here.
2. This situation isn't good for Johnny, the rest of the class, or me.
3. He doesn't seem to respond the way most other kids do.
4. Oh well, I know I'm not the only one with this type of classroom situation. I hear other teachers talking about it all the time.
5. Since I don't like it and I really want things to change, I guess I'll have to do something about it if I want things to be different. Getting upset at myself or at him isn't going to help.
6. He just hasn't learned how to behave appropriately and I'm going to try to teach him how.

7. I don't like this, but he is part of the class, and if I want him to act differently in class I'll have to try some different approaches with him.

8. I think I'll talk to some of the other teachers to see what's worked for them. Maybe I'll talk to the school psychologist.

Feelings: Concerned, Calm

Situation 3.   You are at a teachers meeting and you say something that's on your mind, but you stumble over some of your words.

Thoughts

Teacher A	Teacher B
1. I made a fool of myself.	1. I'm not sure that sounded right.
2. I shouldn't have said anything.	2. Oh well, everyone makes mistakes because we're all human.
3. Everyone will probably be laughing at me.	3. Since everyone makes mistakes, most people probably won't think that what I did was very important.
4. I'm so dumb.	4. And if they do—if they laugh, so what?
5. I'm so embarrassed.	5. I can usually express myself alright.
6. I never do anything right.	6. I'm not going to get myself upset about something so unimportant.
7. I'm never gonna say anything at a meeting again.	

Feelings: Depressed, Anxious   Calm, Confident

CONSEQUENCES OF TEACHER STRESS

Some degree of stress in the work environment is probably inevitable and may lead to positive, constructive, creative responses. However, the research on occupational stress and teacher stress has focused on the numerous negative consequences of chronic stressors.

Physiological Effects. In a study of physical symptoms associated with teacher stress, Needle, Griffin, and Svendsen (1981) found that the most frequently reported complaints were feeling completely worn out at the end of the day, difficulty getting up in the morning, feeling nervous or fidgety and tense, and headaches. Other somatic complaints included back pains, difficulty getting to and staying asleep, becoming easily fatigued, stiffness, swelling or aching joints and muscles, coughing or heavy chest colds, stomach pains, and fast heart rate. In a study of burned-out teachers, Belcastro (1982) reported that somatic complaints included abdominal pain, difficulty in breathing, eczema, hives, tinnitus, occupational injuries, bowel difficulties, and tearfulness. Several illnesses and chronic conditions also have been related to teacher stress. These include high blood pressure, kidney or bladder trouble, arthritis, lung or breathing problems, gall bladder disorders, cardiovascular disorders, insomnia, gastritis, stomach ulcers, anemia, asthma, and colitis (Belcastro, 1982; Needle et al., 1981).

Psychological Effects. Typical psychological reactions to teacher stress include frustration and anxiety (Dunham, 1976), emotional exhaustion (Hargreaves, 1978), depression (Hammen & deMayo, 1982), job dissatisfaction (Kyriacou & Sutcliffe, 1979), and burnout (Maslach, 1978). Other specific symptoms reported by teachers under stress include lack of self-confidence, hypersensitivity to criticism, excessive worry and guilt, inability to relax, feelings of alienation, anger and resentment, moodiness, forgetfulness, and difficulty in concentrating and making decisions (Dunham, 1976; Kyriacou & Sutcliffe, 1978; Spanoil & Caputo, 1979). In addition, teachers under stress may have negative and cynical attitudes toward students, parents, and other school staff (Cunningham, 1983).

Behavioral Effects. Several studies that have examined the behaviors of high-anxiety teachers seem to suggest that teacher anxiety may have a detrimental effect on teacher performance. High teacher anxiety has been found to be related to low verbal support to students, hostile speech and behavior (Petrusich, 1967), low teacher warmth in relating to students (Kracht & Casey, 1968), ineffective use of reward and punishment (Harootunian & Koon, 1970), and dogmatic and authoritarian behavior (Krasno, 1972). In addition, low job satisfaction in teachers has been linked to low opportunity for student discussion (Greenwood & Soar, 1973). Other behavioral consequences of teacher stress frequently mentioned in the literature include absenteeism, tardiness, and turnover (Kyriacou, 1980; Phillips & Lee, 1980).

Effects on Students.   In investigating the connection between teacher stress and student outcomes, researchers have concentrated on one stress response—teacher anxiety. High anxiety teachers have been found to have more disruptive students than low anxiety teachers (Moskowitz & Hayman, 1974; Petrusich, 1966). In addition, a positive relationship has been found between teacher anxiety and student test anxiety (Doyal & Forsyth, 1973). Also, students of high anxiety teachers have been found to have low achievement (Washbourne & Heil, 1960).

RATIONAL-EMOTIVE STRESS MANAGEMENT INTERVENTIONS

Although numerous surveys and studies have been done on incidence, causes, and effects of teacher stress, few studies have examined the effects of teacher stress management interventions, despite the fact that these programs have proliferated in the past few years in attempts to deal with the problem. Teacher stress management interventions having the most evidence of effectiveness contain components that address cognitive control.

Forman and Forman (1980) described a rational-emotive staff development program consisting of 10 1½-hour sessions. Content focused on: (a) how emotions work, (b) identification of thoughts, (c) definition of rational, (d) identification and disputation of irrational beliefs, (e) dealing with anger, (f) dealing with fear and anxiety, (g) dealing with guilt, and (h) building new thought habits. From pretest to posttest, course participants were found to significantly decrease in belief irrationality.

Later studies investigating use of rational-emotive therapy procedures with teachers have included these techniques as part of a broader program of stress-inoculation training. Originally conceptualized by Meichenbaum (1977), this intervention was adapted for use with teachers and other school personnel by Forman (1983). Stress-inoculation training consists of three phases: (a) an educational phase during which a conceptual framework for understanding stress is provided, (b) a skill acquisition phase during which cognitive and behavioral coping techniques are taught, and (c) an application phase during which opportunity for practice of coping skills is provided. Forman and Cecil (1986) described a six-session teacher stress management program based on stress-inoculation training.

During the first session of the program trainees discussed definitions of stress, causes of school stress, and effects of stress on school staff and students. Participants were then asked to identify specific situations that were stressful for them during the school day and to describe their physical, cognitive, emotional, and behavioral reactions to these situations. The Lazarus (1966) model of stress, described earlier, was emphasized and provided a rationale for use of cognitive coping strategies. The idea that emotional responses have both physiological and cognitive components was discussed, and the effects of relaxation and cognitive restructuring were explained. These techniques, which were to be trained in later sessions, were presented with a coping orientation, with personal responsibility for use of the procedures emphasized. Trainees were informed that in order for the training to be effective, daily practice of the procedures was necessary, and that homework assignments would be given each week. After this session, the homework assignment was to record self-assessed level of stress each school day.

The second session focused on relaxation training that included deep muscle relaxation and cue-controlled relaxation (Guzicki, Coates, & Goodwin, 1980). After practicing deep muscle relaxation and breathing while using the cue word, "relax," trainees practiced cue-controlled relaxation while imagining themselves in stress-producing school-related situations. Homework after this session included daily practice in muscle relaxation, daily practice of cue-controlled relaxation in response to imagined stress-producing scenes, daily practice of cue-controlled relaxation in real stress-producing situations during the school day, and self-assessment of stress level for each school day.

Rational restructuring (Goldfried, 1977) was introduced during the third session. Rational restructuring incorporates principles of RET with behavioral procedures through four phases: (a) helping individuals recognize that cognitions mediate emotions, (b) helping individuals recognize the irrationality of certain beliefs, (c) helping individuals recognize that their own irrational cognitions mediate their own inappropriate emotions, and (d) helping individuals change their irrational cognitions. The session began with the trainer explaining that emotions are not the direct result of objective events, but are influenced by the view an individual takes of the event. Ellis', (1962) ABC model of emotions was presented along with numerous illustrations using school situations. Participants were taught to identify the cognitions or self-statements that contributed to their negative reactions to stressors. Homework after this session included daily practice of cue-controlled relaxation, completion of an ABC analysis on a school-related stressful situation, and self-assessment of stress levels for each school day.

During the fourth session, Ellis' (1962) basic irrational beliefs were introduced and participants discussed how these beliefs influenced their feelings and behavior during the work day. In addition, five questions developed by Maultsby (1975) to determine if a thought is rational were presented and discussed. These include the following:

1. Is the thought true?
2. Does it help protect my life or health?
3. Does it help me obtain my goals?
4. Does it help me to feel the way I want to feel?
5. Does it keep me out of trouble?

Homework after this session included daily practice of cue-controlled relaxation, completion of an ABC analysis of a stress situation along with identification of the thoughts as rational or irrational, and self-assessment of stress level for each school day.

The fifth session focused on application. Participants were taught to develop "stress scripts" that, in a written format, provide cognitive, emotional, and behavioral plans for constructive responses to stressors. Thoughts, feelings, and behaviors are identified for specific stress situations and alternative rational thoughts, feelings, and behaviors are devised that will lead to better coping. Table 5.1 and 5.2 show examples of stress scripts.

After the stress script was introduced, participants developed scripts for dealing with specific school-related stress situations, first as a large group activity, later as a small group activity, and finally, individually. In addition, rational-emotive imagery procedures (Maultsby, 1977) were presented. This is a rehearsal procedure through which rational thinking can be practiced by: (a) relaxing, (b) imagining the stress situation, and (c) thinking rational thoughts and rehearsing rational emotional and behavioral responses while imagining oneself in the potentially stressful situation. Homework after this session consisted of daily practice of a stress script through rational emotive imagery, daily real-life practice of rational thinking in stressful situations, completion of stress script, and self-assessment of stress.

During the last session, participants developed additional stress scripts and engaged in rehearsal activities similar to the "barb" technique described by Kaufman and Wagner (1972). In a dyad activity, one partner presented a situation that he or she thought would probably be stressful. The other partner had to verbally respond with constructive self-statements that would help reduce negative stress reactions. Finally, the importance of continued practice of the coping skills that had been learned was emphasized. The stress-inoculation approach has shown evidence of effectiveness in a number of studies. Forman (1982) found that urban secondary school teachers who completed an 18-hour training program exhibited a significant reduction in self-reported stress and anxiety, as well as observed motoric manifestations of anxiety in the classroom, when compared to a no-treatment control group. However, the training did not have an effect on types of teacher classroom verbalization (e.g., praise, criticism). Six-week follow-up data revealed further decreases in self-reported stress and anxiety for those who participated in the program. In an additional study with school psychologists, Forman (1981) found that those who participated in stress-inoculation training showed decreases in self-reported anxiety and increases in job satisfaction, whereas a no-treatment control group of school psychologists did not.

Sharp and Forman (1985) compared the effects of a 16-hour stress-inoculation training program and a behavior modification skills training program on teacher stress. Behavior modification skills training was examined because problems in dealing with disruptive students has been identified as a major source of teacher

TABLE 5.1
Stress Script (Forman & Cecil, 1986, p. 220)

Situation: You get a message from the principal that says he's going to be observing your class tomorrow.

Stress Producing	Stress Reducing
Thoughts	
1. There must be something wrong.	1. I don't like having people observe me, but the principal has to observe everyone, so I guess I can get through this as well as anyone else.
2. I must be doing a bad job.	2. I'll make sure I'm prepared tonight and do the best I can.
3. He probably thinks I'm incompetent.	3. I think I've been doing a good job so far and he's never indicated otherwise.
4. He probably doesn't like me.	4. Since I've been doing well all along, there's no reason to think I won't do well tomorrow.
5. I'll be so nervous, I'll do everything wrong.	5. If I relax and stay calm things will go well, just like they have been going.
6. The kids will act up and I don't know what to do.	6. I have always been able to handle this class before, so there's no reason for me not to handle it well tomorrow. Even if a student does become disruptive, if I can remain calm I'll be able to use a classroom management method that will help the situation.
Feelings	
Anxious, Depressed	Calm, Confident
Behavior	
May teach a lesson and interact with students inappropriately.	Will do a good job with the planned lesson and handle any problems that arise.

stress. When compared to a no-treatment control group, participants in both programs showed reduced self-reported stress and anxiety as well as reduced motoric manifestations of anxiety in the classroom setting. Observed positive teacher classroom statements increased for both treatment groups, although negative teacher classroom statements did not change. Changes in self-reports and classroom behavior were maintained at 4-week follow-up.

In an attempt to compare an individual stress management intervention and an organizational stress management intervention, Cecil and Forman (1988) investigated the effects of stress-inoculation training, co-worker support groups, and a no-treatment control. The 9-hour stress-inoculation training program was effective in reducing self-reported teacher stress and improving self-reported coping skills, whereas the co-worker support group was not. However, neither treatment resulted in changes in motoric manifestations of anxiety in the classroom.

TABLE 5.2
Stress Script

Situation: You give a student an assignment.
He looks at you and belligerently says, "I'm not gonna do that."

Stress Producing	*Stress Reducing*
Thoughts	
1. You little monster.	1. He's not a monster.
2. How could he say this to me?	2. I want to know why he said that, so I guess I can talk to him about it.
3. He's getting me really upset.	3. I can stay calm if I want to because I control how I feel. I can relax and then I'll be able to solve this problem better.
4. He's stupid. He doesn't want to learn.	4. Most kids want to do well. He's probably just afraid he can't do the work.
5. This is going to destroy the class.	5. The rest of the class is doing alright. Most kids are smart enough to understand why some kids act out. This class has been going pretty well for 2 months. One comment won't destroy it.
6. Why hasn't he been helped before? He's in high school already! I shouldn't have to deal with these problems in the high school.	6. It would be nice if he had been given remedial help before and it would be more pleasant if I didn't have to deal with this. But just complaining won't make things better. Since I don't like this situation I will decide where to go from here. No one ever said this job would be easy.
7. I've got to find a way to motivate him. I should be able to do it.	7. I'm going to try to find a way to motivate him. But I also want to remember that it's difficult to find motivators for all kids. We don't have complete control over their lives and we have limited amount of materials. I'll just do my best. I'm doing fairly well with the 27 other kids in the class.

(continued)

TABLE 5.2 (*Continued*)

Situation: You give a student an assignment.
He looks at you and belligerently says, "I'm not gonna do that."

Stress Producing	Stress Reducing
8. What should I do?	8. I will calmly consider the options and then decide which is best. I can talk to him about why he doesn't want to do the work. I can give him something that I know he can be successful at. I can reward him for what he does and gradually make his assignments more difficult. I can ask other teachers or special services staff for suggestions.

Feelings	
Anxious	Calm
Angry	Confident
	Somewhat Optimistic

| Behavior ||
| Yell at him. Tell him to leave the class. | Will relax. Will act on the thoughts in Statement 8. |

Changes in stress level and coping skills were maintained at 4-week follow-up assessment.

In another study comparing different types of stress management interventions, Long (1988) examined effects of stress-inoculation training, an exercise program, and stress-inoculation training with an exercise program. Teachers who had participated in stress-inoculation training with the exercise program reported less stress than those who had participated in the exercise program alone.

CONCLUSIONS

Irrational beliefs have been found to be among the cognitive–mediational factors having an impact on teacher stress. Stress management training programs, with a cognitive restructuring component based on principles of rational-emotive therapy, have shown evidence of effectiveness in reducing stress in teachers. Most successful programs have used a stress-inoculation training framework, providing behavioral and cognitive–behavioral coping skills, which can be used to alter psychological responses to potential stressors and negative stress reactions. Effects on classroom behavior found in the Forman (1982) and Sharp and Forman (1985) studies, but not found in the Cecil and Forman (1988) study, may indicate that length of training is an important effectiveness-related variable, and that sufficient time during training must be allowed for rehearsal activities in order to provide an appropriate basis for behavior change.

A number of methodological issues should be addressed in future studies in order to allow more definitive and specific conclusions to be drawn concerning the effectiveness and role of rational-emotive procedures in reducing teacher stress. First, dependent measures should include direct assessment of belief irrationality, training-related knowledge, and utilization of coping skills addressed during training, as well as more traditional measures of self-reported teacher stress and classroom behavior. This will allow for establishment of the link between specific aspects of training and emotional and/or behavioral change. Other design issues that should be considered include use of a placebo control in addition to a no-treatment control, and use of a longer follow-up period. A placebo control would allow for examination of the possible effects of attention and expectancy for change. Follow-up assessment of participants at 6 months posttraining or thereafter would provide information concerning whether cognitive, emotional, and/or behavioral changes are lasting. Finally, it is possible that the effectiveness of various stress management interventions varies according to subject characteristics such as personality factors, types of teaching environment, and/or major sources of stress for the individual. Therefore, future studies should explore the comparative effectiveness of rational-emotive-based stress interventions for teachers with varying personal characteristics and varying work environments.

Individuals working toward reducing stress in school settings should be mindful of the fact that stress reactions are the result of the interaction of environmental events and individual characteristics. Personal stress management strategies such as those described in this chapter can have a positive effect on the stress level of personnel working in school settings. Rational-emotive stress management programs can provide skills to help individuals deal with potentially stressful school situations. However, a comprehensive approach to dealing with teacher stress will also include efforts to reduce or eliminate school organizational characteristics that have been shown to be related to high stress levels.

REFERENCES

Beehr, T. A., & Newman, J. E. (1978). Job stress, employee health, and organizational effectiveness: A facet analysis, model, and literature review. *Personnel Psychology, 31*, 665–699.

Belcastro, P. A. (1982). Burnout and its relationship to teachers' somatic complaints and illnesses. *Psychological reports, 50*, 1045–1046.

Bernard, M. E. (1988). Classroom discipline and the effective self-management of teacher stress. *S. E. T. materials for teachers.* Melbourne: New Zealand/Australian Councils for Educational Research.

Bernard, M. E. (1989). Teacher stress: How to effectively self-manage it. *Primary Education, 20*, 8–11.

Bernard, M. E., & Joyce, M. R. (1984). *Rational-emotive therapy with children and adolescents: Theory treatment strategies, preventive methods.* New York: Wiley.

Bernard, M. E., Joyce, M. R., & Rosewarne, P. M. (1983). Helping teachers cope with stress: A rational-emotive approach. In A. Ellis & M. E. Bernard (Eds.), *Rational-emotive approaches to the problems of childhood* (pp. 415–466). New York: Plenum.

Cecil, M. A., & Forman, S. G. (1988). *Effects of stress inoculation training and coworker support on teacher stress.* Paper presented at meeting of the National Association of School Psychologists, Chicago, IL.

Cichon, D. (1978, March). Statistical look at stress survey reveals consistency. *Chicago Union Teacher,* p. 1.

Coates, T. J., & Thoresen, C. E. (1976). Teacher anxiety: A review with recommendations. *Review of Educational Research, 46,* 159–164.

Cunningham, W. G. (1983). Teacher burnout—Solutions for the 1980s: A review of the literature. *The Urban Review, 15*(1), 37–51.

Doyal, G. T., & Forsyth, R. A. (1973). Relationship between teacher and student anxiety levels. *Psychology in the Schools, 10,* 231–233.

Dunham, J. (1976). Stress situations and responses. In National Association of Schoolmasters and Union of Women Teachers (Eds.), *Stress in schools* (pp. 19–47). England: Hemel Hempstead.

Elliott, G. R., & Eisdorfer, C. (Eds.). (1982). *Stress and human health: Analysis and implications of research.* New York: Springer.

Ellis, A. (1962). *Reason and emotion in psychotherapy.* New York: Lyle Stuart.

Ellis, A. (1978). What people can do for themselves to cope with stress. In C. Cooper & R. Payne (Eds.), *Stress at work* (pp. 209–222). New York: Wiley.

Forman, S. G. (1981). Stress management training: Evaluation of effects on school psychological services. *Journal of School Psychology, 19,* 233–241.

Forman, S. G. (1982). Stress management for teachers: A cognitive-behavioral program. *Journal of School Psychology, 20,* 180–187.

Forman, S. G. (1983). Occupational stress management: Cognitive-behavioral approaches. *Children and Youth Services Review, 5,* 277–287.

Forman, S. G., & Cecil, M. A. (1986). Teacher stress: Causes, effects, interventions. In T. R. Kratochwill (Ed.), *Advances in school psychology* (Vol. 5, pp. 203–229). Hillsdale, NJ: Lawrence Erlbaum Associates.

Forman, S. G., & Forman, B. D. (1978). A rational-emotive therapy approach to consultation. *Psychology in the Schools, 15,* 400–406.

Forman, S. G., & Forman, B. D. (1980). Rational-emotive staff development. *Psychology in the Schools, 17,* 90–96.

Goldfried, M. R. (1977). The use of relaxation and cognitive relabeling as coping skills. In R. B. Stuart (Ed.), *Behavioral self-management* (pp. 82–116). New York: Brunner/Mazel.

Greenberg, S. F. (1984). *Stress and the teaching profession.* Baltimore, MD: Paul H. Brookes.

Greenwood, G. E., & Soar, R. D. (1973). Some relationships between teacher morale and teacher behavior. *Journal of Educational Psychology, 64,* 105–108.

Guzicki, J. A., Coates, T. J., & Goodwin, D. L. (1980). Reductions in anxiety and improvements in teaching associated with cue-controlled relaxation training. *Journal of School Psychology, 18,* 17–24.

Hammen, C. L., & deMayo, R. (1982). Cognitive correlates of teacher stress and depressive symptoms: Implications for attributional models of depression. *Journal of Abnormal Psychology, 91,* 96–101.

Hargreaves, D. (1978). What teaching does to teachers. *New Society, 43,* 540–542.

Harootunian, B., & Koon, J. R. (1970). *The reinforcement behaviors of teachers-in-training.* Paper presented at the meeting of the American Educational Research Association, Minneapolis. (ERIC Document Reproduction Service No. ED 033 064).

Harris, K., Halpin, G., & Halpin, G. (1985). Teacher characteristics and stress. *Journal of Educational Research, 78*(6), 346–350.

Kahn, R. L. (1981). *Work and health.* New York: Wiley Interscience.

Kaufman, L. M., & Wagner, B. R. (1972). Barb: A systematic treatment technology for temper control disorders. *Behavior Therapy, 3,* 84–90.

Kracht, C. R., & Casey, I. P. (1968). Attitudes, anxieties, and student teaching performance. *Peabody Journal of Education, 45,* 214–217.

Krasno, R. M. (1972). Initial rapport and survival in teaching as a function of the educational attitudes of beginning teachers. *Dissertation abstracts international, 32,* 791-A. (University Microfilms No. 71-19715)

Kyriacou, C. (1980). Sources of stress among British teachers: The contribution of job factors and personality factors. In C. L. Cooper & J. Marshall (Eds.), *White collar and professional stress* (pp. 113–128). New York: Wiley.

Kyriacou, C. (1987). Teacher stress and burnout: An international review. *Educational Research, 29,* 146–152.

Kyriacou, C., & Pratt, J. (1985). Teacher stress and psychoneurotic symptoms. *British Journal of Educational Psychology, 55*(1), 61–64.

Kyriacou, C., & Sutcliffe, J. (1978). A model of teacher stress. *Educational Studies, 4*(1), 1–6.

Kyriacou, C., & Sutcliffe, Jr. (1979). Teacher stress and satisfaction. *Educational Research, 21,* 89–96.

Lazarus, R. S. (1966). *Psychological stress and the coping process.* New York: McGraw-Hill.

Leach, D. J. (1984). Model of teacher stress and its implications for management. *The Journal of Educational Administration, 22*(2), 157–173.

Long, B. (1988). Stress management for school personnel: Stress-inoculation training and exercise. *Psychology in the Schools, 25,* 314–324.

Maslach, C. (1978). Job burnout: How people cope. *Public Welfare, 36*(2), 56–58.

Maultsby, M. C., Jr. (1975). *Help yourself to happiness.* New York: Institute for Rational Living.

McInerney, J. F. (1983). Working with the parents and teachers of exceptional children. In A. Ellis & M. E. Bernard (Eds.), *Rational-emotive approaches to the problems of childhood* (pp. 387–414). New York: Plenum.

Meichenbaum, D. (1977). *Cognitive behavior modification.* New York: Plenum Press.

Moracco, J. C., & McFadden, H. (1981). Principal and counselors: Collaborative roles in reducing teacher stress. *NASP Bulletin, 65*(477), 41–46.

Moskowitz, G., & Hayman, J. L. (1974). Interaction patterns of first year, typical, and "best" teachers in inner-city schools. *Journal of Educational Research, 67,* 224–230.

Needle, R. H., Griffin, T., & Svendsen, R. (1981). Occupational stress: Coping and health problems of teachers. *The Journal of School Health, 51,* 175–181.

New York State Teachers Association. (1979). *Teacher stress survey.* Albany, NY: New York State United Teachers Research and Educational Service.

Petrusich, M. M. (1966). Some relationships between anxiety and the classroom behavior of student teachers. *Dissertation Abstracts International, 27,* 1691-A. (University Microfilms No. 66-12038)

Petrusich, M. M. (1967). Separation anxiety as a factor in the student teaching experience. *Peabody Journal of Education, 44,* 353–356.

Pettegrew, L. S., & Wolf, G. E. (1982). Validating measures of teacher stress. *American Educational Research Journal, 19,* 373–396.

Phillips, B. N., & Lee, M. (1980). The changing role of the American teacher: Current and future sources of stress. In C. L. Cooper & J. Marshall (Eds.), *White collar and professional stress* (pp. 93–111). New York: Wiley.

Poll probes teacher dissatisfaction. (1980, September). *NEA Reporter,* p. 2.

Sharp, J. J., & Forman, S. G. (1985). A comparison of two approaches to anxiety management for teachers. *Behavior Therapy, 16*, 370–383.

Spanoil, L., & Caputo, G. G. (1979). *Professional burnout: A personal survival kit.* Lexington, MA: Human Services Associates.

Truch, S. (1980). *Teacher burnout and what to do about it.* Novato, CA: Academic Therapy.

Turk, D. C., Meeks, S., & Turk, L. M. (1982). Factors contributing to teacher stress: Implications for research, prevention, and remediation. *Behavioral Counseling Quarterly, 2*(1), 3–25.

Vance, V. S., & Schlechty, P. G. (1982). The distribution of academic ability in the teaching force: Policy implications. *Phi Delta Kappan*, 22–27.

Washbourne, C., & Heil, M. (1960). What characteristics of teacher affect children's growth? *The School Review, 4*, 420–428.

6 Rational-Emotive Consultation: A Model for Implementing Rational-Emotive Education

Ann Vernon
University of Northern Iowa

Recently, increasing concern has arisen over the socioemotional development of children. This has been coupled with the realization that prevention is the treatment of choice to address the mental health needs of children who confront not only the typical childhood developmental milestones, but the demands and pressures of a contemporary society as well.

Furthermore, there is now greater recognition that giving children experiences designed to enhance socioemotional growth will eliminate, or at least minimize, potential problems related to self-esteem, interpersonal relationships, communication, stress, expression of feelings, and decision making (Bernard & Joyce, 1984).

Edelsohn and Williams (1985) noted that numerous opportunities exist in schools for both preventative and remedial interventions. And, as the concern for children's emotional needs has increased, more attempts to introduce prevention into schools have occurred. Although it would be ideal if all educators routinely incorporated preventative mental health experiences into their curriculums, many teachers, counselors, or school psychologists lack the adequate training and preparation in affective education. They feel overwhelmed with yet another role as mental health educators. Thus, even though schools represent a "captured audience" for preventative emotional education, greater emphasis is still needed in this area given the preponderance of childhood problems that appear to be increasingly complex.

To assure increased delivery of preventative emotional education programs, a consultation model can effectively be applied to educate teachers and other school personnel. This chapter describes how rational-emotive consultation (REC) can be employed with professionals interested in applying the primary

129

prevention skills emphasized in rational-emotive education (REE). REE is an emotional education program that has been identified as a successful primary prevention intervention strategy for school-age children (Hooper & Layne, 1985).

RATIONAL-EMOTIVE EDUCATION: AN OVERVIEW

Rational-emotive education is based on rational-emotive therapy (RET), a cognitive, behavioral, and emotive approach to therapy developed by Dr. Albert Ellis. The major premise of RET is that emotional upset results from irrational thinking. Therefore, the goal of RET is to help the client identify and dispute her or his irrational thinking in order to adopt healthier beliefs and to eliminate, or minimize, intense negative emotions.

Because RET emphasizes critical thinking and is educative in nature, its principles can be incorporated systematically into an educational setting to facilitate positive attitudinal and behavioral change. Although REE is philosophically identical to RET, REE places greater emphasis on experiential learning as a vehicle for introducing rational concepts to help children gain emotional insight and to acquire problem-solving skills.

Most significantly, REE is a preventative program used with children of all ages to help them manage their feelings and their behaviors. Typically, REE is presented through a structured sequence of lessons, based around major thematic concepts, emphasizing experiential learning, and an active-directive approach. The information learned from the lessons can be applied to handle present problems and, more importantly, can provide children with knowledge and insight to use as future difficulties arise. In this manner, children are acquiring skills that become tools to help them cope more effectively with an increasingly demanding environment.

Although it is certainly not possible to eliminate all problems, the preventive approach equips children with information that may minimize the extent of the problem or help them reach new understandings and resolutions. REE helps build foundation concepts that can be drawn on to help children "get better." As Ellis (cited in Knaus, 1974) stressed, one of the main goals of rational-emotive education is to "help a youngster understand, at an early age, the general principles of emotional health and to teach him or her to consistently apply these principles to and with self and others" (p. xii).

Rational-Emotive Education Concepts

As Knaus (1974) asserted, children can lead more self-determined, self-actualizing lives by learning a systematic approach that will help them accept themselves more fully; cope more effectively with problems related to outside events; minimize their negative emotions such as guilt, fear, anger, anxiety, and frustration; and challenge their irrational beliefs. The major concepts subsequently described represent the key constructs of RET from which REE is derived.

Self-Acceptance.   Children need to develop a realistic self-concept, including an awareness of their weaknesses as well as their strengths. Accepting imperfection and acknowledging oneself as a fallible human being are central concepts. Although RET posits that unconditional self-acceptance is essential, children also come to understand that a person is a complex whole consisting of many characteristics. In other words, who one is, is not to be equated with what one does. A person's self-worth is not affected by his or her performance in any given area. In addition, self-acceptance is viewed as a trait independent of others' approval.

Feelings.   Understanding the connection among thoughts, feelings, and behaviors is the essence of REE; feelings originate from thoughts and are not the direct result of an activating event. In REE, it is important to develop a feeling vocabulary, deal with emotional overreactions, assess intensity of feelings, and develop appropriate ways to express feelings. REE stresses that it is natural to have feelings and that feelings change. The same event can result in different feelings depending on who experiences it and how that person perceives it.

Beliefs and Behaviors.   A key component of REE is the acknowledgment of both rational and irrational beliefs. Irrational beliefs result in negative emotions that disturb people. Waters (1982) developed irrational beliefs for children, basing them on the core beliefs that Ellis developed:

1. It's awful if others don't like me.
2. I'm bad if I make a mistake.
3. Everything should go my way; I should always get what I want.
4. Things should come easily to me.
5. The world should be fair, and bad people must be punished.
6. I shouldn't show my feelings.
7. Adults should be perfect.
8. There's only one right answer.
9. I must win.
10. I shouldn't have to wait for anything. (p. 572)

For adolescents, Waters (1981) identified the following irrational beliefs:

1. It would be awful if peers didn't like me. It would be awful to be a social loser.
2. I shouldn't make mistakes, especially social mistakes.

3. It's my parents' fault that I'm so miserable.
4. I can't help it, that's just the way I am, and I guess I'll always be this way.
5. The world should be fair and just.
6. It's awful when things don't go my way.
7. It's better to avoid challenges than to risk failure.
8. I must conform to my peers.
9. I can't stand to be criticized.
10. Others should always be responsible. (p. 6)

As children and adolescents are taught to differentiate between rational and irrational beliefs, the connection between beliefs and behaviors is emphasized. Irrational beliefs typically involve demands, patterns of awfulizing and over-generalizing, and self-downing that result in self-defeating behaviors and negative emotions. Extreme characteristics are suicide, eating disorders, alcohol abuse, and aggression.

Many problems children and adolescents experience are related to their irrational beliefs. They must be taught to recognize the pervasiveness of the beliefs, challenge them, and replace them with rational beliefs. The "challenging" process involves asking questions to help dispute the irrational beliefs, providing children with rational self-statements, or helping children reframe their thinking. Ultimately, children should be able to do a good deal of their own disputing, depending on their age and the amount of training they have had with the disputation process.

The following example illustrates the process of helping a youngster challenge irrational beliefs that lead to emotional upset (Vernon, 1983):

> An 11-year-old, Roxanne, came to the counselor upset because one of her friends had not been sitting by her and was ignoring her. Thus, Roxanne became angry, and hit and pushed her friend in retaliation. As the counselor worked with Roxanne, it became apparent that the angry feelings resulted from the demands Roxanne was placing on the friendship. Once she was helped to separate facts ("My friend didn't sit by me") from beliefs ("She's ignoring me because she no longer likes me"), Roxanne's feelings changed from anger to disappointment. She realized that there was no reason that her friend should always sit by her. By replacing her irrational demands with more reasonable beliefs, she could see that it wasn't the end of the world if one friend ignored her. After all, Roxanne did have other friends, and maybe if she stopped pushing, this friend might even like her better. (p. 470)

As this case exemplifies, it is important that children differentiate between facts and assumptions. Acting on assumptions without checking out the facts can lead to negative consequences.

Problem Solving.   Learning effective problem-solving skills is an important emphasis in REE. Given the nature of today's society, children are frequently forced to make decisions and to solve problems before they are developmentally prepared to do so. Some of these problems include elementary school-age children experimenting with alcohol and drugs; young children "parenting their parents" because of problems manifested in dysfunctional family systems; more youngsters experimenting sexually, and an increasing number of teenage pregnancies (Hash & Vernon, 1987). Other problems occur when children model parents—who themselves have difficulty adjusting—and the same unhealthy patterns are repeated. Undoubtedly, the lives of many children are dramatically affected because they did not have the ability to sort through the consequences or did not know how to look at alternatives to deal more effectively with the problems. In addition, ineffective problem solving creates a new set of circumstances with new challenges. Without problem-solving skills, the difficulties are perpetuated.

In REE, children are taught to think objectively, and to examine the impact of their beliefs on their behaviors. They learn to look at alternative ways of solving problems by challenging irrational thoughts, recognizing consequences, identifying alternative behaviors, and employing new behavioral strategies.

Frustration Tolerance.   Learning to tolerate frustration and to delay gratification is a core REE concept. It is particularly relevant in a society characterized by "instant access" and a "fast food" mentality. Low frustration tolerance implies that one shouldn't have to wait for anything, nor expend much effort in attaining what one desires. It is important to help children see that there is "no gain without pain," that everything doesn't have to happen immediately and that they can survive if it doesn't. Through REE, children also learn to deal with frustration by challenging beliefs.

The following section describes how these major concepts of rational-emotive therapy can be integrated into an emotional education program for children and adolescents.

IMPLEMENTING RATIONAL-EMOTIVE EDUCATION

Emotional Education Lessons

Rational-emotive education is typically implemented through a series of structured emotional education lessons presented to small groups of students or to a class. Several REE programs have been developed and the lessons have been used extensively throughout the United States (Gerald & Eyman, 1981; Knaus, 1974; Vernon, 1989a, 1989b, 1989c). Lessons are organized around a theme with a specific objective that relates to one of the core concepts described earlier: self-acceptance, feelings, beliefs and behavior, problem solving, and frustration tolerance. The lessons are experientially based, allowing for a good deal of student involvement and group interaction. The lesson format typically includes a short stimulus activity such as role-playing, bibliotherapy, simulation games, imagery activities, small group discussion, problem-solving tasks, art activities, or writing assignments. The stimulus activity usually lasts 15 to 25 minutes, depending on the age of the children and the time allotment. Students then engage in a directed discussion about the content presented in the stimulus activity. It is important that the discussion be structured around two types of questions: content questions that emphasize the cognitive learnings from the activity, and personalization questions that help the students apply the learnings to their own experiences. This discussion is actually the heart of the lesson and generally lasts 15 to 20 minutes or longer, again depending on the children's ages and the time available.

The goal of these lessons is to teach the principles of rational thinking and to apply the concepts to common concerns and issues that children encounter in the course of normal development. The following is an example of an emotional education lesson for first and second graders taken from the Beliefs and Behavior chapter of *Thinking, Feeling, Behaving: An Emotional Education Curriculum for Children* (Vernon, 1989b):

I HAVE TO HAVE MY WAY

Objective: To explore the negative effects of demanding
Materials: Story "Sid and the Baseball Game"
Procedure: Read the story, then discuss

Sid and the Baseball Game

Sid sat on the curb, waiting for the rest of the kids to come and play ball. When Sally came, she said she'd bat first. Sid stamped his foot on the ground and whined, "I won't play if I can't be first." So the kids let Sid bat first.

The first ball Sid hit was a foul, and so was the next one. Sid yelled that the umpire was cheating and if his foul ball didn't get counted as a run he'd quit. But by this time the kids all said, "OK, quit."

So, as Sid walked away, he yelled, "You'll be sorry. I don't ever want to play with cheaters again." None of the kids responded. They were having a great time and were glad to have someone like Sid out of the game.

Discussion: Content Questions

1. What do you think about Sid's behavior? (Discuss the fact that much of Sid's behavior was demanding that things be the way he wanted them to be.)
2. What does the word *demanding* mean?
3. What were some of the demands that Sid made?

4. What was the result of Sid's demanding? Did it make him happy? How did the others respond?

Discussion: Personalization Questions

1. Have you ever acted like Sid? Share some examples of times that you have been demanding. Do you like acting in a demanding way?
2. Do you think people should have their way all of the time? If you are demanding, you probably think that you should have your way. Is this possible?
3. Next time you find yourself beginning to demand, what can you do instead?

To the Leader: Demanding has negative payoffs, and students need to realize that they don't have to be demanding. Although this is difficult for youngsters to do, they can stop and ask themselves "Is it possible for me to always have my way?" "Is it so awful if I don't get exactly what I want?" and "Can't I just accept things the way they are?" Changing children's thinking is a way of altering their demanding behavior.

For Grades 7 and 8, the following example is taken from the Feelings chapter of *Thinking, Feeling, Behaving: An Emotional Education Curriculum for Adolescents* (Vernon, 1989c):

Chain Reactions

Objective: To recognize the chain effect of negative emotions.

Materials: A paper chain with the words mad, inferior, and guilty written on the first three loops. The chain should have at least 12 more loops.

Procedure:

1. Show the paper chain and discuss the concept of a "chain reaction," where one event can trigger others, or in this case, one situation triggers a chain of emotions.
2. Share the following situation: *Someone didn't invite you to a party.* Then read the word on the first chain, *mad*. (Ask if the students would have any other feelings and write those feelings also on the first chain.) Read the following thought: *"If only I were more popular."* Then read the next feeling on the chain which is *inferior.* Read the third thought: *"If only I'd said"* . . . and the next word on the chain, *guilty*.
3. As a group, try to identify another event, a feeling (write on the chain), a subsequent thought and feeling (write on the chain), and another thought if applicable. Do several examples to demonstrate the concept.

4. Take the same chain and try reversing the thoughts. For example: Someone didn't invite you to a party. Ask students how they might feel if their thought was: "So what? I'm busy that night anyway." Discuss how this initial thought would influence the entire chain.

Discussion: Content Questions

1. As demonstrated by this activity, what is the connection between events, thoughts, and feelings?
2. Do you think that it is quite common to have a chain reaction of negative thoughts and feelings?
3. What can be done to break negative cycles?

Discussion: Personalization Questions

1. Have you experienced a negative chain reaction before?
2. If you have experienced this, what was the result? Did it go on for a long time? How did you "break' the cycle?
3. Was it helpful to continue to think negative thoughts and feelings?

To the Leader: Awareness of the chain reaction tendency is important, as is the knowledge that this cycle can be brought under control by changing one's thoughts and subsequently, one's feelings. Refer to the previous activities about self-talk and anger management for additional reinforcement of concepts related to this activity.

Lessons such as these represent a viable approach to preventing or lessening the severity of emotional and behavioral problems. It is recommended that they be implemented on a regular basis for primary and secondary level children. The topics should be developed in sequence to the concepts presented, therefore, assuring that core ideas are introduced and reinforced as developmentally appropriate. For further information the reader is referred to Vernon (1989b, 1989c).

Although the structured emotional education lesson is the most common method of introducing rational-emotive education, three other approaches can complement the systematic presentation of the lessons.

Informal Reinforcement

Informal reinforcement capitalizes on the "teachable moment" in order to reinforce concepts related to emotional well-being. As children experience situations and need assistance working through issues, adults provide guidance to help them deal with the present problem, and to apply these skills to similar events.

For example, a child who is frustrated in class as he or she is learning something new might resort to throwing down the pencil, crumbling up the paper, and repeatedly starting the task again. In this situation, it is apparent that the child may think everything should come easily right away, that the work shouldn't be so hard, that he or she shouldn't make mistakes, and that it's no use trying because it'll never be any good anyway. In such a situation, self-defeating behaviors and attitudes prevail, making it difficult for the child to complete a task. If an adult can intervene and help the child recognize that there is frustration in learning something new and that everything doesn't come easily, then the adult can work with the child to identify constructive ways to deal with the frustration and complete the task. In this approach, both present and future events can be dealt with much more effectively.

Another example might involve helping a student deal with anxiety about playing in a recital. First, the teacher would help the child identify where the anxious feelings were coming from, specifying thoughts such as: "I will fail; I'll make too many mistakes; everyone will laugh; I can't stand being a fool." In working through this problem, the teacher might say something like "Suppose you would make mistakes . . . what does that say about you? That you're no good? Have you ever known anyone else who made a mistake during a recital? Did that person live through it? Do you think that just because you make a mistake, or several mistakes, that *everyone* will laugh? Are you a *fool* just because you make a mistake?" Questions of this nature can help the child put the problem in better perspective and develop a strategy for approaching the problem once the anxiety connected with the irrational thinking is diminished.

Although adult intervention may initially be needed to present the concepts and to help the youngster work through the issue, the intent is for this to be a self-help approach that children can use independently as needed.

Integration into Curriculum

Integrating REE concepts into existing subject matter curriculum represents another method of implementation. This approach involves identifying specific topics related to the REE concepts (self-acceptance, feelings, beliefs and behaviors, problem solving, and frustration tolerance) and introducing them into appropriate curricular areas. When teaching literature, for example, stories could be selected that present characters solving problems rationally or expressing feelings in a healthy manner. In a writing class, theme topics could be related to tolerating frustration, eliminating self-defeating behaviors, making mistakes, or tolerating differences in others. Feeling word vocabularies could be used as spelling lists. Social studies classes could focus on the concept of fairness. Topics such as assertiveness and stress management, which both contain rational thinking as an integral part of the process, could be introduced in personal health classes.

Although integrating REE concepts into a curriculum is less direct than a structured lesson, it represents another way of reinforcing concepts and can contribute to emotional education.

Classroom Structure

The value of more deliberate approaches to emotional education is diminished if classroom procedures do not support rational concepts. This implies that school personnel be familiar with these principles in order to integrate them into the environment. In particular, to facilitate sound emotional growth, classroom teachers must reinforce *improvement* rather than evaluating students solely on the "perfect" product. It is essential to structure practice sessions where children can work to correct mistakes, to discuss the fact that poor performance doesn't make one a bad person, and to individualize assignments so all children can experience some success. Equally important is the introduction of some assignments that may involve frustration. These assignments can allocate time to teach students how to break down a task into smaller parts so as not to be overwhelmed. .Discussing the fact that there are always frustrations to deal with helps dispel the belief that nothing should ever be frustrating.

Through modeling by the teacher, students can learn such rational concepts as: it's natural to make mistakes, human beings are fallible and don't do all things well all the time, there are always alternative ways to handle problems, and one can choose whether or not to become upset by various activating events.

Risk taking can also be encouraged: rewarding children for trying new things, pairing low risk takers with high risk takers for various activities, and utilizing guest speakers who are positive examples of risk taking and other rational principles as well.

Ideally, children of all ages will participate in structured emotional education lessons designed to teach rational thinking principles to help prevent psychological problems and to enhance psychological growth. Coupled with informal reinforcement, integration into curriculum is appropriate, and a classroom structure based on rational concepts, sound emotional adjustment of children will be more certain. According to Bernard and Joyce (1984), "the full utility of RET with younger populations is yet to be determined" (p. 31), but they conclude that children of all ages can learn the content of REE lessons and can apply the content to modify beliefs. This supports earlier research that indicated that children are not only capable of acquiring rational-emotive principles, but that the modification of irrational self-statements contributes to improved emotional and behavioral adjustment (DiGiuseppe, Miller, & Trexler, 1979).

Our goal as educators is not only to teach the basic skills, but also to help children cope more effectively in a society where childhood problems are more complex. Thus, it appears that support personnel must become more actively involved in facilitating the implementation of rational-emotive education concepts through the consultation process. The following sections provide an overview of consultation and specifically describe how the consultant can help promote rational emotive education concepts within an educational setting.

THE CONSULTATION PROCESS

According to Brown, Kurpius, and Morris (1988), consultation is a relatively new function, both in theory and practice. In light of this, it is not easy to define the process. It is difficult partly because consultants may assume various roles in a complex process that encompasses a wide range of skills and a variety of knowledge bases.

Consultation is regarded as a triadic process in which the consultant works with a consultee to develop strategies for eliminating or preventing problems with a client. An important goal of the consultation relationship is to empower the consultee so that he or she is able to deal more effectively in the future with similar issues in different clients (Brown et al., 1988).

A unique aspect of consultation is the equitable power relationship between consultee and consultant. The goal is to improve the consultee's functioning. In some cases, this comes about in a direct teaching/modeling process, and in other instances it occurs more indirectly when the consultant helps the consultee assess and mobilize strengths and utilize resources in a different way.

Consultation is considered a collaborative problem-solving process focusing on altering the consultees' and clients' behaviors. Through consultation, consultees can learn new strategies for working with clients on an individual or a group basis, thus remediating or improving their professional functioning that impacts the client.

Although the significance of consultation has yet to be determined, Brown et al. (1988) noted that consultation may be superior to counseling. Consultation is not only more cost effective and efficient, but the ability to have an impact on the client may be greater. Given that the mental health needs of school-age children are greater than ever before, and that prevention is considered a necessity not a luxury, rational-emotive consultation (REC) is an appropriate vehicle for enhancing the socioemotional development of children.

Rational-Emotive Consultation

Although RET has been widely employed with educators as well as parents in the prevention and remediation of childhood problems, there is little description of the rational-emotive consultative process. For the purposes of this chapter, REC is discussed as an indirect service to the client; the focus is on the consultant working with the consultee to teach rational-emotive education concepts that in turn can be implemented with clients in the prevention of mental health problems as well as current problem resolution.

The following sections describe specific procedures of applying the REC process to facilitate preventive mental health practices and rational problem resolution methods.

CONSULTATION: RATIONAL-EMOTIVE EDUCATION

Although consultation often involves a one-to-one collaborative interaction between consultant and consultee, Lippitt and Lippitt (1978) noted that consultants assume multiple roles depending on the degree of activity. Among those roles identified are trainer/educator, which involves imparting knowledge to the consultee about the problem.

As a trainer/educator, the consultant is involved in presenting basic principles of rational-emotive education to teachers and other school personnel in an in-service format. The purpose is to promote the emotional growth of children through one of the methods of implementation previously reviewed: structured lessons, informal reinforcement, integration through curriculum, and classroom structure. It is suggested that the consultant present the model subsequently described either as a response to general concerns teachers express about children or as a proactive means of meeting student needs. The following outline is divided into five $1^{1}/_{2}$- to 2-hour sessions, or it could be presented in one all-day block.

Rational-Emotive Education In-Service Model Outline

Session 1.   As a general rule, educators are more likely to implement ideas if they see a reason for doing so, or as Bernard and Joyce (1984) suggested, "teachers can be much more motivated to employ procedures we suggest if they can see how they relate to the psychology of the child" (p. 353). Therefore, it is important to introduce the session by involving participants in a small group brainstorming activity and asking them to identify and record some of the current problems children experience that they as teachers are concerned about and feel inadequate to deal with.

Having done this with several groups of teachers, a common array of problems generally emerges, falling into several broad categories: lack of self-esteem or perfectionism; interpersonal relationship issues such as rejection, name-calling, or teasing; inadequate conflict resolution strategies; frustration over task completion; and aggressive behavior and management of negative feelings such as anger, anxiety, or fear. Problems of a more serious nature such as depression, suicidal behavior, abuse, family relationships, and chemical dependency are also frequently included.

After problems have been identified in small groups, have the first group share its list. The leader should write the responses on the board as they are read so that as other groups share, new items can be added. Once this process has been completed, the whole group may want to add to the list and discuss some of their concerns in greater detail.

Using the lists as a reference, the consultant then states that although many of these problems must be dealt with through extensive counseling, it is also imperative that teachers begin equipping children with emotional "information" that can be used preventatively. The rationale is that children can learn to solve their own problems to a large extent, but need "tools" to help them attain a positive mental health status. Although most children are very adaptable, many cannot cope successfully with situational and developmental stressors that they encounter as they mature. Wouldn't it be advisable to anticipate the problems and prepare children to cope *before* the problems arise? Such is the philosophy of preventative emotional education programs.

Session 2.   In this session, rational-emotive education is introduced as an emotional education program proven to be effective in teaching positive mental health concepts to children. The consultant explains that REE presents a sound theoretical basis and an approach that can help children create positive attitude and behavior changes that enable them to deal more effectively with their concerns. As a means of presenting the core concepts, the consultant should explain that REE is based on rational-emotive therapy, emphasizing the following: Emotional upset does not occur because of an activating event, which in RET is called the "A," but rather is influenced by a person's beliefs. Beliefs are classified as rational or irrational. Irrational beliefs are characterized by demanding, self-downing, overgeneralizing and awfulizing, and having low levels of frustration tolerance. Irrational beliefs create negative feelings and behaviors. Although the goal of RET is not to eliminate feelings, the purpose is to lessen the intensity of the negative emotion and, thus, to modify the self-defeating behaviors that often accompany this type of emotional overreaction.

To illustrate this concept, the consultant can list some examples of irrational beliefs on the board, such as "If I don't do a good job with this inservice, I'm a rotten person"; "If my spouse doesn't ask me immediately upon entering the house how my day was, it must mean he or she doesn't care about me"; or "I can't stand teaching here; I never get any positive reinforcement and everyone is always demanding things of me."

Next, divide participants into triads and have them generate personal examples of their own irrational beliefs, either personal or professional. Invite volunteers to share and discuss the concept of irrationality, emphasizing that irrational beliefs result in negative emotions and represent the core of emotional disturbance. Share examples of irrational beliefs of children and adolescents, and have them re-group into pairs to discuss application of these concepts to their individual students.

In closing, review the essence of emotional disturbance by presenting the ABCs of emotion using an example such as the following:

A child complains that others are teasing him, calling him "stupid pig" and "idiot." (This is the "A," activating event). When asked how he feels, the child says that he feels angry and worthless and that he wants to "beat the kids up." (This is the "C," the emotional and behavioral consequence.) Then the counselor tries to help the child identify his beliefs: that others *shouldn't* call him names, and that if they do, he can't stand it and whatever they say must be true.

To help the child, the counselor asks some disputing questions such as: "Just because they called you names, are you what they say you are?" "Even though it isn't very nice to have people call you names, can you control what other kids do? Sure, you'd prefer that they didn't call you names, but is it really so awful that you can't stand it? If you know that you're not a stupid pig, why let them get to you?"

Questions of this nature represent the "D" in the RET schema and enable the child to replace the irrational beliefs with rational ones, which in turn will result in a less intense negative emotion, or a new effect (the "E" in the ABCDE paradigm).

As a homework assignment prior to the next meeting, invite teachers to identify children's irrational beliefs and to try to help them dispute them, utilizing the skills presented during the session.

Session 3.   Begin this session with a review of the homework assignment and respond to questions about the ABCs. Next, present the basic concepts of REE by listing the following headings across the board: self-acceptance, feelings, beliefs and behavior, problem solving, and low frustration tolerance. As concepts are explained according to the information previously outlined, key words illustrating the concepts can be written under each heading to clarify the ideas. Whenever possible, illustrate with examples.

After responding to questions about the concepts, divide participants into groups of five and assign each group one of the five concept areas. Their task is to select two people in each group to role-play a teacher and a student. The student will present a problem that illustrates that concept. For example, under self-acceptance, the "student's problem" may be that he or she puts him or herself down because he or she made a mistake. The person who plays the teacher will attempt to help resolve the issue by asking disputing questions. Other participants serve as observers, giving feedback and suggestions after a 10- to 15-minute role-play period.

As a homework assignment, participants are to analyze student problems according to these core concepts.

Session 4.   After a few minutes are spent discussing the homework assignment, introduce the first method of implementing rational-emotive education: the structured lesson format. This is by far the most effective REE intervention strategy. If lessons are presented consistently and the REE concepts are sequentially developed, children will get involved in the activities, gain emotional insight, and learn basic problem-solving skills.

In explaining the essence of this approach to teachers, it is important to stress that emotional education lessons are presented in much the same manner as a social studies or reading lesson, except there might be more involvement and emphasis on experiential learning. Each lesson is structured around a stimulus activity related to a specific objective. Through a directed discussion, the objective is achieved through content questions that relate to the information presented in the activity, and through personalization questions that encourage transfer of learning as the child applies the rational information to his or her own experiences.

Teachers will need to know how often to conduct REE lessons. Ideally, two to three weekly sessions of 30 minutes would be introduced, but once a week may be all that is feasible. In high school settings, emotional education classes might be structured into study hall periods or through an advisor–advisee system where a teacher meets with a core group of students for one period per week. Basic to conducting lessons is a nonjudgmental attitude and a nonthreatening classroom atmosphere where respect and acceptance of each other's ideas are valued.

In addition to sharing examples of materials that have been developed (Bernard & Joyce, 1984; Gerald & Eyman, 1981; Knaus, 1974; Vernon, 1989a, 1989b, 1989c), a demonstration lesson is recommended to clearly illustrate the process. This could be done with a group of students, or teachers themselves could role-play and participate as students.

Although structured lessons represent the most systematic method of REE implementation, three other approaches are presented in the next session.

Session 5.   In this final session, the emphasis is on less formal, but equally important, methods of introducing REE concepts: informal reinforcement, integration into the curriculum, and classroom structure. As Knaus (1974) noted:

> Because didactically presented concepts may or may not help children deal with some of their everyday problems, it is important for the teacher to be on the alert for live classroom situations in which the concepts may be advantageously illustrated. This kind of experiential use of rational concepts will not only serve to improve problem-solving skills, but it will also emphasize that there are many ways to solve problems. (pp. 4–5)

In presenting these approaches, the consultant first quickly involves the group in generating a list of everyday concerns that they as teachers might have to help children deal with: performance anxiety, acting-out behavior, test-taking concerns, or name calling. Next, divide participants into triads and have one person role-play the student with the problem and another role-play the teacher. The third person observes and coaches the teacher on how to help the "child" deal with the concern by employing rational principles. After 15 minutes, pull groups together and process the role-play, discussing questions and concerns about this method.

Integration into the curriculum represents another viable way to expose students to rational concepts. Teachers could be divided into groups representing various subject matter areas and allowed to brainstorm specific ways to incorporate REE principles. Limited only by time and creativity, this approach tends to come more readily as teachers become more familiar with REE concepts and begin to see application as they select new materials and develop lesson plans. During an in-service session that I conducted, one teacher shared that she had read a story to her third graders from *Color Us Rational* (Waters, 1979). During their writing period, she asked them to write their own rational stories. One student wrote that he thought it was the end of the world when he found out that his parents were getting a divorce, but that when he thought about what could be worse, he realized that it would be worse if one of his parents died. He concluded that even though he didn't like the situation, he could learn to live with it.

Another creative curriculum integration was related by a high school English teacher who developed a unit on individual differences. Students read novels about the elderly, mentally retarded, and the physically handicapped. They interviewed people who worked with these individuals, did research on problems these people faced, and spent time interacting with elderly, physically handicapped, and mentally retarded people. As a final project, the students wrote an essay on these people's outlook on life and what they had told themselves in order to cope with difficult situations.

Sharing examples such as these during the in-service presentation and being available on an individual basis to consult with teachers as they work to incorporate rational concepts into their curriculum can be an effective means of integrating a sound philosophy of life into existing content.

Emphasizing the importance of classroom structure consistent with REE principles is the final implementation method. To illustrate this procedure, divide participants into pairs and give each pair one of the following descriptors: responsibility, grading, exams, group participation, school performances, risk taking. Each pair is to generate one practice relative to the descriptor that is consistent with rational concepts.

For instance, responsibility might mean having a contract system where the student sets his or her own goals and is responsible for the consequences. The rational components relate to the student owning the responsibility, not projecting blame onto others if he or she fails to complete work, and setting appropriate goals. Risk taking could involve sending out invitations encouraging students to try out for cheerleading, a part in a play, or a spot on an athletic team. The announcement could indicate what it means if students don't get the part or make the team (that they are not incompetent or less worthy, but that everyone cannot be chosen), what it says about them because they tried (that they do have courage and are willing to risk), and how they can deal with their disappointment (acknowledge that they are disappointed but recognize that it isn't the end of the world). This procedure elicits the fears that prevent risk taking and helps to allay some of the concerns.

When pairs have completed the task, invite them to share ideas and to discuss practices that they may already be employing. Reinforce the notion that every day opportunities occur to introduce rational thinking. This promotes the likelihood that teachers will begin looking for opportunities as they become more knowledgeable about the theory.

Consultation Interventions

The trainer/educator consultation role that incorporates an in-service model involves imparting knowledge to the consultee to affect change in clients. In this case, the consultant shares his or her expertise in rational-emotive education with teachers, who in turn can implement concepts to promote rational thinking and emotional growth in children as a preventative mental health strategy.

Following the in-service presentation, the consultant may assume a more collaborative role, working with individual teachers upon request to model REE lessons, helping to develop sequential lessons plans, and adapting existing materials to meet the needs of specific populations, a child or a classroom situation. In the latter case, the consultee (teacher) would share the concern with the consultant. Together they would discuss the concern, collect further data as needed, accurately define the problem, and then work together to generate possible solutions. Once solutions have been identified and selected, a specific plan of action is formulated and the procedure is implemented. Evaluation and follow-up are an integral part of the process.

To illustrate, after an in-service presentation was delivered to one group of teachers, several of them began immediately to conduct REE lessons in their guidance classes. After several weeks, one teacher contacted the consultant for additional ideas concerning an adolescent who shared during an REE class that she was extremely upset because she wasn't selected for National Honor Society. The student was apparently telling everyone that she was no good, that the selection process was unfair, that other students who were selected shouldn't have been nominated because she was better than they were, and that this would ruin her chances for college scholarships. As the teacher shared his concerns about the student with the consultant, the consultant utilized the ABC format to help the teacher identify the feelings and irrational beliefs held by the adolescent. Second, the consultant worked with the teacher to generate some examples of disputing questions that could be used to help alleviate some of the irrational beliefs. Next, they discussed how to approach the student to discuss the concern and what further assistance the teacher might need. In a follow-up evaluation session, the teacher reported that the procedure had gone well and that he had utilized some of the same sorts of questions with another student experiencing a similar problem. This, of course, is the essence of the consultation process: improved client functioning *and* increased skill on the part of the consultee that assures more effective interventions with large numbers of clients.

CONCLUSION

The goal of REE is to help children acquire coping strategies that will enable them to independently solve problems. Given the developmental problems that children encounter in the normal course of maturation, coupled with situational crises, it can be argued that permitting

> a youngster to down himself or herself, and to become afflicted with needless anxiety, depression, guilt, hostility, and lack of discipline, and then taking that individual later in life and attempting to intensively "therapize" him or her in one-to-one encounters or small groups, is indeed a wasteful, tragically inefficient procedure. Far better, if it can be truly done is to help this youngster to understand, at an early age, some of the general principles of emotional health and to teach him or her to consistently apply these principles to and with self and others. This is now one of the main goals of RET. (Knaus, 1974, p. xii)

Rational-emotive consultation has been described as an effective procedure for working indirectly with children by teaching consultees how to apply rational-emotive education as a primary prevention strategy. The consultation process offers an intervention method that can potentially produce change that perhaps no other mental health service provides. The implications of such a model are far-reaching, and the impact on client behavior may be considerable.

REFERENCES

Bernard, M. E., & Joyce, M. R. (1984). *Rational-emotive therapy with children and adolescents.* New York: Wiley.

Brown, D., Kurpius, D. J., & Morris, J. R. (1988). *Handbook of consultation with individuals and small groups.* Alexandria, VA: Association for Counselor Education and Supervision.

DiGiuseppe, R., A., Miller, N. J., & Trexler, L. D. (1979). A review of rational-emotive psychotherapy outcomes studies. In A. Ellis & J. M. Whitely (Eds.), *Theoretical and empirical foundations of rational-emotive therapy* (pp. 125–139). Monterey, CA: Brooks/Cole.

Edelsohn, G. A., & Williams, J. C. (1985). Child psychiatry consultation to a public high school: A development perspective. *Journal of Child and Adolescent Psychotherapy, 2,* 105–109.

Gerald, M., & Eyman, W. (1981). *Thinking straight and talking sense.* New York: Institute for Rational Living.

Hash, V., & Vernon, A. (1987). Helping early adolescents deal with stress. *Middle School Journal, 18*(4), 22–23.

Hooper, S. R., & Layne, C. C. (1985). Rational-emotive education as a short term primary prevention technique. *A Journal for Remedial Education and Counseling, 1,* 264–269.

Knaus, W. J. (1974). *Rational-emotive education: A manual for elementary school teachers.* New York: Institute for Rational Living.

Lippitt, G., & Lippitt, R. (1978). *The consulting process in action.* San Diego, CA: University Associates.

Vernon, A. (1983). Rational-emotive education. In A. Ellis & M. E. Bernard (Eds.), *Rational-emotive approaches to the problems of childhood.* New York: Plenum Press.

Vernon, A. (1989a). *Help yourself to a healthier you: A handbook of emotional education exercises for children.* Minneapolis, MN: Burgess.

Vernon, A. (1989b). *Thinking, feeling, behaving: An emotional education curriculum for children.* Champaign, IL: Research Press.

Vernon, A. (1989c). *Thinking, feeling, behaving: An emotional education curriculum for adolescents.* Champaign, IL: Research Press.

Waters, V. (1979). *Color us rational.* New York: Institute for Rational Living.

Waters, V. (1981). *The living school.* RET work, 1,1.

Waters, V. (1982). Therapies for children: Rational-emotive therapy. In C. R. Reynolds & T. B. Gutkin (Eds.), *Handbook of school psychology.* New York: Wiley.

7

A Rational Perspective on the Problems of Students

Marilyn Rothschild
School Psychologist
Denver Public Schools

It may surprise you to know that parents and teachers, for the most part, hold common goals for children. Some practitioners who read this may strongly doubt me, but nevertheless, except in unusual circumstances, teachers and parents want the same things for their children: good mental health, achievement in school, comfortable relationships, self-discipline, independent work habits, and so forth. What often differs between parents and teachers are the methods by which and the circumstances under which each tries to help children and adolescents accomplish these goals.

In addition, I have found that many parents and teachers prefer to help children themselves, without referral to outside sources, if this is possible and if they are able to provide help. In a survey of teachers about what kind of interventions they preferred when children have difficulties, the majority indicated they wanted strategies to use on their own in the classroom without disrupting the class too much, and without referral to a principal, a parent, or for disciplinary action outside the classroom (Martens, Peterson, Witt, & Cirone, 1986). I have also found that many of the problems children and adolescents have can be helped significantly by parents and teachers, provided they (the adults) are committed to helping, have a good general philosophy to guide them, and strategies to use in applying this philosophy. A philosophy is necessary because it will help solve many problems on a long-term as well as short-term basis.

The system of rational-emotive therapy (RET) by Albert Ellis (1962) provides such a working philosophy. It is systematic, focused on understanding and coping with emotional upset, and challenges the notion that adults and children are helpless in the face of adversity. It has been used as a self-help system for adults (Ellis & Harper, 1975), and can be used to prevent serious emotional disturbances in children as well, provided the language level is modified appropriately (Ellis, 1969; Knaus, 1974; Lafferty, Denneral, & Rettich, 1964).

What makes RET an even more desirable system is that its major premises are basic for helping children and adolescents gain and maintain good mental health. What I believe this means is that because we cannot expect their lives to be problem-free, we would want to help them develop the sense that they can handle most problems, if not all. The basic qualities we want children to have to develop this sense would be an internal locus of control, self-acceptance and unconditional acceptance of others, thinking and communicating skills, ability to problem solve effectively, and ability to engage in activities that are in their best interests even when doing so is difficult.

A child or adolescent who possesses an internal locus of control operates with the attitude that rewards in life are for the most part dependent on his or her behavior. The child believes, for example, that he or she earned an A that he or she received. The child or adolescent with an external locus of control believes rewards happen because of persons or factors outside him or herself (Rothbaum, Wolfer, & Visentainer, 1979; Rotter, 1966). The child believes he or she received the A because of luck or because of the teacher's good graces. According to research the student with an internal locus of control feels more in control of him or herself and the things that happen to him or her than the child with an external locus (Bialer, 1960; Crandall, Katakovsky, & Crandall, 1965; Morgan, 1986; Nowicki & Strickland, 1973). Learning and accepting the major premise of RET theory—emotional difficulties are self-created and can be self-uncreated—is learning to develop an internal locus of control.

Research findings indicate that having an internal locus of control empowers adults and children. The internally oriented person exhibits less delay in decision making (Strickland, 1972), ability to forget failure (Pearl, Bryan, & Donahue, 1980), less conformity and more ability to resist subtle social influence (Massari & Rosenblum, 1972), and higher risk-taking behaviors (Rothbaum et al., 1979). Children who believe their own behaviors are responsible for their success or failure make greater academic gains than those with an external locus of control. They learn more from experiences that they feel they have the power to influence (Brown, 1980; Cervantes, 1976; Massari & Rosenblum, 1972; Morgan, 1986).

Unconditional self-acceptance and unconditional acceptance of others is another pivotal construct of RET (Ellis, 1974). Unconditional self-acceptance means accepting oneself as human, with all one's imperfections and assets, without "ifs" or "buts." (e.g., If only I were thinner, then I would be okay). Unconditional acceptance of others means accepting others as human. In neither case does it mean liking one's (or another's) imperfections; it means not putting oneself or others down for being human. This philosophical position enables a child or adolescent to take responsibility for his or her own problematic feelings while maintaining feelings of worthwhileness, and to build and maintain relationships. This area is discussed in more detail later in this chapter.

Communicating and thinking both involve language. Although feelings can be communicated with body language, these signs can easily be misinterpreted. It is often hard to tell just by looking whether a person is upset or whether his or her feet hurt. After 38 years of marriage, I still cannot tell whether my husband is tired or angry simply from the expression on his face. The clearest way to express feelings is by verbalizing them. RET strategies, with their emphasis on developing appropriate inner speech, serve to encourage children and adolescents to verbalize thoughts and feelings rather than act them out. Furthermore, it encourages them to use private speech to organize, understand, and gain control over their behavior, things that are essential to problem solving and achievement (Berk, 1980; Vygotsky, 1962).

Problems are another word for living. They are natural and normal in an imperfect world filled with imperfect people. So we might as well accept them when they come along, and try to reduce our distress over them so we can do our best to solve them. Then we can go on and enjoy the rest of life. But before we can begin to solve problems, we have to engage in clear thinking about them and the options available. Strong emotions like rage, anxiety, helplessness, and depression interfere with clear thinking and effective problem solving, and are often the first reactions children and adolescents have when frustrated by problems. Helping children and adolescents learn techniques for reducing strong emotions when they encounter problems, as you see here, is part and parcel of the RET system.

Children and adolescents tend to be pleasure-seeking, and often will follow the line of least resistance in conflictual or problematic situations. In these times, many suffer from low frustration tolerance, and many are overconcerned with acceptance, particularly peer acceptance. Some children's feelings about peer disapproval or rejection border on the extreme. Bright students have told me, with little hesitation, that they would jump off a roof if a friend threatened to reject them if they didn't. Pursuing their own best interests is not a high priority for young people, particularly if they perceive frustration or rejection as a possibility.

Helping children and adolescents to deal with the irrational beliefs that underlie difficulties such as low frustration tolerance, passivity, and fear of rejection, is basic to RET. By learning its systems and strategies, parents and teachers can help children learn to change their thinking, feelings, and behaviors, and enable them to pursue what is best for them. Such a pursuit is basic not only to survival, but to achieving the good life.

Helping Children Develop Responsibility for Their Feelings and Behaviors

Understanding the causal relationship between thinking and feeling and accepting responsibility for one's own emotional disturbance may seem, at first blush, too great a burden for children and adolescents, given their state of cognitive development. But although it is difficult, children and adolescents do come to understand the sense of it, and once they do, I have seen that not only do they accept it, but they practice it with considerable enthusiasm. They seem to view it as empowering them, rather than as burdening them. It helps them reduce their feelings of helplessness and rage, feelings that are engendered when they blame most of their difficulties, failures, and discomforts on chance, other persons, or other external factors over which they have little control.

This increased sense of power, or the development of a more internally oriented locus of control, can happen even for young children. For example, one physically strong, bright, 6-year-old first-grade boy was having temper tantrums frequently at school. During the tantrum he would throw anything (chairs, tables, etc.) that was nearby, and was otherwise uncontrollable. He was able to learn to control his anger cognitively after being told that if he was able to make his anger "big" he could make it smaller if he tried. He was helped in this visually. He was instructed to watch the psychologist's outstretched arms and reduce his anger as they got close together. He was then reinforced for this control with time to talk. Each time his anger recurred, as he spoke about what happened, the signal was reinstituted and he calmed himself down. The tantrum problem was not only resolved for that day but also decreased over the school year with relatively little contact. During a follow-up session, when the child was asked how he learned to become less angry when something happened, he said, "I think this way," and gestured with his arms.

This procedure has been helpful as well for older children, helping them to understand that they can reduce their emotional distress by thinking. It can also be used as a visual signal to remind an angry or distressed student to calm down. Visual signaling by teachers is often effective for behavioral control. It could be useful for parents as well in some social situations, such as during meals at home or out, when a verbal reminder may be less desirable. But it should be used, as in the case with all signaling, only if there is a prior agreement with the student and if its message is clearly understood by the child.

The idea that they are responsible for creating and uncreating their emotional distress is not easy for children to buy. The media, other people (peers particularly), and their own emotional reactions may do much to support the opposite idea, that the causes of their emotional disturbance (i.e., anger, depression, etc.) are external to them (e.g., other people, teasing, certain things happening). To help them accept this new but perhaps unpopular concept, it is important that:

1. The parents or teachers understand it, accept it, and practice it themselves.

2. The children have time and opportunity to discuss it and disagree with it without condemnation.

3. The children are given evidence or proof of the concept and help refuting the concept that their emotional difficulties are externally caused.

4. The children are given time and encouragement to think about it and to test it out.

Not only would these activities help persuade them that feelings come from thinking and that this position empowers them; it would also help demonstrate that scientific thinking and proof or evidence is needed before one accepts any belief (idea) as true or sensible.

How do you prove to children that feelings come from thoughts? I have found the following strategies and exercises helpful.

1. Question their thinking. Wouldn't it be true that if feelings came from events, then everybody would feel the same about an event? Has it been their experience that everybody feels the same way about parties, going to the dentist, being teased, and so on? If they say yes, suggest they do an experiment to check it out. Survey their friends' or classmates' feelings about birthday parties, teasing, the teacher, and so forth, and keep a record of their feelings. They probably will not have to do this activity, but many want to. Sum up by indicating that not everybody feels the same way about the same things, and that not even one person may always feel the same way about one thing or one person. Help them understand that this means that it isn't an event that causes most of a person's feelings.

2. Have them do the following exercise (adapted from Knaus, 1974, p. 20). Close their eyes and imagine they are on a crowded elevator or bus. Then they feel someone poking them in their backs. Ask them how they would feel. You'll probably get anger in many forms, like hitting, killing, whining, annoyance. Accept them all and tell them to keep feeling that way. Then ask them to close their eyes again and pretend they turned around and can see that the person who poked them is blind. Ask how they feel now. They will probably respond with less anger and even sorrow and guilt. Ask where their anger went, and why did it change? Explain the idea that being poked was annoying and irritating, but getting mad about it was due to the way they evaluated it. When they changed their evaluation of what happened, it reduced their angry feelings or got rid of their anger entirely!

3. Teach them that what other people may do, or not having what you want, or teasing, is annoying, irritating, or frustrating. But we make ourselves feel *very* angry, depressed, anxious, or inferior by the way we think, and these big feelings cause us trouble. Explain that they would want to change their thinking to change their feelings so they can try to solve problems, perform better, get those troublesome persons off their backs, and go after things that are best for them even when they find them difficult, irritating, boring, or frustrating. They don't have to make those little pains into a big deal; even if they do, they can stop. Stress that they are not helpless to control their feelings. I usually add something like, "That's real power, isn't it?" to know you can do that. Then give them oppor-

tunities to discuss this after they think about it, so they demonstrate understanding. Many children act as if they understand things when they really don't.

4. Many children and adolescents, even when they can identify and verbalize their feelings, have difficulty identifying and, particularly, challenging or disputing the irrational thoughts behind them. This has also been the finding of other practitioners (Bernard & Joyce, 1984). Because of this, I have found it helpful to construct and reinforce rational self-statements and rational poems that are appropriate to a problem area. Following are some poems I created that have been helpful with children and adolescents in calming themselves or in preventing them from getting so upset when unpleasant things happen. The poems may not be well understood; their meanings or some words may need to be clarified. To help them understand and remember the rational ideas in the poems, I have had children make posters with illustrations. These can be hung around the house or classroom. This will remind teachers and parents of the concept as well.

> Sensible thinking each day,
> Will help keep —————— away!
> (fill in the blank with undesirable feelings, people, behaviors, etc.)
>
> If you think before you do your thing,
> Then you probably won't act like a ding-a-ling.
>
> When trouble comes, don't act the fool,
> Think sensibly and you'll stay cool
>
> If you exaggerate what happens to you
> Then you'll cry and rage and stew.
> But if you think, "it's not so bad,"
> Then you'll feel less worried, angry, sad.
>
> When you feel anxious, mad, or down,
> When a bad thing happens to you,
> It's not because of what happened,
> But due to your point of view.
> You can help yourself to feel better,
> And become more effective,
> If you challenge your irrational thoughts,
> And develop a realistic perspective.
>
> When things are not comfortable or fine,
> And people act badly with no gratitude,
> It is best not to get mad or whine,
> But to try to change things or your attitude.

5. Two humorous stories by Virginia Waters (1980) that explain these things more fully are "Fasha, Sasha, and Dasha" and "Cornelia Cardinal Learns to Cope." These can be read to children or read by them. They are two of six

amusing, well-written children's stories by Waters that deal with feelings and problems from an RET point of view. A series of pamphlets for parents covering the same areas accompanies the stories. The parental material can be easily adapted for use by teachers.

6. There is also a pamphlet entitled *Rational Counseling Primer,* by Howard Young, which is useful with older children and adolescents and even adults. It is an excellent, easy-to-read introduction to the basic principles of RET.

Toward Unconditional Self-Acceptance

One emphasis of RET is on the development of unconditional self-acceptance and its corollary, unconditional acceptance of others (Ellis, 1962, 1974). Such a position is a change from the usual notions of self-concept. The terms *self-concept* or *self-esteem* imply that adults and children hold global evaluations of their value, self-worth, goodness, and badness. They believe as well that self-concept is enhanced or lowered by success or failure, approval or disapproval.

Many of us, particularly our children, have learned this way of thinking from our society. But forming such global conceptions of ourselves is hazardous to our mental health, creating many built-in problems. Among these are:

1. Events and the unpredictable actions of others cause frequent ups and downs in how people rate themselves.

2. Self-evaluations, rather than being flexible, become fixed, something especially undesirable when the evaluations are negative. It is my experience that children (and adults) who are good actors maintain negative self-concepts much of the time because their focus is only on their negative traits and behaviors.

3. Most importantly, it is not possible to evaluate so complicated a thing as the total self at any time and with any accuracy. A global self-concept, in my estimation, is pure trouble.

How do you dislike one of your traits without putting yourself down for it? How do you dislike someone's behavior without putting him or her down for it? The answer is to completely give up rating your *self* or others' *selves* as a totality. Not accepting your *self* or putting your *self* down and rejecting your humanness is not rational!

Why is it irrational? People are complex, not simple; not just one thing, but many things. We have innumerable characteristics and behaviors, and it doesn't make sense to judge *all* of them by any *one* of them. If we fail at doing something, especially something important, then presto! We become total failures. Our past successes are ignored or forgotten. A child who fails a test or gets a bad grade is magically changed into a total disappointment. I have been told by many students that when they bring home report cards with a bad grade, their parents often fail to notice the good grades, so narrowly are the parents focused.

Does personal worth or one's value as a human being change with performance? Let's explore this hypothetically through a procedure similar to one devised by Knaus (1974). If a student were to get 100% on a test, he or she would get an A for the performance, but what grade would the teacher be able to give him or her for personal worth? Can this be determined? No! On the next test the student gets 75% and a C. Again the teacher cannot rate the student's value. On a third test, the student achieved 35% and received an F. What *now* is the student's value? Could the student be evaluated as a good person because he or she got an A or a bad person because he or she got an F? No! Clearly, the human value of a person is never in question and does not change with performance.

What are the emotional consequences of someone blaming him or herself for being human? Any time the person makes a mistake, does wrong, fails, and so forth, he or she will become angry at him or herself and others. The person may develop feelings of depression, worthlessness, guilt, or anxiety, as well as a strong tendency to self-down and to put others down. And with such emotional difficulties, the ability to solve problems, correct mistakes, and achieve is greatly diminished.

However, you can realistically rate one of your traits or performances. You may want to do this to try to change something you don't like about yourself, or to correct an error, improve a test performance, reduce your weight, decrease your anger, increase your skills, improve your teaching style, and so forth. You can teach children to rate what they do and not themselves, and when they fail or do something bad, you can work at helping them not to make the same mistakes again. It would be wise to remember and teach children not only that humans are not perfect but that we are not totally imperfect either. It would be wise to remember and to teach children that there are no good or bad people, only people who do good and bad things. It would be wise to remember and teach children that there are no better human beings than you or them . . . *anywhere*. We are all equally worthwhile. Our worthwhileness is not measurable and never at stake when we do things. Working toward the goal of accepting yourself and others unconditionally and helping your children to do the same makes tremendous sense, does it not?

These are some things that I have used successfully to assist parents and teachers to help children and adolescents develop self-acceptance. They are adapted from material written by Ellis, Wolfe, and Moseley (1966); Waters (1980); Young (1975); Knaus (1974, 1977); and Hauck (1967, 1977).

1. Model for children that you are working on accepting yourself unconditionally, that you can accept responsibility for creating your own feelings, making mistakes, acting poorly at times without blaming yourself or putting yourself down. Teach children to take responsibility for their feelings and actions and to

avoid blaming themselves or others when things go wrong. (Waters, 1980, pp. 64–68).

2. Demonstrate how you are trying *not* to equate your performance with your self-worth. Think out loud such ideas as, "I did a bad job but it doesn't make me all bad." The idea is to remind yourself and to teach children that you and they are too complicated to be rated by one thing. Help them to understand by indicating that you wouldn't sell your house just because the roof leaked or trash your car if it had a flat tire, so why do it to oneself? In addition, don't tell your children they are good or bad when they have done something good or bad. Telling this to children tends to support the idea that performance equals self-worth (Young, 1975, pp. 7–9); (Waters, 1980, pp. 7–9)

3. To help a child or students understand they are never all good or bad, have them construct a "Me" circle or list (Knaus, 1974). This should contain at least four things about themselves they consider good qualities, and an equal number of "bad" qualities. Traits such as friendly or kind, feelings such as anger, behaviors such as "have failed tests" or "gotten an A," and likes/dislikes can be included. In my experience, children and adolescents find it easy to indicate their negative qualities, but have great trouble citing their positive traits. They will need your help with this. (This will also remind you of their positive qualities if you have forgotten them.) Have them write these with qualifying words such as "sometimes" or "often," especially those involving negative feelings and behaviors, to remind them (and yourself) that they don't have negative feelings or behavior all the time.

When the "Me" circle or list is complete, have them look at all of it and ask "Are you just one thing?" Have them pick a bad item and ask "Does that make you all bad? Why not?" Remind them, if necessary, of the rest of their qualities that still exist when they do something bad. Ask them, "Can you ever be all bad?" and have them answer. When this activity is done in the classroom, have children volunteer rather than to choose them to respond. You will probably find that after a while most of them will be clamoring to respond. Their "Me" circle or list is to be kept by them and looked at frequently, especially when they get in trouble. Looking at it will help to keep their perspective of themselves more realistic and keep them from denigrating themselves (Knaus, 1974, pp. 28–31).

4. Work at accepting others, your children, your spouse, or even your parents or in-laws (who, beliefs to the contrary, are not totally imperfect either). Instead of judging, blaming and putting them down for their behavior, work at changing your thinking about them. Remember, they too are complex human beings and do good things as well as bad ones. You don't have to like them, just accept them in order to keep your dealings with them calmer, and possibly to help them change their attitudes and behaviors. Encourage your children to accept others as just humans, especially when they have to endure annoying adults and peers (Ellis et al., 1966, pp. 78–79).

5. Help children not to be so concerned about making mistakes. Encourage them to speak up in class even when they are unsure of their answers, assert themselves with their peers, try new things. The idea is to help them discover that they will not curl up and die if they make a mistake, are laughed at, or fail. Learning and growing up is enhanced by risk taking and making mistakes.

6. Show children that you are aware of and accepting of your positive traits and the good things you do. Verbalize aloud nice things about your performances and do things to give yourself pleasure. Pay attention to the children's positive behaviors and respond to them with as much interest and emotion as you might to their negative behaviors. This will help them be more accepting of their positive qualities (Waters, 1980, pp. 65–66).

7. When you discipline, focus your disciplining on children's specific undesirable behaviors and help them to change these behaviors without blaming them for them, or creating guilt and shame because of them. Statements like "Why can't you do anything right without being told," or "You will drive me crazy if you keep that up," puts children down as well as make them responsible for *your* feelings. These communications are like throwing out the baby because of the dirty bath water (Hauck, 1977, pp. 415–418).

8. Following are some rational poems that I have composed to remind children to think differently about themselves. Teaching children or adolescents to understand and remember these poems will help to encourage self-acceptance when they have problems.

> When I make a goof or fail at school,
> I'm just being human, not bad or a fool!
>
> There are no bad or good kids around,
> Only kids who do good and bad things are found.
> So it makes no sense to rate them or you,
> Try to accept your mistakes and theirs too.
>
> Even when I goof up or get very mad,
> I know the real me is never all bad!
>
> No matter where I look or who I see,
> I'll never find anyone better than me!
>
> No matter where I look or who I see,
> I'll always remember it's great to be me!

Dealing with Performance Anxiety

Worrying or feeling anxious is a very common problem for children, despite what many parents and teachers may believe. We used to think of childhood and adolescence as a pretty carefree time, as "the best time," but we know from many sources that often young people feel highly anxious about problems of living in general and of achieving in particular. Many children I have seen, even very young ones, describe themselves as chronic worriers, who feel nervous about everything, especially things like going to school, taking tests, or speaking up in class. Others who don't perform well and who verbalize an angry "I don't care," frequently respond this way in an attempt to cover very strong feelings of concern.

Parents and teachers might believe that it is a good thing to feel anxious about taking a test or doing a good job, and to some extent this is true. There is research that indicates that some highly anxious people are able to use anxiety to help motivate them during test taking and to help them concentrate! But many other studies indicate the contrary: that academic failure is as much as four times greater in highly anxious persons as compared with low anxious persons. A high level of anxiety generally disrupts and disorganizes performance. It interferes with a person's ability to think clearly, express what he or she knows, and do his or her best (Oliver, 1975).

Performance anxiety is experienced as stage fright, freezing up, falling apart, blocking or forgetting what has been studied, and failure to read instructions carefully or to understand them even when they are carefully read. Older and younger children have told me that often they worry about how they are going to do while studying or while taking a test, and this interferes with their concentration. They say things to themselves, mostly negative things, like expressions of inadequacy ("I can't do this"), fears of failure ("Oh God, what if I fail?"), lack of self-acceptance ("I'm so stupid"), and self-blame ("I should've studied—I deserve to fail"). They also compare themselves with others ("He's almost done—why am I so slow?").

It is not the test or activity itself that causes performance anxiety; rather, it is the fear of some consequence of the performance and the fear of being helpless in the face of the consequence that does it. Some children believe something horrible or disastrous will happen if they have to do something they don't like or if they don't perform well. They think "I'll just die if I fail," "Everybody will laugh at me and I couldn't take it," "I can't stand being bored," and turn an annoying event into a life or death situation. It's like they take 1 + 1 and get 2,000, according to Young (1975). This catastrophic thinking creates so much anxiety in them that children and adolescents may not even do things they'd like to do (e.g., trying out for a team or a part in a play), as well as things they have to do (e.g., attending school).

Oliver (1975) identified four main components of performance anxiety. The first one that children and adolescents catastrophize about when taking a test or doing something risky is *failing*. Many believe they must succeed at whatever they do, and judge their value as a person by whether they pass or fail. It is like they put their entire being or complete reputation on the line every time they take a test or use a skill.

Making mistakes is a second component. Many students believe they must never make mistakes or must always be the best. Anything less than perfection is considered failure. They tend to catastrophize about making mistakes in their daily performances as well as on tests, and often focus on what they couldn't do or on the mistakes they have made. They ignore or disdain their successes (e.g., "It was too easy"). Perfection-seeking often accounts for low motivation and dropping out of school; the safety of not trying is preferred to the risk of making errors.

Fear of disapproval and criticism is a third concern. Many children worry extensively about what their parents, friends, and teachers will think of them if they fail, whether they will continue to be acceptable. They catastrophize about criticism and disapproval and accept it as proof of their worthlessness. Even when some children and adolescents have stopped demanding they be successful or perfect, they continue to maintain and defend their disastrous thinking about disapproval and criticism. The irrational belief that one must have acceptance and approval from important persons for everything one does, may be especially hard to shake in children and adolescents, perhaps because of their realistically dependent status.

Worrying about getting nervous is a fourth component of performance anxiety. Some children and adolescents believe they should not get nervous and worry about getting nervous as much as they do about doing well. The student thinks something like, "I know I'll be very nervous; I always get nervous. I can't help it," and feels helpless, unable to do anything about his or her emotions, much less about passing the test. This may result in self-criticism, feelings of guilt and depression, and a pattern of avoidance. That is, because of concerns about being discomforted by anxiety, they may avoid situations they think would produce anxiety, like attending a difficult class or pursuing a goal that involves some risk of criticism or failure. The avoidance or passivity gives them temporary relief from their discomfort anxiety (Ellis, 1979, 1980).

Helping children and adolescents reduce their performance anxiety begins with helping them talk about their anxiety, or at least to acknowledge it. Many students are not used to verbalizing their feelings with adults, even their parents, and many who do often minimize their anxious feelings, especially older children and adolescents. Prompting or guessing with them about how you think they might have felt often helps them to talk about/acknowledge anxiety. I have found it helpful, especially with a taciturn child, to talk about my own anxious feelings in a similar situation. The idea is to demonstrate by this that you understand and are willing to listen to their concerns, to accept them and their feelings, and to convey that they can trust you not to criticize or blame them for their poor performance or their feelings of anxiety. Talking about one's own feelings and behaviors also seems to help children identify their feelings, understand that it isn't terrible to feel the way they do, and learn they can do something to reduce anxiety and improve their performance next time.

If an adult finds he or she is unable to accept the child or adolescent's anxiety, or has negative feelings, or is overreacting to the child's poor performance, it would likely be because of personal problems about achievement. The adult may hold demanding or catastrophic beliefs about the child or his or her own failures. It would be wise, before talking with the child, for the adult to challenge this thinking and to reduce the strength of feelings, or at least to suppress overreactions. Otherwise the adult's emotional difficulties could reinforce the child's own fears and anxieties (Bernard & Joyce, 1984).

I often urge adults who are perfectionistic because of their anxiety about making mistakes, to start working on this problem openly. If necessary, they are even asked to make mistakes on purpose so they can verbalize rational statements about them in earshot of their children or students. "Oops! I goofed! It's okay— I'm human. I don't have to get bent out of shape over it. Now let me see how I can fix it." This is the sort of statement several teachers used in front of their classes with good effect. They reported that it helped the students view the teacher more realistically, relaxed some students, and helped several timid ones increase their risk-taking behaviors in class. Parent feedback has also been positive.

After identifying that performance anxiety is present about taking a test, for example, the parent or teacher would want to help children and adolescents to understand that it is how they think about the test, and not the test itself, that is causing their anxiety. Explain that if they think something terrible will happen if they fail or make mistakes, then they will worry a lot or get so nervous during a test that they will not be able to pay attention to what they are doing. But if they think failing or making mistakes is unpleasant but not disastrous, they won't feel so bad. Indicate to them that it is important to believe this because it means they can calm themselves down by rethinking even during a test. Methods of demonstrating this for children and for proving this basic concept about feelings have been previously discussed.

When discussing fears or anxieties with children or adolescents, parents and teachers may want to use a strategy I have used with children and adolescents, individually or in groups. A child or a group is asked to compare and rank experiences that are commonly thought to be unpleasant, like taking tests or going to the dentist, with things thought to be more devastating, like serious illness, tornadoes, hurricanes, nuclear disasters, and so on. It has quickly helped those involved to understand what is meant by catastrophic thinking, and to develop more realistic perspectives on their concerns.

I have found that children and adolescents, particularly the latter, often spend much more time worrying about failing than they do studying. Although it clearly would be better if they suffered studying instead of suffering worrying, this may be difficult to accomplish. The next best thing is to try and help them control their worrying.

There are two strategies I have found useful in reducing worrying and worrying about worrying. The first is a thought-stopping strategy. It consists of having the worrying child say the word "stop" forcefully to him or herself, or to picture a very large stop sign or red stop light, whenever worrying begins. These have worked particularly well when paired with thoughts like, "Worrying is a bad habit. It does nothing but waste my time."

The second strategy, one for the older child or adolescent who insists on worrying, is to urge him or her to restrict worrying to short periods, like 10 or 15 minutes per day, using a timer or alarm clock. This gives oneself permission to worry, but only in a controlled and limited way.

To help children and adolescents think more rationally about the possibilities of failure, mistake making, disapproval, and nervousness about being nervous, and to prevent or reduce performance anxiety, I help them construct and reinforce rational self-statements appropriate to their anxiety area to remember and repeat to themselves. Some of these self-statements and poems that I have used over time are presented here under the four components of performance anxiety discussed earlier. Clearly, the rational ideas in each overlap each other and other emotional areas. Both the sentences and poems were structured to be catchy, sloganlike, corny, and humorous when possible. I know from the students' responses that I succeeded most of the time in being corny.

Failure

Relax, calm down, just do your best,
Remember, it's not the end of the world,
It's just a test.

Failing this test won't make you a total failure. Nothing can do that.

Doing my best is like eating roast beef (or cake, cookies, etc., whatever is favored),
Getting a good grade is like the gravy (or frosting, nuts, etc.),
I can enjoy roast beef without gravy (or frosting, etc.).

If I don't pass this time, I can try again.

I don't know if I will pass, but I can sure try!

Making Mistakes

Everybody makes mistakes, but nobody, not even me, is totally imperfect.

Mistakes help me learn.

Goofing up is not dumb—it's human!

Doing a dumb thing doesn't make me a total dummy.

If I make a mistake, I'm just mistaken—not stupid.

Better to try and risk a mistake,
Than not to try, 'cause *that's* a mistake.

When you goof up at what you try,
Or make mistakes at home or school,
You need not get mad at anyone or cry,
You're just being human—not bad or a fool.

Disapproval

I won't curl up and die if my friends tease me about failing. After all, I know I can stand teasing, since I have already.

I won't like it if my parents are disappointed with me for failing. It won't be easy, but I can stand it!

I'd like to be liked by everyone in the class, but I don't need to to be okay.

I don't like being criticized or corrected, but I can take it. Maybe if I don't get myself too mad about it, I can learn something from it.

I made a mistake which is my problem. Now the others are making a mistake by teasing me, and that is their problem.

Getting Nervous About Getting Nervous

I don't have to worry about getting nervous because I'm in charge of my feelings and can change them by thinking differently.

If I get nervous, I can tell myself that nothing super bad will happen if I fail, and that will help me calm down.

So what if I get nervous. I can still do it.

How come I'm letting the butterflies in my stomach tell me what to do when my mind is the boss? I can change that.

Overcoming School Phobia

Some children and adolescents suffer specific fears or phobias. One, related to attending/remaining in school, is known as *school phobia* (Ellis et al., 1966). The student may show fearfulness or resistance to attending classes or attending school at all, and may develop physical symptoms like stomachaches or headaches. Some younger children may cry, throw temper tantrums, insist on leaving, or run home after arriving at school. One second-grade girl would come to school but then spend much of her time in the nurse's office. A high school student would only walk in the halls when few students were present, and she would hug the walls even then.

Several types of specific fears underlie school phobia. One involves anxiety about separating from the parent(s) rather than a fear of school itself. The parent is perceived as undependable by the child and is not trusted to be at home after school. This perception may be due to things like parental illness, separation or divorce, frequent moving, a new sibling, or parent's occasional threats to leave the child. These problems may be real or fantasized, but these children believe something catastrophic will happen to their parents or to themselves if they are not at home to care for their parents or to control the situation. Their fearfulness may be reinforced by well-meaning but overprotective parents who keep the students home when they have minor aches and pains or when they show resistance to going to school.

Concerns related to school and schoolwork also underlie school phobia. The school environment is perceived as unsafe, or peers and teachers as threatening, and the child or adolescent believes harm would befall him or her if he or she attended. These fears also could be based on real problems or on exaggerated or fantasized difficulties. One fourth-grade boy refused to come to school because the previous year he had had a teacher who criticized and physically abused him. The child firmly believed all teachers would be as bad. In addition, he believed he would be powerless to do anything about it. He continually fantasized that he would be dragged to school by a monster who wanted him hurt, and he would hide in various places in the mornings. Another 14-year-old, a student with a learning disability, missed more than two thirds of a school year because he believed he could not cope with the frustrations of schoolwork.

In these instances, and others in which the school situation is viewed as unsafe, the essential element is that the student engages in catastrophic thinking about school. As a result, the student believes unrealistically that he or she is helpless or inadequate to cope with school, and there is no one to help him or her cope.

Many students I have seen with specific fear syndromes like school phobia turn out to be children who are anxious about many things. They view the world as a threatening place, have a hard time developing trust in persons other than family, generalize negative experiences to similar situations and predict insurmountable difficulty, tend to be vulnerable to the opinions and fears of others, and think of themselves as helpless in the face of these fears. Recently, I was consulted by a teacher about a 6-year-old child who had developed what seemed to be a phobia about the wind. He had refused to go out at recess because he was afraid he would be blown away, and began to cry when he saw the trees blowing. He began to refuse to do schoolwork, which previously he had liked, because he was afraid to make errors; and he began to express negative feelings about peers, school, and teachers, although he had liked all of these before. His parents also reported that he had become "nervous" at home and was expressing reluctance to do his chores and to attend school.

Helping a child who is phobic requires that the helper, parent or teacher, not overreact, become overwhelmed, or be angered by the child's fearfulness and resistive behaviors. This can happen easily because the child's fear seems unreasonable, and his or her stubborn refusal to believe reassurances is often very frustrating. The first step in helping the phobic child is, of course, for the parents and teachers to deal with their own emotional reactions, and to challenge any irrational beliefs that are behind their emotionality. Examples of such beliefs are that the child should not have such fears, that the child is bad or inadequate because of them, that the parent/teacher is bad or inadequate because he or she is not able to help the child, and that the helper cannot stand the annoyance or inconvenience of the problem. Dealing with one's own disturbance will help the parents or teacher accept the child's fears, calm down, and facilitate problem solving.

Strategies to help students with phobias vary depending on whether the student wants to solve his or her problem and will discuss his or her fears. Some students, especially younger ones (but older ones as well), are so overwhelmed by their fears that they can do little more than repeat their fears over and over, and remain overwhelmed by their emotions. Others, such as the fourth-grade boy who would not come to school because he feared teacher intimidation/abuse, were able to engage in fairly calm discussions and could think sensibly. With most students I have counseled, however, behavioral management strategies expedited the solutions.

A gradual return program was instituted to desensitize the fourth-grade student. It began by his attending weekly counseling sessions only at school, followed by attendance at his class's halloween party, then half days in class, then finally full days for longer periods of time. The teacher and parent both participated in the process and helped by reinforcing the child's appropriate behaviors. No pressure was used to bring him to counseling or to school, as is sometimes used with younger children. Instead, he was urged to force himself back to school, because he knew that, although returning would be difficult, it would be in his best interests to do so. He practiced rational self-statements to help his resolve, such as "Last year's teacher was a pill, but how do I know this new one is?". This challenged his belief that all teachers were out to abuse him. "If the teacher yells at me for being away from school so long, it would be unpleasant, not terrible, and I can take it," challenged his belief about his helplessness in the face of difficulty. Reinforcers, supplied by the parent and a social worker, were chosen from a menu devised with the child. These included one special reinforcement, tickets to a football game, which he earned after attending school full time for a month. There were no further difficulties during the school year. When the student transferred, his mother expressed confidence that she could help him if the symptoms recurred.

Facing his fears and behavioral management were the techniques used by the teacher and parents to help the 6-year-old child with the wind phobia. Any discussion about his fears produced prolonged bouts of crying and anger. The teacher began helping him deal with fears directly by accompanying him to the playground, holding his hand and talking calmly and pleasantly with the child, assuring his safety. The teacher's goal was to help the student understand what the wind was and to "make friends" with it. She used a windmill to help with this. She also empowered him to cope with changes in wind velocity and direction by problem solving what he could do if the wind bothered him. Options discussed were that he could turn around, grab onto something, ignore it, call another person, and so on. After a while she brought him to his friends on the playground, watched as he played, and finally left him with them. He accepted this easily and happily. His parents were encouraged to remain calm in the face of his fears, and also to help him face them. They began taking him for walks when it was windy and to bring him to school every day. His complaining and crying were ignored, but he was immediately reinforced for his coping efforts with stickers, praise, and recognition. These efforts were quite successful, and by the end of the year he was also more comfortable when in class.

However, it has been my experience that those students who have learned to reduce their fearfulness by changing their thinking, have sustained their gains and had fewer recurrences of their problems than those helped only through behavioral management techniques.

Work Avoidance and Procrastination

Many children and adolescents tend to be pleasure seeking and work avoidant. They put off tasks that they define as unpleasant, boring, difficult, or anxiety-provoking. Procrastination allows them temporary relief of their displeasure and stress reactions (Ellis & Knaus, 1977, p. 7–8).

Older children and adolescents demonstrate two patterns of procrastination. The first is related to getting started, and the second to getting finished. Both derive from their propensity to exaggerate the awfulness of things they don't like to do (like cleaning their room or doing homework), and their helplessness in the face of temptation (like partying). They tend to believe they can't stand doing the work or not partying with friends. Some intelligent, highly competent high school students procrastinate because they find it difficult to start or complete work that they tell themselves they have to do exceedingly well. Otherwise, they believe, all sorts of catastrophes would befall them that they could not handle. Feelings of guilt, shame, and anxiety often accompany avoidance or procrastination.

One senior high school student believed he should work during all of his spare time. He would alternate between periods of furious work and little or no work, both of which distressed him. He constantly denigrated himself for not having any fun and for not doing enough work. He worried a great deal about his procrastination as well.

With counseling he accepted himself as worthwhile even if he didn't work constantly, and he became less depressed and stressed, but he continued to procrastinate and to worry about procrastinating. Although he knew he felt great satisfaction when he worked (as well as less guilt and anxiety), the feeling was not strong enough to motivate him to work on a regular basis.

Parental encouragement and reinforcement, and support from teachers, did not work either. As is often the case with older children and adolescents, such efforts on the part of adults are viewed as pressure, and thus are resisted. What did help in this case and many others was to leave the forcing and reinforcing to the students themselves.

I have found that assisting students to develop a flexible, written daily schedule for themselves, one that included time for leisure activities as well as short periods of working, has been helpful. It is important that serious planning for leisure time be involved, because otherwise the procrastinating student will surely steal it. Most older students and adolescents I have seen with this problem have given themselves, and me, any number of wonderful reasons for why they did not or could not study or do their chores at home.

Once a schedule is completed, students are urged not to permit themselves to do the leisure activities until they complete the amount of work planned (an amount deemed reasonable by themselves). They are to say to themselves something like, "Just do an hour's work, then leave") to initiate or continue work. They are also instructed to remind themselves they could fix up their work later if necessary. After working the allotted time, they are then instructed to reinforce themselves with a pleasant activity not marred by worry or guilt. Almost all students had indicated that they were rarely free of concern or guilt when they did little or no work.

The parent or teacher might offer to withhold access to the leisure activity until the student shows proof that he or she has earned it, or to provide additional reinforcement, but this should be purely voluntary.

Ellis, the developer of RET and author of several creative self-enforcement strategies, suggests that to help people get themselves to do something that is difficult or disliked, they might put money on the line. That is, he or she is to take a meaningful amount of money and put it in an envelope, stamped and addressed to a detested group or person. Then he or she is to give it to a reliable person with instructions to mail it or burn it the first time he or she does not do the promised work. (Ellis & Harper, 1975; Ellis & Knaus, 1977). Or a procrastinator wanting help might give a promissory note to a parent or teacher to do extra work after school, to baby-sit, to wash dishes, or to perform some other voluntary service that is disliked intensely, for the next time he or she procrastinates.

I have had no takers from students on these tactics, but I have found that a system of self-imposed rewards and punishments in a milder form has been quite successful.

Although developing a schedule helped the previously mentioned high school student to procrastinate less, it did not help him to reduce his worry or guilt when he did procrastinate, or to reduce his worrying about possibly procrastinating in the future. A rationally oriented worry stopper was devised for him that went, "Stop worrying about procrastination; procrastinate about worrying instead." He said it made him laugh as well as reminded him that he was in charge of his emotions and behaviors and not helpless in the face of them. He kicked the worry habit considerably, continued to work fairly well through the school year, and graduated on time.

The following rational poems were written to help students procrastinate less. Parents and teachers might want to use them and the system of self-enforcement and reinforcements to help themselves or their children or students who are work-avoidant.

If you put off doing stuff that's hard or a bore,
Then tomorrow it'll still be there and probably more.
Then it'll be two days work, guilt, and a poor grade,
And angry parents, teachers, maybe yourself I'm afraid.
So THINK—while doing the work today might be rough,
Tomorrow it will be at least twice as tough!

Do!—
Don't stew!

Just an hour each day will keep the schoolwork at bay!

If I don't do exceptionally well,
Will I really die and go to—?
NO, it'll just be a pain in the—
Not being at the head of the class.
So I'll keep trying just to do my best,
And won't worry 'bout beating the rest.
I'll work some each day getting the work done
Then it'll be time to go for the fun.

Oh I wish I were perfect,
Never did the wrong thing,
Never had any defect,
Never just took a fling,
Never made any goof,
Never failed any test,
Then I'd have proof,
That I am the best.
The only problem I fear,
With this entire plan,
Is that I wouldn't be here,
But in Never-Never-Land.

Other self-statements and poems dealing with perfection, mistake making, and self-acceptance presented elsewhere, are suggested for use when children and adolescents procrastinate because of perfectionistic inclinations.

Frustration and Anger

Many people believe that anger is a natural reaction to frustration and poor treatment, and that the expression of anger is important for good mental health. Many parents I have encountered encouraged their children to express anger with phrases like, "Don't take anything from anybody," "Always defend yourself," "You have to get even," or "Show 'em who's boss." Many advocate physical fighting and are upset when their children don't fight back. Children often take this parental encouragement to mean they should act aggressively whenever they have a disagreement.

Although there might be something positive said for fighting to defend oneself or as an expression of overwhelming anger, most of the time getting angry causes children (and adults) trouble, more trouble than they had in the first place (i.e., referral, detention, grounding, pain, etc.). Fighting rarely helps them get what they want or get others to like them. Anger, especially big anger (rage), like other strong emotions, interferes with sensible thinking and problem solving. To paraphrase one psychologist, intelligent behavior is reduced as a function of the intensity of emotions (Rothschild, personal communication, 1985). If you doubt this, watch two very angry people trying to settle a disagreement.

What or who causes anger? As with other overpowering emotions, it is not another person or event, but one's belief or attitude about the person or event. If, for example, a child or adolescent *demands* to have what he or she wants, and doesn't get it; or that others act a certain way, and they don't; or that the world be a certain way, and it isn't; then that person will become frustrated and enraged, blaming and punishing toward others. If the child insists he or she must never make mistakes, and he or she goofs up, the child will likely grow angry at him or herself. If the child frequently exhibits frustration and anger, one can assume that demanding beliefs are present. Helping the child to reduce anger and blaming really means helping him or her change his or her demanding beliefs to more realistic ones (Knaus, 1974).

Demanding attitudes are reflected in the words we use in thought or speech, such as "should" or "must," "need" or "gotta have," "can't stand it when." I often refer to these as the real profanity in our language, because when we are serious about them, more often than not they get us in trouble. They are demand or blame words that contain ideas that function like unbreakable laws in our thinking. They tell us that things or people shouldn't be the way they are but the way we want them to be. According to Young (1975), it is something like insisting red should be blue. He also indicated that when the word "need" is used by some adolescents, the intent is so strong that the implication is that they will "curl up and die" if they don't get or achieve what they want. A need is really something one can't survive without, like food or water. So it is no surprise that when wants are elevated to the level of needs by one's thinking and are left unfulfilled, intense frustration and anger result (Ellis, 1962, p. 21).

In helping children learn to reduce anger and frustration, it will first be necessary for parents and teachers to reduce their own emotions over the child's behavior. Acting out of anger and low frustration tolerance are among the most common and difficult problems that young people have, and often these are met with anger and frustration on the part of the adults dealing with them.

Reducing one's own anger is an important prerequisite for helping children cope with their anger. It is very easy for adults to blame a child or adolescent for acting like a child, and to put the child down for annoying childish behavior (Ellis et al., 1966). It is also easy to think of an angry child, who frequently gets into trouble, as a bad child, forgetting that he or she also has good behaviors. In my experience, if an adult can develop a more realistic perspective about the child or adolescent and evaluate only the child's behavior rather than the whole child, the adult quickly becomes able to reduce his or her anger.

Parents and teachers will want to reduce their anger when dealing with children or adolescents for other important reasons. First, it will help them not to be too punitive when they discipline, which could otherwise be destructive to them and their relationship with the child (and particularly with an adolescent). The goal of good discipline, at home and school, is to be calm and kind, but firm and consistent (Hauck, 1977), so the child learns the adults mean what they say but don't hate him or her for goofing up. Second, parents and teachers won't provide a model that shows it is okay for adults to get very angry when something bugs them. Rather, the adults would model appropriate feelings when they are frustrated. Third, the adults will be able to think clearly so they can help a child accept the responsibility for and the consequences of his or her behavior without putting him or herself down. And finally, not getting angry will support parent and teacher efforts to help the children learn to reduce their anger and prevent a recurrence of the problem or problems.

I have taught many children and adolescents, both individually and in groups, to understand what causes anger and how to reduce it. Most can already identify angry feelings, and given half a chance (plus a sympathetic ear that won't criticize or castigate) will talk easily about how much trouble they get into because of their tempers. By and large that is as far as they can go. However, when they are given suggestions about what they might be thinking, they agree that they are thinking demanding and blaming thoughts. (They usually reject those suggestions that are not what they believe.) "He shouldn't have called my mother a name," "I can't stand it when he looks at me that way," "He shouldn't get away with that stuff," "I'll show him," "I can't stand my teacher," are the demanding and blaming beliefs most commonly expressed.

To help children differentiate between demand and nondemand words (which are realistic and which aren't), parents and teachers might use a strategy suggested by Knaus (1974). It involves mixing up sentences, some with demand words and some with nondemand words, and asking children to tell which is which. I have also found it useful to ask the children how they think the people who used each kind of sentence would feel if they didn't get what they wanted.

Another of Knaus' methods of teaching kids the difference between *need* and *want* consists of presenting the following problem to them:

Supposing you and some others were going to a desert island. What would you need to bring along to survive a long time? The child or group is asked to name things, and all responses are listed. Then the children discuss the list and cross off all but the essentials (food, water, etc.).

The discussion is often lively, for some children insist they can't live without friends, hair dryers, stereos, and television sets. The presenter then stresses (a) that we do not need as many things as we think we do to survive; (b) that we want things because they're nice to have, not because they're necessary; (c) that not having things we want is annoying, frustrating, or saddening, which are realistic feelings; (d) that believing we *must* have what we want to survive and be happy causes much more anger than believing it would be *nice* to have things.

A good tactic that has helped children and adolescents reduce anger and develop a more appropriate perspective on people who they blame, hate, or can't stand, is to have them conduct an experiment to try to identify at least five things about the undesirable person that are not so bad or are even likable. Have them list these traits alongside five of the person's perceived bad traits. Then, before they express their litany of complaints about the person, have them state the not-so-bad traits. This will temper their condemnation of the person and help them view him or her as human with good and bad traits. The effect of this on children and adolescents has been not only to improve their relationships with the people they investigated but also to improve their concentration in class and to do more of their work. I have used it similarly with students who have generally negative attitudes about school.

I have found that children and adolescents whose thinking skills are not well developed can respond to and use prepared rational statements that counter their irrational thinking. For example: a 13-year-old student who was short for his age responded to teasing by becoming enraged and fighting, no matter what the size of the teaser. As a result, he was often hurt and/or suspended for fighting. He was first helped to understand that he was overreacting, not because of the teasing, but because of his irrational beliefs about the teasing. One of the ideas suggested to him was that he believed he should not be teased, that peers had no right to tease him. He agreed (but expressed it in much stronger language). He was also helped to understand that his anger was just what the teasers wanted, so he was encouraging them rather than intimidating them with his anger. He thought this might be true, because when he teased others, he wanted them to get mad and to feel put down. He decided he would participate in an experiment to see if he could change his feelings. He was to say, "Sticks and stone may break my bones but names can never hurt me—unless I let them" to himself, inside his head, when teased, and report back. When he returned the following week he indicated that not only did he feel calmer when teased, he didn't even get angry.

"It made me laugh a lot." There were no fights or suspensions that week, the first time since starting school. He also said, "You know, I felt in charge of myself." He laughed. "And like 10 feet tall—no, about 6 feet." A follow-up study showed there were few fighting problems during the rest of his stay at the school.

Other rational self-statements or poems that I have encouraged children and adolescents to think about and to remember, are to follow. Corny as they are, they are all thoughts that when used, have helped children avoid overreacting with anger when something annoying or frustrating happens at home or in school.

> Stop! Don't get yourself mad,
> Re-think and get yourself glad.
> (Or at least less mad.)

> "It's awful!" "I can't stand it!" "I gotta have my way."
> Are my flipped-out thoughts that make my mad come and stay!
> "It's a pain, but I can stand it." "I wish I could have my way."
> Are my cooler thoughts that chase most of my mad away.

> I don't like it but I CAN stand not having my way.

> I don't like not having it but I can live without it.

> Is he (she) really all bad? No! Nobody's all bad, not even my teacher
> (parent, sister, brother, classmate, teaser).

> When trouble comes don't act the fool,
> Think sensibly and you'll keep cool.

> I am powerful because I can control my temper!

> Who's the boss of my temper—I am!

> When things are not comfortable or fine,
> And people act badly, with no gratitude,
> It's best not to get yourself mad or whine,
> But to try to change things or your attitude.

About Teasing

A common and often difficult problem that many children regularly have in school is coping with teasing and name calling. It seems to be a favorite sport of siblings and school children and one that has been around as long as children have. In my experience and the experience of teachers and parents, there seems to be no age level or grade at which it does not occur, but its frequency and intensity seems to increase in the upper elementary and middle-school years (fifth through eighth grade) and decrease thereafter. Bernard (1989) working in Australia also found this sort of pattern. However, recently I have counseled a 17-year-old high school senior who reported that he was experiencing name calling and was seeing it a lot among his peers.

It also seems there are no specific characteristics that are focused on by teasers, although students with academic problems and those who are overweight seem to be the targets of teasers somewhat more often than others. In the past several years I have counseled students who were teased for being short and tall, obese and thin, poor achievers and very good achievers, unattractive and attractive, and ethnically different and not ethnically different. The teasing, often on a daily basis, was highly stressful for them and they exhibited a variety of symptoms including poor achievement, anxiety, physical symptoms (stomachache, headaches), aggressive behaviors, school phobia, and, in several cases, depression and suicidal feelings. One student who exhibited these latter symptoms believed that not only would the teasing never cease but that he would never be able to cope with it.

Parents and teachers have had some success helping children who have difficulty coping with teasing by doing any or all of several things. They have advised the child or student to ignore the teasing, to stand up to it (even physically if necessary), and to stay away from the teaser. Teachers or counselors have met with a teaser in an attempt to discourage further teasing and encourage or reinforce more friendly behaviors toward a victim, or brought the teaser and victim together to talk and problem solve. When the teasing of a child is widespread in the class or in the school, teachers and parents have been able to arrange to change the victims or the teasers' classes, or, as has happened in several instances, to change their schools.

But there are problems with these strategies. For one thing they are often short-term solutions, even when classes or schools are changed. The problems of both the victim and the teaser are internal, that is, based on beliefs they have about themselves and others and the whole nature of teasing. For another, as for example in physically standing up to the teaser, the solution (e.g., fighting) often causes worse problems, not the least of which is that someone may get hurt. For a third, although ignoring is a good strategy, it is often extremely difficult for many of the victims of teasing. They get themselves very upset and angry when teased, and manifest it in their facial and bodily expressions even if they don't respond overtly. They fool neither themselves nor the teaser. However, I and others (Bernard, 1989; Ellis et al., 1966) have found that helping a child to truly ignore teasing by not taking it seriously and increasing "tease tolerance" (Bernard, 1989) or "emotional toughness" is the most successful strategy on a long-term basis.

How do you help children to not take teasing so seriously, to build internal toughness?

To begin, an adult needs to understand a child's point of view about teasing. Many teachers and parents view the problem of teasing as relatively inconsequential compared to other problems, but from a child's perspective it is a major difficulty. To get in touch with how it feels, you might want to remember your own painful experiences with being teased and particularly how you coped with teasing. If you were among the fortunate who did not experience much teasing, then try to imagine how it would feel if, every day when you go to work, you expect to face criticism and derision from your boss or colleagues. This is how a bright, obese 14-year-old girl described her school situation. But don't go overboard in your sympathy for the victims! The idea is to help toughen them, not to encourage them to feel sorry for themselves, and to convey that they are not helpless in the face of teasing.

As in dealing with other problems, strengthening a student so he or she can cope with teasing begins with developing their understanding that much of their disturbance comes not from the teasing itself but from their point of view about it. Once they accept that they create their own emotional disturbance, they also can begin to understand that they can alleviate their distress about teasing and not take it so seriously, even if it continues.

It would also be wise to help children develop a different perspective about teasing. Parents and teachers can help a child understand that teasing is just words. It is actually air waves, or a lot of "hot air" that really can't hurt them unless the teasee lets it. It is at the most another person's opinion and it is not a fact or the truth. Even if it is a trait they have that they don't like, it doesn't mean the victims are all bad people or unlikable because of it. After all, who is perfect? Certainly not the teaser, who is behaving badly by doing the teasing. Using the "Me" circle to help remind victims that they are complex, more than just one thing, and cannot be rated as a total anything, can aid in this endeavor.

In addition, it would help children to know and accept that just because someone calls them or their relatives bad names, it doesn't make them or the relative into that name. Encourage them to practice saying this to themselves every day.

To offer proof of the concept that is not the teasing but one's point of view about what is said that makes them angry, ask or have them do some research on the following two questions: Does everybody they know get so upset, angry, or depressed when they are teased? Are there any children they know who like to be teased. I remember well getting very angry and frustrated when I was a sixth grader and teased by my brothers for being obese, but not minding it so much when an attractive boy did it. His attention was even enjoyed, negative as it was. Help the children conclude from their research that it is how one thinks about teasing and not the teasing itself that is upsetting them.

Help children and adolescents understand that realistically, teasing at worst is annoying, irritating, frustrating, saddening. It is not:

1. Terrible, awful, horrible
2. Can't standable, curl up and dieable. (Victims can stand it even though they don't like it. After all, they already have stood a great deal of it.)
3. It doesn't have to drive them up a wall
4. It doesn't make they or the teaser horrible, awful, or terrible (blameworthy)

Children and some parents and teachers may not go along at all with Item 4, but it will help all enormously if they can change their perspective on the teaser. Much of the anger generated by those teased comes from blaming or self-righteous indignation about being teased. "He/she *should* not tease me" is something I've heard many times from children who felt like killing, or at least maiming, their tormentors. But children do tease, and the fact that they do engage in this annoying behavior does not warrant their total condemnation. Does it?

Teasers, like their victims, sometimes operate because of problems they have, but a teaser is not a totally bad person. Some of the reasons they tease are that they want to be liked and see teasing as a fun game, they want to appear smarter, they feel inadequate and putting others down makes them feel temporarily better about themselves, they only feel worthwhile if they continually prove they are better than someone else. Many teasers report that they "hate" to be teased; they often get teased and pushed around by older siblings. Many victims report that they like to tease others. Thus, it appears that teasers and teasees often have the same problems; their emotional reactions are like the two sides of a coin and what helps one often helps the other. Constructing a "You" circle with the teaser in mind can help remind the victim and you that the teaser is also a complex human being, cannot be rated only by the teasing, and is not totally imperfect.

Once they have a different perspective about teasing and the teaser, then it would be wise to help victims practice thinking rational self-statements. Instead of thinking irrational things which anger or upset them, like "I can't stand being teased," when the teasing happens, help them to practice thinking things like, "I don't like being teased but I'm tough and I *can* stand it," or "I won't like it but I won't curl up and die if it continues," or "Teasing can't hurt me unless I let it." Help them to learn and understand the concept behind "Sticks and stones will break my bones but names will never hurt me." I usually suggest they add, when repeating this old saying to themselves, ". . . unless I let them." Encourage them to think things about the teaser when teased, such as, "I wonder what _____'s problem is today." "I'm not gonna take _____'s teasing seriously and make it my problem." "He/She wants to put me down to get a charge. I'm not gonna play his/her game and give him what he wants."

"Just because _____ calls me _____ (e.g., dumb), it doesn't make me _____."

"_____ is not in charge of my angry feelings—I am."

There is another important reason to help your child or student reduce his or her emotional reactions to teasing. It is because the victim's emotional reaction reinforces the teaser's behavior. Overt reactions are what teasers want. If the victim stops taking it seriously and does not get upset (cry, get mad, tease back, tell, or fight), and continues to do so even when the teaser keeps trying, the teasing will probably lessen or stop entirely. This is based on the principle of reinforcement.

The exercise that follows, adapted from Hauck (1967, p. 125), will help make the nature of the reinforcement principle clear:

With an individual or in a classroom situation, have the child or children close their eyes and imagine they own a boat and fish for a living, and all are very successful at it. Have them see themselves in their mind's eye, taking their boat out to a certain place, throwing their nets in and catching lots of fish, which they sell and eat at home. Have them imagine that on one day, when they go to this place and throw their nets in, they catch no fish. Decide with them that it's only a bad day and have them see themselves returning to the same spot the next day. Again they catch no fish. Have them envision themselves returning the next day, the day after that, and the next, but catching no fish. Have them open their eyes, and ask them, "What are you finally going to do to catch some fish?" When the child or someone in the class states that they will go to another pond, reinforce this enthusiastically.

Conclude the following:

Teasing is like fishing. Teasers tease to get a response, catch a fish. If you do not take the teasing seriously and really ignore it because you don't mind it so much, it will not satisfy the teasers. They may not believe you for a while, but if you keep up this mental muscle, what will the teaser have to do to get satisfied? Go to another pond, that is, try teasing someone else. It is possible, too, that once the teasing has stopped, the two might become friends and the victim may even want to help the teaser develop mental muscle and stop teasing so he or she can feel better about him or herself.

Following are two poems I wrote about teasing that contain rational messages that, when understood and repeated to themselves, have helped children change their emotional reactions to teasing.

> People tease to get others mad,
> Because inside they may feel bad.
> They want other to feel the same,
> Putting people down seems to be their game.
> Playing their game won't help them or you,
> Not taking their words seriously is the thing to do!

> Were you caught today when teased at school,
> Or did you think sensibly and keep yourself cool?
> Remember teasing is just a lot of words,
> And getting mad at them—that's for the birds!

Other Social and Relationship Problems

In addition to teasing, other social relationship problems such as shyness, response to peer pressure, difficulty with authority, and aggressiveness, comprise what seems to be the most frequently occurring groups of social problems of children and adolescents. For some, they start early, even as early as preschool, and persist through high school, and often throughout life. For others they begin around the fourth or fifth grade, the preteen and early teen years, when there is increased emphasis on establishing and maintaining close friendships among and between boys and girls. Rivalries between children for "best" friends, boy-friends, and girlfriends develop among triads or larger groups of students, rivalries that often stimulate continuing problems. One insidious relationship game I have encountered is a rumoring game, best described as "He/She said that So and So said that _____ said about you that . . . ." The goal of the teller is to cause a rift in the relationship or fighting between the listener and a third person. The listener and the third person usually oblige and the teller stands aside and witnesses the action. Hurt feelings, anxiety, and feelings of loneliness and depression may result from this game. Fortunately this game tends, like teasing, to decrease by about Grade 10.

There seems to be some central irrational beliefs that tend to underlie most of the relationship difficulties children and adolescents have with peers and adults. The first concerns the belief that they must do well and have the love, approval, and acceptance of others to be acceptable and to be worthwhile (Ellis et al., 1966). Self-acceptance is thus made conditional on social acceptance. Slightings, criticism, teasing, rejection, are seen as proof they are unlovable and therefore worthless. To gain approval, some do almost anything they can to please their peers and adults, even things that they know are not in their best interests. They will put up with blatant manipulation and intimidation from "friends" at times to maintain approval and acceptance. To keep in the good graces of one "friend," a fifth grader stole money from home to purchase goodies for this person. She participated in things like witchcraft and sexual activities so that she could appear "cool" and "adult" to an older sister and to others.

Children and adolescents who are shy and sensitive, who acquiesce to peer pressure, and who have problems with dating, operate from this irrational position. Making mistakes, particularly social mistakes, is viewed as catastrophic. Some of their self-statements are as follows:

"I gotta be liked (loved) by others (friends, teachers, parents) in order to be okay (worthwhile)."

"It would be awful if I didn't have friends who cared for me."

"I'm a total nerd because I goofed up."

"If I said the wrong thing they would laugh at me and think I'm dumb. I couldn't stand that.

"Supposing if I tried to date _____ and she didn't want to date me. Oh, God! I couldn't stand to be rejected! It would prove how awful I am."

"Nobody likes me. I'm just no good."

"I'll never have any friends—I might as well be dead."

"It's awful that my teacher (parent) doesn't even like me."

Although lack of self-acceptance and feelings of worthlessness are also involved when children act socially aggressive or have problems dealing with authority figures, aggressive acting out seems to stem largely from a second irrational belief: that peers and adults should act a certain way—their way. When they don't they should be blamed and punished. They demand that others treat them well and that they not be frustrated, be subjected to unfairness, or rejected. They insist on having their way, and when someone thwarts them, authority figure or peer, they engage in resistive or revengeful behavior (Bernard & Joyce, 1984, pp. 150–155). Some of the self-statements expressed by children who act out aggressively are:

"He shouldn't have said that to me. It's not right. I'll show him."

"I can't stand the teacher. She can't make me do that. Nobody can make me do anything I don't want to do."

"He had no right to push me even if it was an accident. He should've been more careful. That'll (hitting) teach him."

"Nobody's allowed to push me around. I'll show him who's boss."

"That teacher picks on me. It isn't fair. She's just no good."

"I don't steal from people—just stores. They'll never miss it. They steal from us with their high prices anyway—so why shouldn't I take what I want."

Involved in most social problems as well is a third irrational notion. Children and adolescents often seem to believe they should not be discomforted, that things should come easily and that life should always be interesting and fun (Bernard & Joyce, 1984, p. 129). The thought of having social discomfort or frustration or difficulty doing tasks produces anxiety, anger, and depression. They believe that any discomfort or annoyance is terrible or awful and they will be unable to tolerate it.

Some children's self-statements expressing this third belief have been:

"It's awful not to have a friend—to be by myself. I just can't stand being alone."

"The teacher is boring. I can't stand being bored—it's worse than anything."

"I couldn't stand it if she turned me down (for a date)."

"I have to get a date for the prom. I couldn't face my friends if I didn't. Me—not having a date. They'd all make fun of me and I couldn't stand that."

The three irrational notions that seem to cause children to have most of their social and relationship problems may be summarized as follows:

1. I must have others' acceptance and approval to be okay.
2. I must get what I want and be treated well by others.
3. I must always be comfortable and have fun.

Teaching children and adolescents methods for disputing these ideas and working or applying them, along with helping them learn appropriate social skills when needed, seems to be the most desirable plan for helping them deal with their social and relationship problems.

Ways for parents and teachers to help children and adolescents learn to challenge their irrational ideas have been discussed elsewhere in this chapter (i.e., sections discussing self-acceptance, anxiety, and anger). However, there is a strategy for identifying and challenging irrational thinking about social and relationship problems that I have found useful for producing positive short-term and sometimes long-term effects. It begins by listening for the use of words that contain gross exaggeration or predictions of the future in their complaints: "Nobody likes me!", "I'll never have friends," "I always fight," "The teacher is awful!". Other words, like profanity, may be substituted to convey the meaning that something or someone is perceived as more than 100% bad or totally negative. These words indicate clearly that their thinking about themselves and others is unrealistic and is incrementing their feelings in the situation.

Challenging such terms (thinking) can be fairly easy. To illustrate is the case of a girl who had recently arrived at high school. She was resisting attending classes because she believed adamantly that nobody liked her. She appeared quite depressed and felt she didn't want to continue attending school. Her records indicated there was a history of social problems.

The student and the school psychologist agreed to focus on her concern that 100% of those in her classes disliked her. She was persuaded to attend two classes at least for several weeks to conduct an experiment. She was to count how many students she thought showed that they actually disliked her, how many she wasn't sure about, and how many she didn't know about. The following week she indicated reluctantly that she had reduced the 100% to about 95%. She agreed to continue the study and to attend some other classes and to include in her report a count of how many student she liked or would like to know better. The third week, smilingly, she brought it down to 50% or less and also acknowledged she had made a friend. The idea involved was to help the student (a) challenge her absurd idea of "nobody" liking her when she hardly knew those in her classes and (b) to focus her on her own feelings about others. The project also empowered her to become active in the face of her concerns.

Another situation concerned an 8-year-old boy who was obese and when teased would become very angry and fight. He was in a special class and had made no friends. He was often depressed and would voice wishes to be dead and suicidal feelings. He was helped through behavioral management to control his fighting somewhat, but he remained angered and depressed because of the teasing. There was little progress in counseling until he expressed his belief that his problems would never cease and that he would never have friends.

This prediction of never-ending teasing and loneliness seemed the key to his depressed feelings. It was challenged. Through discussion he was asked how he could tell about the future, how could he predict that the teasing would never stop and that he would never make a friend. He agreed that he could not predict the future. He was also asked how he knew for sure that if he learned not to take the teasing so seriously and become less worried and angry about it, that the teasing wouldn't lessen or stop. Was it not possible that he could then make friends? He agreed he could not tell about that. He then said, "You mean that if I stopped being mad and fighting today, the teasing could even stop tomorrow." He was told, "It's possible, but it's not likely to happen quite so soon." "Well," he said excitedly, "if I kill myself then I won't be there to see it stop—right?" "Right!" "Well, it would be dumb to kill myself or even think of it any more, right?" "Right!" Challenging his concept of "never" challenged his beliefs about the hopelessness of his problems and his helplessness in the face of them, and he became active in working on problems. It is these irrational beliefs, when maintained, that change unhappiness about a situation into depression for children, and adults as well (Knaus, 1974, p. 81).

Helping children and adolescents to relate better to authority figures, such as teachers, parents, and others with whom they may have to or wish to continue a relationship, is often accomplished by a similar technique. Often students express strong and only negative feelings about a teacher who they feel is "mean," picks on them, hates them, and they "can't stand" being in that class. They may not work, or they may act out, or resist it by not attending or by arriving late. I urge these children and adolescents singly or in groups to check their all-negative perspective by the investigative process described in an earlier section of this chapter. Developing a more human, realistic perspective about the adult in question has helped many students reduce their angry or hurt feelings, to act less aggressively and to behave less resistively with teachers.

This change in the child's behavior may in turn change the adult's view of the child and the way the adult behaves toward him or her. Whether or not such a change is forthcoming, the child is in a better position to problem solve about the situation, make the best of an unchangeable, difficult circumstance, and, in the case of a class, learn in spite of the relationship difficulty.

When helping children and adolescents overcome shyness, inhibited behavior, passivity, and blind acquiescence to peer pressure, parents and teachers should bear in mind that these children often are self-deprecating and highly anxious. Although they may want friends, they are frightened that social contacts may result in rejection. They are concerned about mistakes, particularly social mistakes, and thus are nonassertive in relationships. They also tend to hold negative views of themselves and to blame themselves when things go wrong in relationships. In addition, they often feel negative about others and resist suggestions about how to go about making friends (Ellis et al., 1966; Grieger & Boyd, 1984). Therefore, it will be important to help them understand and learn rational ideas and self-statements they can verbalize to themselves when attempting to overcome their shyness or avoidance of people.

Rational statements that have succeeded in helping children reduce their level of anxiety and have allowed them to take risks have been given elsewhere in this chapter. Other rational self-statements and poems that have been useful in helping children and adolescents deal specifically with social relationship difficulties are presented here.

If _____ doesn't like me, it doesn't mean I'm a nerd.

I don't know why _____ doesn't like me. Maybe it's her problem, not mine.

The dating game is not a self-rating game.

I'd like the teacher to like me, but I can stand it if she doesn't.

I don't like it when people push me around (name call, boss me, etc.), but I don't have to lose my cool over it.

I won't die from boredom, maybe just get a little sick of it.

I'm worthwhile whether I have friends or not.

Be fair and share,
It shows you care. (Courtesy of a third grader.)

I like to be liked,
It makes my day,
But even when I'm not,
I'm still okay!

Problems of shyness and inability to assert themselves are, in my opinion, some of the main reasons children and adolescents do drugs and alcohol and are overly sensitive and responsive to peer pressure. In addition to their irrational thinking about themselves and others, they often lack both the basic understanding about people and the social skills to help them relate more comfortably and to resist social influence. Some strategies that parents and teachers would find helpful in assisting shy and inhibited youngsters develop better relationships and social skills are as follows.

1. Help them to change their focus about relationships from being liked and accepted by others to liking and accepting others. The way they feel and act toward peers they like is in their control for the most part, and they can change these things if they wish. Help them understand that having friends and winning approval is desirable and pleasant, but it won't make them more acceptable and worthwhile than they already are. By relaxing about having friends and showing more positive feelings to others, they will increase the likelihood of making friends and maintaining close friendships.

2. Gently but firmly encourage them to do something they fear, such as approaching another student or speaking up in class about something they know or asserting themselves with a friend. Have them determine who they want to

approach and what they want to say. Urge them to force themselves. Start them simply, in one class, making simple statements to one student they like or would like to know. Assure them you will help them deal with it no matter what happens and to try it again even if it doesn't work out the way they wish. To support their effort, accept their fear but remind them that they have nothing to lose and everything to gain. That is, at worst, they will not feel much worse than they do already. In fact, they will learn they will survive even a negative reaction, whatever it is, though they won't like it.

3. Before they try it, a parent or teacher might practice with them and rehearse what they plan to do or say. Parents might want to talk about a problem they have had when they were young and what happened and how it was handled, stressing they didn't like it but managed. With a very shy or inhibited young child, role playing about the new situation, with each taking turns being the child, would be helpful.

4. Help them to problem solve about their social difficulties and other problems. This means helping them to identify what they are afraid of and what they would like and those emotions that are standing in the way. It means helping them develop options other than withdrawing or acquiescing or being alone or worrying. Shy children and those acquiescing to peer pressure often feel they have no other recourse and that they are helpless to do anything other than what they are doing. Just helping children and adolescents learn that most problems are solvable and getting them started talking about and proposing options has been successful in mobilizing more assertive activity.

5. The parent or teacher, in helping shy or acquiescent children, may become aware that their children or students lack adequate social skills. Helping them develop these skills may involve teaching and modeling for them basic things like facing a person when talking, establishing eye contact, and using an appropriate tone of voice. It may involve teaching and demonstrating skills in conversation and friendship skills such as active listening, making new friends, forming groups, conversing, or skills for getting along such as sharing, when and when not to interrupt, accepting and saying thanks, accepting and giving complements or criticism appropriately. They may want to help them develop such skills as asking for help or feedback, how to negotiate, be persuasive and give help.

Shy and acquiescent children and adolescents as well as those with problems of aggressiveness will probably find assertiveness training very helpful. Such training is focused on asserting oneself or expressing feelings and desire appropriately. Assertiveness is quite different from aggression. Aggression reflects demanding rather than asking and is often hostile and primitive in quality.

Teaching social skills and assertiveness to children may be a large order for either parents or teacher in many cases. A professional program may be more appropriate to help very shy, inhibited children or aggressive acter-outers. Such programs are often found in schools or at mental health clinics or hospitals, possibly ·as part of group therapy programs for children and adolescents.

There are two children's stories that I have found useful in stimulating discussions about feelings and social problems with children. These are:

Homer the Homely Hound Dog, by E. J. Garcia and N. Pellegrini (1974). This book discusses how Homer is helped to overcome shyness, passivity, and self-deprecation.

I Have Feelings by T. Berger (1971). This book is for younger children, 4 to 9 years. It presents 17 feelings illustrated by photographs and explanations from a rational-emotive perspective.

Conclusion

It is hoped that this chapter enables practitioners of RET, in their role of consultants, to make issues of causality and methods of remediation clear to parents, teachers, and others working directly with children. Parents and teachers often find it difficult to understand and accept the idea that irrational beliefs underlie children's emotional and behavioral difficulties and not the past, others, or external conditions, and that remediation depends on helping children replace these beliefs with rational or sensible ones.

It is hoped, too, that consultants will help their consultees to accept some other notions that are implicit in the chapter. The first is that there is much that they can do to help children and adolescents develop and maintain good mental health, increase achievement, accept themselves and others as worthwhile human beings, engage in problem solving, and enjoy positive relationships with peers and adults. In other words, they can help their children and students be happier and more productive despite some very complex and often difficult circumstances.

The second is that the task is not an easy one and will require commitment and patience on the part of teachers and parents. Changes in thinking and behavior occur slowly at best, as do changes in any habits, and setbacks or regressions are normal and to be expected. But they are to take heart, because persistence, encouragement, and support and reinforcing the efforts of the young persons to change will pay off eventually.

The third is that many secondary benefits will accrue to the teacher and parent who helps their children and students. In addition to being something that many parents and teachers want to do, it will change their focus to working positively to change things rather than spending their time disciplining, punishing, and putting out brush fires. In addition, it is likely the RET philosophy and strategies they learn to help the children and adolescents will also help them to better cope with their own problems and lead happier and more productive lives.

It is felt that much of the material in this chapter is suitable for reading (and re-reading) by parents or teachers and would help their understanding and efforts to assist children and adolescents with problems. A consultant working with them is therefore encouraged to reproduce suitable portions of this chapter (with credit to the author, of course), when it is considered appropriate and beneficial.

There will be problems that will need much more help than parents and teachers can give, as in cases of severe or persistent emotional problems (e.g., withdrawal, running away, depression, aggressiveness, suicidal feelings, etc.) and more intensive intervention by the consultant or other professional will be necessary. But the understanding the parents and teachers have gained through their own efforts to assist children will help them participate in and perhaps expedite the therapeutic process and thereafter.

REFERENCES

Berger, T. (1971). *I have feelings*. New York: Human Sciences Press.

Berk, L. E. (1980). Why children talk to themselves. *Young Children, 40*(5), 46–52.

Bernard, M. E. (1989). *Increasing your child's tease tolerance*. Unpublished paper, University of Melbourne, Australia.

Bernard, M. E., & Joyce, M. R. (1984). *Rational-emotive therapy with children and adolescents*. New York: Wiley.

Bialer, I. (1960). Conceptualization of success and failure in mentally retarded and normal children. *Journal of Personality, 29*, 303–320.

Brown, R. (1980). Locus of control and its relationship to intelligence and achievement. *Psychological Reports, 46*, 1249–1250.

Cervantes, R. A. (1976). *Self concept, locus of control, and achievement in Mexican-American pupils*. Paper presented to the third annual Conference of Bilingual-Bicultural Education, San Francisco.

Crandall, V., Katakovsky, W., & Crandall, V. J. (1965). Children's beliefs in their own control of reinforcement in intellectual and academic achievement situations. *Child Development, 36*, 91–109.

Ellis, A. (1962). *Reason and emotion in psychotherapy*. Secaucus, NJ: Lyle Stuart.

Ellis, A. (1969). Teaching rational-emotive education in the classroom. *School Health Review, 1*, 10–14.

Ellis, A. (1974). *Humanistic psychotherapy*. New York: McGraw-Hill.

Ellis, A. (1979). Discomfort anxiety: A new cognitive-behavioral construct (part I). *Rational Living, 14*(2), 3–7.

Ellis, A. (1980). Discomfort anxiety: a new cognitive-behavioral construct (Part II). *Rational Living, 15*(1), 25–30.

Ellis, A., & Harper, R. A. (1975). *A new guide to rational living*. North Hollywood, CA: Wilshire Books.

Ellis, A., & Knaus, W. J. (1977). *Overcoming procrastination*. New York: Institute for Rational Living.

Ellis, A., Wolfe, J. L., & Moseley, S. (1966). *How to raise an emotionally healthy, happy child*. North Hollywood, CA: Wilshire Books.

Garcia, E. J., & Pellegrini, N. (1974). *Homer the homely hound dog*. New York: Institute for Rational Living.

Grieger, R. M., & Boyd, J. D. (1983). Childhood anxieties, fears and phobias: A cognitive-behavioral psychosituational approach. In M. E. Bernard & M. Joyce (Eds.), *Rational-emotive therapy with children and adolescents* (pp. 146–147). New York: Wiley.

Hauck, P. A. (1967). *The rational management of children.* New York: Libra.

Hauck, P. A. (1977). Irrational parenting styles. In A. Ellis & R. Grieger (Eds.), *Handbook of rational-emotive therapy* (pp. 409–418). New York: Springer.

Knaus, W. J. (1974). *Rational-emotive education: A manual for elementary school teachers.* New York: Institute for Rational Living.

Knaus, W. J. (1977). Rational-emotive education In A. Ellis & R. Grieger (Eds.), *Handbook of rational-emotive therapy* (pp. 398–408). New York: Springer.

Lafferty, J. C., Denneral, D., & Rettich, P. A. (1964). Creative school mental health programs. *The National Elementary School Principal, 43,* 28–35.

Martens, B. K., Peterson, R. L., Witt, J. C., & Cirone, S. (1986). Teacher perception of school-based interventions. *Exceptional Children, 5,* 213–223.

Massari, D. J., & Rosenblum, D. C. (1972). Locus of control, interpersonal trust and academic achievement. *Psychological Reports, 31,* 355–360.

Morgan, S. R. (1986). Locus of control and achievement in emotionally disturbed children in segregated classes. *Journal of Child and Adolescent Psychotherapy, 3,* 17–21.

Nowicki, S. Jr., & Strickland, B. R. (1973). A locus of control scale for children. *Journal of Consulting and Clinical Psychology, 40,* 148–154.

Oliver, R. (1975). Overcoming test anxiety. *Rational Living, 10*(1), 6–12.

Pearl, R., Bryan, T., & Donahue, M. (1980). Learning disabled children's attributions for success and failure. *Learning Disabilities Quarterly, 3,* 3–9.

Rothbaum, F., Wolfer, J., & Visentainer, M. (1979). Coping behavior and locus of control in children. *Journal of Personality, 47,* 118–135.

Rotter, J. (1966). Generalized expectancies for internal versus external control of reinforcement. *Psychological Monographs, 80* (1, whole no.609).

Strickland, B. R. (1972). Locus of control and competence in children. *Journal of Consulting and Clinical Psychology, 40,* 148–154.

Vygotsky, L. S. (1962). *Thought and language.* Cambridge, MA: MIT Press.

Waters, V. (1980). *Rational stories for children.* New York: Institute for Rational Living.

Young, H. S. (1974). *Rational counseling primer.* New York: Institute for Rational Living.

Young, H. S. (1975). *Counseling strategies with working class adolescents.* New York: Institute for Rational Living.

8 A Rational-Emotive Model of Organizational Consultation

Raymond DiGiuseppe
St. John's University
and
Institute for Rational Emotive Therapy

Alfred R. Miller
Institute for Cognitive Development

Psychologists have a long history of consulting educational, public service, and business managers to operate organizations effectively. The principles of each generation of psychologist have services as the basis for consultation strategies to increase organizational effectiveness.

As early as 1962, Sofer (1962) suggested that organizational consultants need the same clinical skills as psychotherapist. Dickson and Roethlisberger (1966) suggested that consultants need behavioral science and research knowledge, but that clinical skills were essential. Organizational psychology has flourished by taking the then current theories of individual psychotherapy and applying them to problems in the workplace. The psychological theories of personality assessment, motivation, job satisfaction, creativity, and team development have all been applied by organizational psychologists to help improve work performance. Many in organizational psychology stress the systemic aspects of the field. However, the history of the practice of organizational consultation shows a great reliance on clinical psychotherapy skills. Our conversations with many consultants suggest that they believe their "clinical" skills are most crucial to their success. This chapter focuses on the application of the principals of Rational Emotive Therapy (RET) to foster the systemic change in organizations by promoting emotional adjustment.

Although, organizational psychologists have utilized theories concerning the individual to construct interventions, they have also recognized that people function in social systems. The structure of social systems significantly influences the behavior of individuals. All groups and organizations have their own set of rules, norms, structures, and procedures. These elements greatly influence the behavior of individuals who work in groups. The use of the term *corporate culture* suggests the advance in our knowledge in this area. For example, some educational organizations reinforce staff for getting their paperwork in on time, whereas others are more concerned with the quality of instruction.

Organizational consultants wishing to improve the functioning of individuals in an organization are concerned with the skills of individuals. They may introduce interventions such as motivational programs, procedures for assessing the appropriate candidate for each job, training in communication skills, and possibly removing emotional blocks to communicating or performing a task.

Those organizational consultants who wish to reorganize an organization to improve the functioning of its members may use a systems perspective. They may focus on such issues as the lines of communication, the specific structure of supervision (who takes responsible for tasks and employees), the clarity of boundaries, the incentives for certain behaviors, the alliances within the organization, or the flexibility of individuals to reach goals in a method of their choice.

Schmuck (1990) identified four primary interventions used by organizational consultants. They are training, data collection and feedback, confrontation, and process observation. Some of these interventions rely on improving the skills and functioning of individuals, whereas others involve restructuring the organization. For example, training involves teaching employees new skills that are necessary to do their jobs and accomplish new goals set by the organization. Training teachers in a new instructional method of reading, training support staff in word processing, teaching supervisors to do performance appraisals, or providing stress management seminars are examples of training activities.

Data collection and feedback involve the systematic collection of data to help generate solutions to the problems faced by the organization. Suppose a school district experienced a rapid and high turnover in teaching staff resulting in an inexperienced staff and inadequate instruction. An organizational consultant could design a job satisfaction questionnaire for teachers to assess their reasons for leaving. Also, one could observe teachers at work to see which tasks they are assigned and how these differ from their expectations. With this information, the consultant and the administration could design different structures and procedures aimed at reducing the turn over.

In confrontation interventions, the consultant gathers different groups in an organization and encourages them to express their thoughts concerning how they could work more effectively. The result would be to pinpoint what each group would like from the other. These activities sound a great deal like behavioral family therapy. People are asked to problem solve about how they could work together by asking for specific changes in the procedure, behaviors, and attitudes of their colleagues.

In process observation, the consultant observes how people in the organization interact in group activities and offers feedback on their interaction styles. This type of intervention, also known as T groups, has been popular in organization consulting and greatly resembles group therapy.

There has been a long debate in the social science whether the object of study, assessment, and the target of intervention should be the individual or the social group. Psychology has usually taken the position to target the individual, whereas sociology and family systems theories have focused more on the structural aspects of the group. Of the interventions mentioned by Schmuck, training and process interventions appear aimed at changing the individual, data collection and feedback appear aimed at changing the organization's procedures, norms, and structure. Confrontation appears aimed at changing both. It targets the individuals because specific things that a person does on the job to interfere with others may are discussed. It targets the organizational procedures, norms, and structure, because this type of job hindrance may be revealed in the confrontation.

Our position is that in order to effective organizational consultants psychologists need to consider *both* the individual and the systemic points of view. Focusing only on the new skills employees need to learn or the structure of the organization may not be sufficient for change. The individual's thoughts and emotions may prevent or inhibit the implementation of desired new skills or the structural change. For example, one of us was asked by a metropolitan school district to teach consultation skills to school-based support teams (school psychologist, school social workers and educational evaluators). This intervention was designed to change the structure of the organization because an assessment had suggested that these professionals spend too little time consulting. As a result, too many children were referred to special education services before any other interventions were tried. Thus, the organizational assessment suggested individual skills-based intervention. Although the training of staff was needed, it did not change the behavior of the professionals to do more consultation with teachers for several reasons. First, many school-based support team personnel were reluctant to change their role. They had spent years doing evaluations and making referrals. Now they were being asked to give concrete specific advice to teachers. What if the teacher did not comply? What if the child did not respond? There was quite an emotional response to the new procedures resulting in defensiveness. Also, the procedures and structure of the organization did not support this change in behavior. Structurally, the school-based support teams were assigned to the division of special education. The administrators of this division did not want employees on their pay role working with regular education teachers and children. Procedurally, there was no code to show that consultation took place on the daily work log. Thus, a school psychologist who spent time consulting with teachers appeared to administrators to be doing nothing.

Changes in the structure, procedures and norms of the organization were needed before the staff could change, so a systems perspective was necessary to support change. However, focusing only on the systemic variables such as structure and procedures would have produced useless or no consultation if the staff did not have the skills to do the task. But, teaching the staff the skills would also be insufficient for change if the staff were too emotional defensive to implement what they learned.

Interventions at all levels, organizational structure, skills, and emotional adjustment, would accomplish the goals of the organization. Namely, reducing the number of children referred to special education. However, the administrators were reluctant to make the changes necessary. One psychologist experienced fear of confronting the central board to change the daily work log. They would view her as making waves, and that might upset her plans for promotion. Another administrator thought it was too much of a hassle to confront the conflict of interests that existed in the special education department. How could they have their own employees work to reduce the need for their services? Bringing up such an issue was threatening. People might get mad at him and make work unpleasant for quite awhile. The special education administrator was threatened by any attempt to remove people from under his realm and by that reduce his power. Organizational change was needed if the goals were to be achieved. Everyone agreed with that. However, organizational change is implemented by individuals, and here all the individuals were inhibited from confronting the tasks necessary to foster organizational change because of their emotions of fear, or anger. Individuals often sabotage organizational change for their own idiosyncratic irrational reasons.

RET AND ORGANIZATIONAL CONSULTATION

RET focuses on the role of thoughts in creating emotions. RET is a procedure by which people learn to control their thinking to eliminate disturbed emotions and to replace them with more appropriate adaptive emotions. As a general principle we do not believe that adopting a RET perspective will radically alter the principles and procedures used by an organizational consultant. It will not produce a paradigm shift. However, the adoption of a RET perspective will add an important powerful tool that will add to the many ideas already used in the field.

Perhaps we could display how RET would contribute to consultation using the example of the metropolitan school district that wanted to provide more consultation to reduce the number of children referred to special education. How would an organizational consultant with a RET perspective design an appropriate intervention?

As already noted, some interventions that organizational consultants use are designed to improve the skill level of individuals, and to improve the communications between individuals. There are a few general principles that link all these consultation skills designed to intervene at these levels. If an individual's emotions are blocking performance, the cognitive perspective offered by RET will greatly enhance the stress management programs used to remove these blocks. The use of T groups, and confrontation activities designed to improve awareness and interpersonal skills can be enhanced if one focuses on the emotions being expressed and on the irrational beliefs generating these emotions, teaching the consultee to change the thoughts and the feelings. No empirical data has yet appeared supporting the effectiveness of RET consultation. However, we believe that our effectiveness as consultants has been greatly increased by adding RET to the group activities usually included in the organizational development literature for improving employee effectiveness. In the case study mentioned earlier, the consultant might have recommended that the members of the school-based support teams meet in groups to explore their thoughts and emotions about the change in their role. Helping them develop more rational beliefs about consultation and the possibility of failure might have made them more amenable to the organizational changes.

Many communication problems arise because a person's emotions inhibit him or her from communicating what was intended. Many communication receiver errors result because of the emotional upset of the receiver that distorts the message sent (DiGiuseppe & Zevee, 1986). Communication training often is highly loaded with emotional issues. The addition of a RET component to uncover and alleviate these issues would greatly enhance communications training programs. Skill deficits often result because people have emotional problems that go unrecognized and untreated and prevent them from learning new skills. Employees may be trained to perform new skills only to have those skills blocked by emotions that the new skill provokes. A good example is the area of training supervisors in giving performance reviews. It has been our experience that once supervisors learn the behavioral skills to do performance appraisals, they still do not use the skills. They are inhibited by anxiety that the subordinate will disapprove of them for a poor performance review. Skills training may be enhanced by including an assessment of emotional blocks that might arise once a skill is learned and a RET component to handle these emotions. In the case study mentioned earlier the same principle would apply. Teaching the professional staff how to do consultation did not deal with their emotional reactions of having to do consultation. Their emotions may have interfered with the skills even if the skills were well taught and well learned.

Although these levels of RET consultation provide specific skills for consultants to improve the performance of both clients and consultees, they are designed to influence the performance of individuals in the organization. They are not really an application of RET to organizational psychology. They do not influence the norms, rules, procedures, or structure of organizations. The question remains whether RET has value for organizational psychology's view of the system and what practical value it has for consultants when they are concerned with producing *organizational* change.

Organizational consultation employs many ideas to understand how organizations function and to guide their assessment in determining whether an organization is functioning inefficiently. An organizational consultant can use communications theory and examine how information is transmitted and received within an organization. The consultant can use role theory and examine the roles individual employees perform. The consultant can examine whether there is sufficient clarity in the boundaries of employees' roles and if the hierarchy of managerial responsibility is clear. Consultants can look for conflicting lines of responsibility or interfering alliances within an organization that interferes with productivity and job function. The consultant can also use behavioral theory to examine the reinforcement contingencies that exist and explore those which are likely to meet the organizational goals.

Organizational systems do greatly influence human behavior. Although cultures rarely have a particular person responsible for their design, the same cannot be said for "corporate cultures." Organizational systems are designed and maintained by the people in positions of power. Key executives in organizations set the tone and norms of many aspects of the corporate culture. Key executives, administrators, boards of directors, superintendents, and CEOs do make procedures, structures, and rules that will affect the operations of organizations.

The Missing Element in Organizational Consultation.   Our experience and that of others is that consulting with senior management personnel in business and educational institutions often involves an additional level of consultation. Namely, the reluctance of senior management to consider the alternative structural and procedural recommendations made by the consultant. People usually employ a consultant because of the persistence of the problem that they have been unable to solve. The presenting problem may persist because the consultee does not have the practical skills or knowledge to solve it. Or it may persist because the consultee is blocked from considering various options because of rigid adherence to previous strategies and by irrational beliefs concerning what solutions *should* work.

Many consultants report spending considerable time convincing senior management of the necessity of exploring or adopting different management policies. The senior officials may be rigidly blocked from considering certain solutions because of their own irrational expectations of their subordinates or organizations. Although the consultant may have an excellent plan to solve the organizational problem, that solution must be approved by senior management if it is to be implemented. An organization is only as flexible as its top managers. If their personalities or belief systems limit them from accepting certain alternatives, these alternatives will not be available to the organization.

Sometimes solutions that will solve a problem require the acknowledgement of a broader problem. The senior management may not wish to follow a course, which will openly acknowledge certain problems, because of the fear of disapproval of the community, the electorate, the school board, or the board of directors. Fear of being viewed as incompetent or fear of removal may deter some top administrators from adopting solutions that are in the organizations long-term best interest.

Thus, the consultant may be placed in a role similar to the individual therapist. That is, exploring the philosophies and emotional reactions of the senior management that prevents him or her from considering or implementing new problem-solving strategies.

One recent example of this kind of rigid thinking was with a large multinational firm that had acquired three U.S. manufacturing companies. After the acquisition, all three companies became divisions of the parent company. Immediately after the acquisition, new organizational goals and work practices were established, and new supervisors and managers selected. Two years after the acquisition, all three of the American divisions were plagued with high employee turnover and low productivity. After visiting each organization, evidently there were two main problems: (a) Upper management had a cultural gap in not knowing how to effectively manage U.S. employees. What they apparently took for granted in their own country (i.e., social custom and work values) were not the same in the United States. (b) Most of the first-line supervisors were hired or promoted based on their technical skills and not on their people skills. In addition, none of the supervisors had received any basic supervisory training in how to plan, develop, train, and motivate employees.

Think of yourself as the consultant asked to bring this kind information to upper management. How do you tell executives of a successful multinational company that they made some serious mistakes, especially when they believed that they had a proven track record in manufacturing throughout the world? In a conversation with one key executive, we mentioned that it would be a good idea to get some notion of what employees think of supervisory and managerial work relations. Based on this information it would be clear what needed to be changed and efforts could be started in training and organizational change programs to improve effectiveness. The executive quickly pointed out that the employees were not running the company and if the employees were not responding to current management practices it was a problem with them not with management.

RET makes a distinction between practical problems and emotional problems. Practical problems are the noxious stimuli or negative activating events confronting. These could include failure to attain one's goals, failure at tasks, being confronted by a changing market or more competition, or having to comply with new government relations. Emotional problems are the emotional reactions and evaluations that people have to the practical problems. Emotional problems could be either intense disturbed emotional reactions or irrational demands and rigid expectations about the nature of the practical problem. Practical solutions are the behaviors or problem-solving strategies that the person can use to overcome, react to, or change the activating events. RET also posits that it is best to target emotional problems first before practical problems. This belief is based on the notion that emotional problems will interfere with a person's ability to carry out strategies that achieve goals, interfere with efforts to learn new skills to achieve goals, and interfere with problem-solving to decide which strategies could achieve one's goals.

Replacing the maladaptive emotional reactions with more appropriate emotions is called the *emotional solution*. Most of the strategies that organizational consultants use are practical solutions. They are aimed at target behaviors that clients use to change negative activating events in their organization and eliminate the reason for referral. RET does not believe that these practical organizational solutions are inappropriate, nor does it recommend an either-or approach to target emotions instead of practical problems. RET places primacy on changing emotions *first* and believes that the consultant had better teach clients strategies to more effectively influence their environment. There are two reasons for this position. First, emotional problems will interfere with the execution and learning of such behaviors as noted previously and second, the consultee may be *unable* to change the aversive activating events. If the consultees only learned strategies that help them confront and change events that thwart their goals, they will have no coping strategy for those events which they are unable to change. There are many situations in life that one cannot change. RET adopts the philosophy that one learns to change the things that can be changed, accepts the things that cannot be changed, and develops the wisdom to tell the difference.

In the case study mentioned earlier, the emotional blocks of several administrators were preventing the implementation of structural plans that could help accomplish the goals of placing fewer children in special education. A RET oriented consultant would have addressed these emotional blocks along with the irrational beliefs underlying them. This might have been done by meeting with each individually or by bringing them together as a group to discuss the feelings and objections that they had to any proposed changes.

This aspect of our model does not appear to be one that we see acknowledged in other sources. However, we believe that consensus from many consultants suggests that this is precisely what they often do. There are a few differences between regular therapy and therapy for the CEO as part of consulting. Changing one's emotions is usually part of the implicit or explicit contract between therapists and clients. It usually is not part of the contract between senior management and consultant. As a result, the consultant/therapist must be careful how the agenda is changed. It is important to develop these emotional change goals into the consultative alliance. This can be done by bluntly informing the senior manager that you think that her or his emotions and beliefs are preventing him or her from evaluating alternatives. Fines, clinical acumen, and good clinical judgment are needed in deciding when to offer such a change in the agenda.

ORGANIZATIONAL CONSULTING

We now present some examples of organizational consultation activities similar to those outlined by Schmuck (1990) with a RET component added. We hope that this makes the point just stated. A consultant does not have to shift paradigms of organizational psychology to use RET. The RET model is complimentary with existing systemic organizational interventions. Having an effective strategy to manage the dysfunctional nature of worker and managerial emotions and behaviors can mean the difference between success and failure of consultants engaged in organizational development and training programs. The rationale for the strategy used in each intervention discussed in this section is based on actual case studies.

Employee Attitude Surveys

The use of a survey questionnaire is undoubtedly one of the most reliable and popular methods for obtaining information. Although interviews and observations can be performed, they are often more time consuming, expensive, and less reliable than administering surveys. Interviews are limited by the extent that employees will reveal what they think. They are greatly affected by the biases of those asking the questions, observing and recording employee and work site information. Faced with these problems, it is not surprising that many organizations prefer the lower cost, greater objectivity, and scientific value of a survey.

One critical aspect of establishing a successful survey process is building an awareness and receptivity for the information that the survey provides. All too often, managers are eager to find out what employees think; however, they may become angered by what they find out. As a consequence of their thinking styles and irrational beliefs, managers can vacillate from paralysis to overreaction.

After 11,500 air-traffic controllers walked off the job in 1981, the Federal Aviation Administration (FAA) took a hard look at itself and the way it related to its employees. In an attempt to rebuild employee management relations (A. Miller & DelBalzo, 1989) a survey was developed to assess the supervisory and managerial leadership style. This program differed from other surveys because it was designed to measure leadership effectiveness from an employee perspective and not from an upper management perspective. This approach was based on the fundamental belief that leaders do not manage and supervise in a vacuum.

The history of surveys in the FAA before 1981 was similar to that of many other organizations in that the survey was popular when it was first started. However, after several survey administrations, employee support decreased and the survey received less than a 50% response rate.

Faced with low interest and a low response rate, W. Miller (1986) developed a program where employees, supervisors, and managers at all levels of the organization were actively involved with the questionnaire design and administration.

They received special training sessions on how to use the survey information. All supervisors and managers received a 1-day workshop that provided instruction on how to analyze the survey report on and how to effectively manage discussions and problem-solving sessions with their employees. As part of the workshop, the supervisors and managers received instruction on how to manage their irrational beliefs and dysfunctional emotions related to the employees' assessment of their performance. Based on examples provided by Ellis and Harper (1975) and Walen, DiGiuseppe, and Wessler (1980), training sessions were developed to provide instruction on changing dysfunctional thought patterns. These involved irrational beliefs such as awfulizing, demanding, self and other rating and low frustration tolerance. By disputing these dysfunctional thought patterns, supervisors and managers could avoid developing dysfunctional emotions that might adversely affect their problem-solving ability and work relations with their subordinates.

In the training session, each participant received a sample survey report that showed a very dissatisfied employee rating for six of the nine areas surveyed. The participants were then instructed to imagine that the sample report was their actual report and that they would have to present and discuss the report with their subordinates. After spending a few minutes reviewing the report, the participants were then told to write down their thoughts and feelings about receiving this kind of feedback from their subordinates. The dysfunctional thoughts that were often expressed at the training sessions were:

- I must get a good survey report.
- It would be awful if I received a report as bad as this.
- I'm a failure.
- This survey report is not only unfair. It's awful.
- This report means that I will never succeed as a supervisor.
- They should know what I am up against.
- I'll never turn this around.
- My career is over.

After recording the thoughts and feelings expressed by the participants regarding the sample report, the participants were given a short lecture regarding the effect irrational thinking has in creating emotional distress and its deleterious effect on problem-solving performance (D'Zurilla, 1986). The participants were then put in small groups and instructed to analyze their thinking for irrational thoughts. They had to replace the irrational thoughts with more realistic or rational thoughts using the ABCDE model presented by Walen et al. (1980). After spending about 1 hour in the small groups discussing and challenging their irrational thoughts, the participants reported less emotional distress. In the final phase of the training, the participants received instruction on various ways to facilitate discussion of the survey report with their employees and how to create an effective problem-solving atmosphere.

Although the effect that the survey process had on improving supervisory and managerial effectiveness was not measured directly, the response rate for all three administrations of the survey was more than 94% (A. Miller, 1988). This high response rate was achieved by the enthusiastic support of employee unions and the high value placed on the information it provided by supervisors and managers. The survey process also provided an effective means by which employees could contribute their ideas for improving many of their work relations with their supervisors and managers (DelBalzo & Miller, 1989). Another benefit of the program was the RET training. Many supervisors and managers reported that they felt less threatened by feedback that was critical of their performance and believed they were more effective in solving employee problems. The RET training helped supervisors and managers to modify their style of management and improve their complete performance.

Employee Training and Development

With corporate operating budgets becoming leaner due to lower profits and increased global competition, training for results has become a serious concern for many companies. However, many executives have serious concerns about spending money for training activities. Some important questions they usually ask a consultant are:

How do you know that this training will fix the problem?
Have you considered the cost of the lost productivity if we do this training?
I know we probably need it, but can we afford it?

The Research Institute (W. Miller, 1986) suggests that in 1985 alone companies spent $180 billion for employee training programs. Yet despite this large expenditure, there is little evidence that what is presented in many training sessions is transferred to the work situation (Marx, 1986; Youker, 1985; Zemke & Gunther, 1985).

In trying to obtain greater effectiveness there is a growing trend to move the training from classroom to an adventure-based outdoor experience. Although there is little evidence that these programs provide skills that can be transferred into the workplace, these programs are widely publicized and growing in popularity. The growing pressure for training to more effectively change behaviors and attitudes will no doubt continue to generate increased interest in new ways to provide employee training. Some problems in traditional training seminars are: (a) Some are too academic and do not apply to work situations. (b) Some can be too passive for the participants. (c) There can be a reliance on popular and high-priced celebrity speakers. What a person hears is often misunderstood and easily forgotten. Thus, high-priced celebrity speakers might be entertaining but they usually have minimal effect, if any, in changing the way people behave. (d) Having participants role-play pre-written scripts create an experience that may not be real for the participants. Even if the scripts tend to focus on work situations, they may not elicit the same kinds of behaviors and emotions that occur at work.

DiMattia, Yeager, and Dube (1989) suggested that increased training effect can be accomplished by including emotional management instruction. Using the RET model, the authors outlined the role that thinking plays in determining how we feel and behave. Although there are not many data to support the view that emotional management will improve training outcomes, incorporating a RET dimension to training does have some real advantages. First, focusing on the role that thinking plays in determining emotions and behaviors provides the participants a strategy for changing dysfunctional emotions and behaviors. Second, RET personalizes the training around the needs of the participants by letting them identify their "B" (beliefs) and "C" (consequences) behaviors and emotions associated with specific activating events. The first step in using RET in the training program should start with explaining the ABC model. In step 2, describing the "A," the participants create a list of situations that are generally troublesome for them. Creating this list of problem activating events is very important because it assures that the list will include one or more situations that are troublesome for each participant. In step 3, describing the "C," the participants choose a situation and describe the way they generally behave and feel. In Step 4, describing the "B," the participants analyze their beliefs about the situation "A." In Step 5, the participants form small groups and share what they have written for Steps 2, 3, and 4. The participants analyze each situation presented by each group member for irrational, exaggerated, or faulty thinking. When faulty or troublesome beliefs are found, the group attempts to develop a new way of looking at the situation. This active participation usually creates a great deal of involvement and often contributes to new learning and problem-solving skills.

INTEGRATING RET WITH CONFRONTATION AND PROCESS OBSERVATION STRATEGIES

Similarly, a consultant can integrate RET with the confrontation strategies recommended by Schmuck (1990). The employees can be placed in groups and encouraged to express their thoughts concerning how they could work more effectively together. As they state what each group would like from the other, strong emotions are likely to be felt. The consultant asks group members to share these feelings and the thoughts and beliefs that occur with them. These beliefs are then processed by the consultant to expose any that are irrational. The group members can help each other dispute their irrational beliefs and devolve more rational alternatives. After the group members, emotions are under control, they can problem solve about how they could work together.

Process observation strategies can incorporate RET similarly. The consultant observes how people in the organization interact in group activities and offers feedback. The feedback is likely to elicit strong and perhaps dysfunctional emotions. Perhaps an employee feels angry or hurt about the feedback on his or her style of communication. The beliefs behind these emotions can be processed by RET methods. The result may be a person who is better able to receive critical feedback on his or her communication style and can improve even after the process group ends. Also, the consultant might explore the emotions behind a person's dysfunctional interaction styles. Anger at or fear of other employees might be revealed. The consultant could explore the beliefs associated with these emotions and process and dispute them similarly.

RET Applications for Improving Work Relations.   Both confrontation and process evaluation strategies involve the identification of troublesome interactions between managers, supervisors, and employees. RET would posit that the way a person thinks and feels about his or her personal and work life has important implications for their productivity, morale, job satisfaction, and creativity. If employees are not satisfied, their creativity and productivity will be low ultimately negatively affecting organizational effectiveness and corporate profits. Because work is like most other human activities, employees arrive with their head full of expectations of success and failure, rational and irrational ideas, and various emotional predispositions. In this section, we discuss some topics that could be addressed in RET process and confrontation interventions.

In our years consulting to organizations, we have heard many variations on the patterns that lead to dysfunctional work relationships and poor job morale. Listed here are some troublesome beliefs:

1. "Things have really gotten unbearable around here, nobody gives a damn!"
2. "She should know what has to be done."
3. "People in the front office are brain dead. They never do anything right."
4. "I can't stand working here any more."

If Statement 1 sounds like awfulizing to you, you are right. The statement expresses thinking that is clearly exaggerated. Things might be bad but they are surely tolerable. The part, "nobody gives a damn," is also exaggerated. In our experience, when morale and productivity in organizations are really bad, people do care a great deal. However, they don't always know what to do about it.

If Statement 2 sounds like absolutistic demanding to you, you are right. Because organizations are run by mere mortals, mistakes happen for good reason. Some reasons humans make mistakes include not knowing what to do or how to do it, being too busy, or not feeling well. Although it may be preferable that Mary knows what to do, it is not realistic to think that there is a law in the universe that covers competency. Humans learn by doing and by failing. It would be more effective to think about the reasons why Mary doesn't know what to do, so we can fix them, without getting upset by demanding that she different.

If Statement 3 sounds like an overgeneralized condemnation of others, you are right. One doubts that everyone in the front office is brain dead. It is also unrealistic to think that they never do anything right. A danger here is not only will this kind of thinking create upsetting emotions but it will also severely limit efforts that could correct problems. Thinking of an entire group of people as brain dead may even set up a self-fulfilling prophecy of failure for all future efforts.

If Statement 4 sounds like low frustration tolerance to you, you are right. Although it might very well be better for one to look for another job, it is simply not helpful to tell yourself you can't stand it. You still have to work where you are until the new job starts. Chances are that you can stand it. It would be more effective to remind yourself that although it is difficult, you can handle it, and if things don't improve you will get another job. This latter thinking will move you from a reactive emotional state to a proactive position where you won't be paralyzed by emotional upset and where you can more effectively problem solve.

The same irrational beliefs that relate to emotional disturbance in the psychotherapy office will be found in the workshop ran by the consultant.

The Consulting Relationship: How to Enhance Your Effectiveness

A consulting alliance develops through the purchase of expert information. The client, an individual, supervisor, or manager defines a need. Something that he or she would like changed (e.g., a work practice or a training activity). A consultant is hired to help in causing that change. Some critical aspects related to developing an effective consultative alliance are:

1. Has the consultee accurately identified his or her needs? That is, those areas that need to be changed. Does the consultee have good technical knowledge regarding the area to be changed? Is there a need for the consultant, to gather additional information?

2. Are there adequate resources and time to support the effort?

3. Are there support and adequate resources for the effort?

4. Have other efforts been tried? If so, to what extent were they successful?

5. Is it clear what your role and responsibilities are?

6. Is your consulting relationship collaborative?

7. Has the client worked with a consultant before? Can the client handle negative feedback, for example, being told that he or she may be the problem?

If these areas are not adequately considered, it has been our experience that the effort has a low probability of success. Getting a clear understanding of roles and responsibilities is essential before starting any actual work. Argris (1971) suggested that maintaining objectivity and relative independence from the client's culture is also essential. He believes consultants should have a high degree of self-awareness and self-confidence to effectively take the risks necessary in confronting clients with their own behavior. It is our experience that the consultant will often unwittingly serve as a role model for the client and the organization. RET can be extremely helpful in building an effective relationship with the client and presenting a positive role model. Some irrational thinking that you as a consultant had better guard against might be:

1. I must be brilliant.
2. They must listen to everything I say.
3. They must do everything I say.
4. They must not question or challenge any of my ideas or suggestions.
5. I should be treated with respect.
6. They should like me.

Whether you are an internal (employed by the organization) or an external consultant (on contract) these irrational thoughts are good to guard against. As an external consultant, it is a good practice to coordinate your efforts with internal consultants. They are surely involved in ongoing efforts and can help manage the success of your efforts long after you are gone. Successful, well-adjusted consultants would display good emotional management skills, high frustration tolerance, and nonapproval seeking. She or he would also be tolerant of human foibles.

REFERENCES

Agris, C. (1971). *Management and organizational development: The path from Xa to Xb.* New York: McGraw-Hill.

DelBalzo, J. M., & Miller, A. R. (1989). A new organizational flight pattern. *Training and Development Journal, 43*(3), 40–44.

Dickson, W. J., & Roethlisberger, F. J. (1966). *Counseling in an organization: A sequel to the Hawthorne researches.* Cambridge: Harvard University, School of Business Administration, Division of Research.

DiMattia, D. J., Yeager, R. J., & Dube, I. (1989). Emotional barriers to learning. *Personnel Journal, 68*(11), 86–89.

DiGiuseppe, R., & Zevee, C. (1986). Rational-emotive approaches to marital therapy: An integration with social exchange theory. *Journal of Rational-Emotive and Cognitive-Behavior Therapy, 4*, 22–37.

D'Zurilla, T. J. (1986). *Problem-solving therapy: A social competence approach to clinical intervention.* New York: Springer.

Ellis, A., & Harper, R. A. (1975). *A new guide for rational living*. North Hollywood, CA: Wilshire Books.

Marx, R. (1986). Self-managed skill retention. *Training and Development Journal, 40,* 54–57.

Miller, A. R. (1986). *Enhancing supervisory and managerial effectiveness* (Report No. AEA-10C-1986-1). New York: Eastern Regional Federal Aviation Administration.

Miller, A. R. (1988). *Managerial/supervisory survey scores 94% employee response.* (*Eastern Intercom,* 88–6). New York: Eastern Region Federal Aviation Administration.

Miller, W. H. (1986, November 24). Trouble at home? *Industry Week.* Research Institute Report.

Miller, A. R., & DelBalzo, J. M. (1989, September). *Enhancing supervisory and managerial response to survey feedback.* Paper presented at the annual conference on Creativity and Innovation in Public Service by the American Society of Public Administration, Atlantic City, NJ.

Walen, S. R., DiGiuseppe, R. A., & Wessler, R. L. (1980). *A practitioner's guide to rational-emotive therapy.* New York: Oxford Press.

Schmuck, R. (1990). Organizational development in schools: Contemporary concepts and practices. In T. Gutkin & C. Reynolds (Eds.), *Handbook of school psychology* (2nd Ed., pp. 901–921). New York: Wiley.

Sofer, C. (1962). *The organization from within.* Chicago: Quadrangle Books.

Youker, R. B. (1985). Ten benefits of participant action planning. *Training. 22,* 52–55.

Zemke, R., & Gunther, J. (1985). 28 techniques for transforming training into performance. *Training. 22,* 48–63.

Author Index

Subject Index

A

ABC model, 1, 3, 17, 98, 99, 103, 104,
    105, 119, 120, 142, 145, 198
abcde model, 142, 197
Absolutist demanding, 199
Activating event, 8, 14, 17, 98, 142
Adaptive negative emotional states, 7
ADD (Attention Deficit Disorder), 79
Anger, 10
Anticipatory anxiety, 69
Anxiety
    ego, 69
    discomfort, 70
Approval seeking, 10
Attention deficit hyperactivity disorder,
    54
Attention deficit disorder, 5
Authoritarianism, 111
Authority figure, 10
Awfulizing, 19, 167

B

Behavior management, 45
Behavior modification, 120
Behavioral methods
    cognitive, 17
    emotive, 17
    behavioral, 17
Behavioral consequence, 142
Belief system, 17
    irrational belief system, 160, 171,
    183

Beliefs

Beliefs
    self-defeating, 64
    rational, 98
    emotional, 98
    irrational, 7, 13, 14, 58, 101, 104,
    105, 141, 142, 145, 160, 171, 183,
    192, 195, 196
Biblitherapy, 48

C

Catastrophe scale, 23, 24
Catastrophizing, 38
Classroom management skills, 7
Client consultation, 57
Cognitive mediational factors, 123
Cognitive behavioral approaches, 79
Cognitive personality traits, 14
Confort zone, 50
Confrontation, 188
Consequence, 98
Consultation model, levels of
    Level I, 7
    Level II, 9
    Level III, 9, 10
    Level IV, 11
Consultant, 2, 3, 9, 13, 145, 183, 184,
    187, 192, 201
Consultation methods
    behavioral and organizational, 5, 33
    consultee centered consultation, 13
Consultation process, 1, 3, 139, 140
Consultation skills, 189
Consultative alliance, 3, 13, 17, 18

207